"Michael Cox has long been one of the most intelligent and original scholars of America's grand career on the modern world stage. In this engaging collection of essays, Cox turns his attention to United States foreign policy during the post-Cold War unipolar years, offering a compelling portrait of an unsettled superpower that is at once an empire and a liberal democracy."
G. John Ikenberry, Princeton University

"Represents the decades that Michael Cox has spent thinking about the US and its foreign policies. It is shrewd, insightful and wise on the politics of a global power that claims not to be an empire. A book to be enjoyed."
Caroline Kennedy-Pipe, Loughborough University

"Few observers of America's 'unipolar moment' have a perspective born of both closeness to the debates and detachment from Washington's machinations as Michael Cox. And even fewer afford the United States such fairness of judgement, unencumbered by ideology or vested interest. Cox sheds crucial light on the question of whether the United States can continue to play the role it has for the last 30 years, and what the alternatives are for the rest of us."
Nicholas Kitchen, University of Surrey

"A sweeping, illuminating journey through American grand strategy from the end of the Cold War to the dawn of Biden's presidency. Cox is an astute guide who offers a readable, thoughtful exploration of how the American empire has evolved to reshape the world."
Brian Klaas, University College London

"For many years Michael Cox has been writing articles and books that compel us to reassess fundamental assumptions. Here again, in this book of incisive, powerful essays, he impels readers to rethink America's actions and behaviour in the international arena."
Melvyn P. Leffler, University of Virginia

"Michael Cox's collected essays provide a bounty of smart insights for anyone trying to make sense of the twists and turns in American foreign policy over the past 30 years."
John Mearsheimer, University of Chicago

"A fascinating critique of American foreign policy since the end of the Cold War by one of Britain's leading analysts."
Joseph Nye, Harvard University

"In this empirically rich revisionist study, Michael Cox explains why a self-confident America of the late 20th century has arrived at the critical turning point it finds itself at today."
Brian Schmidt, Carleton University

"With great power comes great responsibility, but as Michael Cox deftly shows in this persuasive account of US foreign policy since the end of the Cold War, only when a country's leaders can turn that power into judicious policy. In an era when American power has outstripped national will, Cox's balanced assessment of the foreign policy missteps, miscalculations and lapses it has wrought makes for essential reading. Scholars and students alike will benefit from these penetrating essays on what ails the American colossus."
Peter Trubowitz, Phelan US Centre at LSE

AGONIES OF EMPIRE

AGONIES OF EMPIRE

American Power from Clinton to Biden

Michael Cox

First published in Great Britain in 2022 by

Bristol University Press
University of Bristol
1-9 Old Park Hill
Bristol
BS2 8BB
UK
t: +44 (0)117 954 5940
e: bup-info@bristol.ac.uk

Details of international sales and distribution partners are available at bristoluniversitypress.co.uk

© Bristol University Press 2022

British Library Cataloguing in Publication Data
A catalogue record for this book is available from the British Library

ISBN 978-1-5292-2153-4 hardcover
ISBN 978-1-5292-2154-1 paperback
ISBN 978-1-5292-2156-5 ePub
ISBN 978-1-5292-2157-2 ePdf

The right of Michael Cox to be identified as author of this work has been asserted by him in accordance with the Copyright, Designs and Patents Act 1988.

All rights reserved: no part of this publication may be reproduced, stored in a retrieval system, or transmitted in any form or by any means, electronic, mechanical, photocopying, recording, or otherwise without the prior permission of Bristol University Press.

Every reasonable effort has been made to obtain permission to reproduce copyrighted material. If, however, anyone knows of an oversight, please contact the publisher.

The statements and opinions contained within this publication are solely those of the author and not of the University of Bristol or Bristol University Press. The University of Bristol and Bristol University Press disclaim responsibility for any injury to persons or property resulting from any material published in this publication.

Bristol University Press works to counter discrimination on grounds of gender, race, disability, age and sexuality.

Cover design and front cover image: Liam Roberts

Bristol University Press uses environmentally responsible print partners.

Printed in Great Britain by CMP, Poole

To Fiona

Contents

About the Author		x
Preface		xi
Introduction: The Rise of an Empire		1

PART I Clinton: Liberal Leviathan — 5
1. From Geopolitics to Geo-Economics? — 7
2. The Wilsonian Moment? Promoting Democracy — 23
3. Failed Crusade? The United States and Post-Communist Russia — 40

PART II Bush Jnr: Empire in an Age of Terror — 55
4. American Power after the Towers — 57
5. Empire, Imperialism and the Bush Doctrine — 63

PART III Obama: Towards a Post-American World? — 77
6. Navigating the Rapids — 79
7. Stresses across the Atlantic — 96
8. Axis of Opposition: China, Russia and the West — 106

PART IV Trump: Turbulence in the Age of Populism — 123
9. Populism, Trump and the Crisis of Globalization — 125
10. Trump's World: The Legacy — 135

PART V Biden: Is America Back? — 151
11. After the Deluge or Whither the Empire? — 153

Notes and References	159
Acknowledgements	183
Index	184

About the Author

Professor Michael Cox joined the London School of Economics and Political Science (LSE) in 2002 where he later helped to establish the Cold War Studies Programme and LSE IDEAS, one of the world's leading university-affiliated think tanks. A prolific author and editor, his most recent publications include a collection of his own essays, *The Post Cold War World* (2018), a third edition of his co-edited best-selling *US Foreign Policy* (2018), a centennial edition of J.M. Keynes's *The Economic Consequences of the Peace* (2019) and a new edition of E.H. Carr's 1945 classic *Nationalism and After* (2021). He is currently working on a history of the LSE titled *The 'School': The LSE and the Shaping of the Modern World.* He holds a Visiting Professorship at the Catholic University of Milan, is an Associate Fellow on the US and Americas Programme at Chatham House, London, and a member of the Scholarly Advisory Board of the Gilder Lehrman Institute of American History, New York.

Preface

The essays collected together in this volume are the result of many years reflecting on a country that is more than just a nation-state but is, what I would prefer to call, an empire. Some would no doubt question this designation. Some would even argue that it makes no sense at all calling the United States an empire when it doesn't control the territory of other countries and has never sent 'settlers' overseas to pacify other nations. My response is not to deny the obvious fact that the United States is not another British Empire or Washington another Rome – though there are some similarities between the two cities and both empires – but simply to observe that in terms of its military reach, its position at the centre of the world economy, its capacity to shape or limit the choices of others, and its promotion of a certain idea of modernity, the United States comes as close as anything in history to resembling what I would call an empire. As one wit once put it, 'if it looks like a duck, swims like a duck and quacks like a duck' then it is almost certainly a duck. Many might prefer that America was not so influential and have been predicting – perhaps even looking forward to – its decline for the better part of half a century. Others even wonder whether we should even call it an empire at all when we have so many other terms at our disposal such as superpower or hegemon. But empire in my view captures something about the sheer power of the United States and the role it purports to perform – with ever-decreasing success – in the wider international system.

Many of the ideas here have benefited from lengthy discussions and debates with a whole range of writers and academics, many but not all American, covering the spectrum from radical to neoconservative, liberal to realist with a dash of 'English School' thrown in for good measure! Some of the thoughts expressed here also build on work I have done at Chatham House over the years, so special thinks must go to it and its directors for indulging me for so long. I have also had the privilege of lecturing in the US at several institutions, and even chanced my arm on at least one occasion teaching a course on America and the world going all the way back to colonial times when that engine of early globalization known as the British Empire first took an interest in the land mass to its West. Whether or not my students much appreciated what I had to say still remains unclear. However, in the process of trying to make sense of the United States, I certainly learned a lot about US history and why that history still remains so contested today.

The volume certainly takes history seriously, and indeed opens with a very brief survey of America's past, and how the republic evolved in the way in which it did to become the most powerful nation on Earth by the late 20th century. However, the primary purpose of the book is less to explore American history – fascinating and important though that is – and more to explain why, in spite of its very great power, successive US presidents since Clinton have found the world so difficult to manage. There are several reasons why this may have been so, not the least important of which was the end of the certainty created by the Cold War itself. If we then add to this the re-emergence of two revisionist powers in the shape of Russia and China, strategic miscalculation (most clearly the decision to go to war with Iraq in 2003), and at least two 'black swan' events – the financial crash of 2008 and the election of Donald Trump being the most catastrophic – it is easy to see why so many pundits today believe America's best days are now behind it. We can only wait and see how much Biden's much-criticized decision to leave Afghanistan in August 2021 adds to America's woes.

Many of the chapters here build on earlier work, though a number are entirely new. Naturally enough, they do not cover everything. But taken together, they do provide what I think is a reasonably comprehensive discussion of US foreign policy as it searched for purpose in an increasingly uncertain world. The volume has no single message to deliver other than the obvious one that overcoming its communist rival created just as many challenges for the United States as opportunities. Victory over the Soviet Union certainly must have tasted very sweet for those present at the time. But it left many questions unanswered, most obviously: what was a single superpower supposed to do if it no longer had a well-defined rival around which to organize its affairs; what should be its new mission; how should it deal with new threats; how should it relate to traditional allies; and finally, for how long would it be willing to carry the 'burden of leadership' imposed on it by its leading position in the hierarchy of states? How in the end presidents as different as Clinton, Bush Jnr, Obama, Trump and Biden tried to answer these questions, forms the basis of what I go on to discuss in this volume.

Michael Cox
London School of Economics and Political Science
January 2022

Introduction:
The Rise of an Empire

> I am persuaded no constitution was ever before so well calculated as ours for extensive empire [...].[1]

The rise of the United States from being part of the first British Empire to becoming a world power by the 1890s, a superpower by the end of the Second World War, and finally the only significant player in the international system by the late 20th century, is one that has been told many times before. Viewed by critic and defender alike as one of the most extraordinary transformative events in modern world history, there is little doubting that this most 'dangerous' of nations, as one writer with impeccable conservative credentials once called it, would in time go on to change the world.[2] Blessed by geography, surrounded by nothing more threatening than Mexicans, Canadians and fish, and with two vast oceans protecting it from the threat of invasion, the United States grew up in what the American international relations scholar Hans J. Morgenthau might have described as a 'security rich' environment.[3] But not only was it secure from external enemies. It also benefited from an abundance of 'free' land (mainly stolen from Native Americans), a surfeit of capital (much of it foreign), a highly profitable system of plantation slavery producing America's most vital commodity (King Cotton), and last but by no means least, one of the largest movements of people in human history which drew nearly 30 million Europeans to American shores between 1850 and 1920. Aided and abetted by a powerful federal state, a raft of measures designed to protect the American economy from foreign competition, and a legal order that treated private enterprise and private property as sacrosanct – 'government should not do for its people what they can best do for themselves' declared one court in 1899[4] – America's rise was about as inevitable as any event in international history was likely to be, but only after it had successfully navigated the most traumatic moment in its history: the Civil War.[5]

The history of the Civil War itself is invariably told in terms of its famous battles, its sometime less than competent generals, the huge losses suffered on both sides, and of course through the biography of the man who led the North to victory: Abraham Lincoln. But the war also forms a crucial watershed moment in America's rise to pre-eminence. Not only did it settle the issue of slavery (albeit rather late in the day), it also guaranteed there would only be one United States of America. Moreover, by marginalizing the Southern Democrats and allowing the Republicans to gain full control of Washington, it accelerated the construction of a new industrial nation.[6] In the process, vast new factories sprang up, railroad construction surged and oil production soared. As a result America became more urban, major cities started to dot the landscape, and huge fortunes were made by dynasties bearing such names as Rockefeller, Mellon, Carnegie and Vanderbilt. Meanwhile, the revolution in transportation opened up the West and in time transformed US agriculture into the most innovative and productive in the world. All this in turn had an impact on America's position in the hierarchy of states. Before the Civil War America had been an up-and-coming power on the margins of an international system still dominated by the Europeans. By the end of the century, however, it was a force to be reckoned with – in control of the world's largest economy by the 1890s, and in possession of something that any self-respecting nation had to have to confer great power status on it: some overseas colonies and a blue-water navy.[7]

Naturally enough, all this frenetic activity on one side of the Atlantic did not go unnoticed on the other. For years, influential thinkers in Europe – perhaps the most famous being Alexis de Tocqueville – had been fascinated with the very exceptional character of America. But it was only after the Civil War that Europeans really began to wonder what the rise of this new economic behemoth would mean for them. Many, of course, found the very idea of America a deeply attractive one, most obviously those described on the base of the Statue of Liberty as your 'tired, your poor, your huddled masses yearning to breathe free'. However, some in Europe were perhaps a little less enamoured with the new republic with its 'commitment to equality and freedom from class restraints'. Indeed, certain elites on a continent where emperors still ruled, looked askance at this vulgar upstart.[8] Some indeed appeared to feel threatened by the rise of what one writer has aptly called this 'great imperium with the outlook of a great emporium'.[9] But as one sympathetic British writer noted at the time, whether the ruling establishments of Europe liked it or not, there was no hiding from what he called 'the greatest political, social, and commercial phenomenon of our times'. Europe might still have larger armies and its policy makers more foreign policy experience; its ancient capitals may have been more beautiful and its galleries and museums full of superior cultural artefacts. But the economic axis of the world was slowly but surely shifting westwards across the Atlantic. The European age was already beginning to come to an end: an American century was about to be born.[10]

One of the many myths that has surrounded the rise of the United States is that so consumed was it with the building of a new nation at home, that it had little time, and even less interest, in becoming involved in the affairs of others. Yet like all dynamic powers in history, as soon as it began to 'rise' America very quickly started to look for new fields to conquer. Indeed, even the United States itself was the result of either conquest or purchase: first, of land once occupied by Native Americans, then of a whole swathe of territory once controlled by France (the Louisiana purchase of 1803), then of those parts of the American land mass originally under Mexican rule, and finally by the relatively peaceful acquisition of Oregon (from the British) and Alaska (from Russia). Moreover, the ideological drive behind all this was really no different from that supporting European expansion elsewhere: namely, a belief in racial hierarchy in which the superior white race was only proving its right to rule by dominating others who were not.[11]

Nor, of course, were US leaders (almost entirely Anglo by heritage) indifferent to the opportunities that lay outside America's original borders. Isolationism is a term frequently used to describe America's world outlook. However, there was nothing particularly isolationist about its behaviour when President Monroe decided in 1823 to lay claim to the whole of South America, or when 30 years later Admiral Perry forced Japan at the point of a gun to open up its markets, or when in 1898 President McKinley enthusiastically waged war against Spain, in the process acquiring the territories of Cuba, Puerto Rico and the Philippines (and Hawaii from the Hawaiians in the same year). Nor, one suspects, would Washington, Hamilton or Jefferson have disapproved of all this muscular activity. Indeed, the once standard tale of an anti-imperial nation born in innocence and reluctant to become 'entangled' in the world turns out on closer examination to be little more than a children's fairy tale served up to the unwary as a means of obscuring what even the Founding Fathers knew to be true: that America was born out of the defeat of one empire and had every intention of creating one of its own. As one of the more original writers on American history has pointed out, 'empire was consistently on the mind of early American state builders'.[12] They may have called it an 'empire of liberty' while others later preferred terms like 'insular' empire or even a forgotten empire without a 'consciousness of itself'.[13] Either way, this was still an empire but with one very obvious difference: many Americans denied it was one.[14]

If the century before 1914 was one in which American leaders were more concerned with constructing a nation (without ever ignoring the opportunities presented to them elsewhere), in the years which followed they had no alternative but to become ever more involved in the international system. Global war, the collapse of the old international order in which the European powers had for long been dominant, and the rise of revolutionary states like Russia championing a distinctly un-American ideology, provided the US both with a huge challenge but an even greater opportunity to enlarge its weight in the world. Here again, though, myth mingles with fact, producing a comforting narrative in which America, we are told, became ever more powerful but without meaning or wanting to. Moreover, having established itself as a major global presence it was, we are told once again, always trying to divest itself of its responsibilities. Few great powers in history have ever refused to be greater still. However, in the American case, it seems it either had greatness thrust on it, or, like the British Empire, acquired its power in a fit of absent-mindedness. Indeed, if we are to believe more orthodox accounts, America has been one of the most reluctant great powers in history with few ambitions of its own other than to stay at home and tend to its own garden.[15]

How and why this particular narrative ever became as influential as it did is an interesting story in its own right, as interesting perhaps as to why it came under sustained attack by an up-and-coming generation of more critical historians writing in the 1960s. But both schools of thought did, and presumably still do, agree on one thing: that the outcomes of the three great wars of the 20th century were not only determined by American intervention but went on to transform America's position in the world as well. Some Americans may have resisted getting pulled into conflicts fought on distant continents. But every time it did so, it invariably emerged stronger.[16] Thus when war broke out in 1914 it was still a debtor nation with little influence in Europe. By 1918 it had become the saviour of the Old World as well as being its banker. In 1940 it was still in the economic doldrums while declaring its neutrality from wars then raging across Asia and Europe. By 1945 with the rest of the world in rubble, and its own economy twice the size of what it had been five years earlier, it found itself sitting astride the globe like some colossus. In 1947 it faced threats and challenges on many fronts. By 1991 it was without peer competitor with its alliances intact, a commanding military lead over all possible rivals, an economy representing close to 30 per cent of world GDP situated in a wider international system which had never been so secure. As one seasoned observer noted 20 years later (when the world was a good deal less secure) what a peculiarly favourable time it was with, among other things, Germany just having been 'reunified peacefully', its 'partners in the European Union' moving toward economic integration', China 'absorbed' at home, and 'Iraq' having been 'humbled by recent defeat in the Gulf War'. By any measure, this was a moment to savour: another American century seemed to beckon, and as we shall see, it initially fell to Bill Clinton a two-term governor of one of America's least populous state – Arkansas – with almost no foreign policy experience to try and realize it.[17]

PART I

Clinton: Liberal Leviathan

I became engaged in thinking about Clinton's foreign policy largely because I could not understand why so many American writers on the subject had very little that was positive to say about what he was attempting to do in a world no longer shaped by the Cold War. 'Incoherent', 'lacking in strategic clarity' and 'without direction' were perhaps some of the more charitable things said about the former governor from Arkansas who was now sitting in the White House. Some of the criticism was reasonable enough. But a good deal of it, I felt, either came from realists who did not much appreciate a liberal running US foreign policy, or Republicans who were unhappy that Bush Snr – a foreign policy president if ever there was one – had lost the election in 1992 to someone who by his own admission had little or no international experience. Either way, what I set out to do was try and make sense of how the Clinton administration tackled some of the big challenges facing the US. Three seemed to me to be critical at the time, the most important of which was how to develop a 'grand strategy' that would allow the United States to compete more effectively in an increasingly globalized economy. Linked to this was a second initiative: the promotion of democracy both as an end in itself but also as a means of achieving international stability and global prosperity. And the third piece of the puzzle – on which Clinton spent an inordinate amount of time – was how to bring about a transition in post-communist Russia so as to prevent it becoming (as it subsequently did under Putin) an authoritarian enemy of the West.

1

From Geopolitics to Geo-Economics?[1]

Ask not what your country can do for you, ask what exporting can do for your country and you.[2]

One of the observations repeatedly made about American foreign policy after the end of the Cold War was that its primary point of reference gradually, but perceptibly, shifted away from a concentration on more traditional security matters to a new agenda, in which the main preoccupation now was less to worry about 'the Soviet bear in the woods' and more to focus on how it could compete more effectively in an increasingly globalized economy. Indeed, according to this view, the United States had previously been unable to do so because of the constraints imposed on it by the superpower conflict. As the US Trade Representative Mickey Kantor observed, prior to 1989 the United States had 'often neglected' its 'economic and trading interests because of foreign policy and defense concerns'.[3] But it would no longer be doing so, he argued, and henceforth would be pursuing its material goals without the Cold War compromising its economic interests.

Naturally enough, in this new environment, the rules of what one economist termed the 'new game' were bound to change.[4] So too were US needs as it quickly became clear that America's main assets in the new world order were not so much rockets, tanks and warheads, as were its trained workers, educated entrepreneurs and high-tech industries. Moreover, the object of the game now was not to prevent the spread of an alien ideology, but rather to maintain and, where possible, increase market share. This, however, did not make it any the less serious as a contest. For if the United States succeeded in 'winning' the economic battle it would mean domestic prosperity and continued influence abroad. But failure could easily lead to decline internationally and rising social tensions at home. The stakes in the post-communist era were every bit as high as they had been during the Cold War itself.[5]

This somewhat oversimplified picture obviously requires some qualification. Military power, after all, did not become completely irrelevant after the end of the Cold War, no more than did the threat posed by the spread of nuclear weapons and what Washington defined as 'backlash states'. Nor, of course, had the United States been indifferent to economic questions before. A powerful case could be made, in fact, that had it not been for American economic strength, containment might not have been successful. However, it was only with the withering away of the superpower conflict that policy makers in general, and the president in particular, were able to focus more completely on economic issues. Indeed, it would have been odd if they had not done so. It was, after all, a short-lived economic recession that delivered Clinton the White House in the first place; it was Clinton's focus on 'the economy, stupid'[6] that made his campaign the successful one it was, and by getting the economy right, Clinton also hoped to guarantee himself more than one term in office. So it was hardly surprising that as president he came to concentrate as intensely as he did on making Americans more prosperous and America more competitive.[7]

In what follows, I attempt to explore the movement from one era defined by 'geopolitics' to another shaped by what I term here as 'geo-economics'. The first part outlines Clinton's political economy. Next, I examine some of the key figures who helped set Clinton's economic agenda. This is followed by a consideration of some of the many practical implications of his approach. Finally, we look at some of the problems involved with implementing his international economic policies.

Clinton's political economy

One of the more enduring myths about Bill Clinton was that because he entered office without much foreign policy experience, he therefore had no clear idea of what he might do when he became president. Nothing could be further from the truth. Indeed, Clinton (like Ronald Reagan) assumed office with a fairly clear view of the world and the sorts of policies he would have to pursue in order to enhance American power. Of course, unlike Reagan, his main interest was not in 'the evil empire' but in the world economy, and the principal means he hoped to use to mobilize Americans behind his policies was not by attacking an enemy that had disappeared anyway by 1991 but 'raw economic self-interest'.[8] Moreover, by linking the material aspirations of ordinary Americans to the pursuit of his wider economic goals, Clinton calculated that he would be able to counter any drift to isolationism. To this degree, his call for America to 'compete, not retreat' had as much a political purpose as an economic one.[9]

Central to the Clinton administration's vision of America's new role in the world was the notion that in an era of geo-economics no distinction could be drawn between domestic politics and foreign policy. If the United States was not economically strong at home, he insisted, it was bound to be 'weaker abroad'. Nations that were 'stagnant', Clinton argued, lost 'the ability to finance military readiness, afford an activist foreign policy, or inspire allies by example'. The primary foreign policy task, therefore, was not to go out and fight unnecessary wars abroad, but instead build the United States from the ground up through a series of well-coordinated economic measures – beginning with deficit reduction, continuing with a marked shift from defence spending to infrastructural investment in education and training, and moving forward over the longer term with government encouragement to key high-technology industries deemed to be vital to US power.

What Clinton referred to as a 'high-wage, high-growth economy' could not be built in isolation, however. From this perspective isolationism as a policy option made no sense whatsoever, especially for a nation that was more closely integrated into the world economy than at any time in its history. When one in seven American jobs was linked to trade, when US investments overseas amounted to several hundred billion dollars and when the country's future prosperity depended very directly on the health of the international economy, the United States could hardly start thinking about distancing itself from the world. The real question for the Clinton administration, therefore, was not how to disentangle the United States from the international system, but rather, how to make itself a more competitive actor in it.[10]

From this logically flowed a renewed emphasis on successfully competing in world markets. Increasing its share of world exports had always been one of America's goals (by the early 1990s it was selling annually well over $400 billion worth of goods and services abroad). But now promoting trade almost seemed to be synonymous with US foreign policy itself. Nor was this a passing fad, involving as it did what one leading official called a 'change in mind set as significant as any that has taken place in [our] nation's history'. Indeed, in the new era, trade policy according to Jeffrey Garten, one of his advisers, was now to be 'linked to virtually all aspects of American life: to jobs, to stable communities, to research and development programs, to new directions in education', even 'to health care reform where lower cost burdens on business [were] so important to competitiveness'.[11]

To be competitive, however, it was vital to rethink the relationship between government and business. For too long, according to the Clinton administration, US business had not received the support it needed or deserved – especially from the Republicans who for ideological reasons had been strongly opposed to the state being a major player in economic matters. But in a cut-throat world economy where governments in other countries were actively promoting business, the United States simply could not afford the luxury of laissez-faire. This might have been feasible when it had been economically preponderant, but was simply counterproductive when it was under serious economic challenge from both Europe and Japan. In this sense, the redistribution of economic power towards its main competitors during the 1970s and 1980s meant that America had no alternative but to construct a more intimate partnership between government and industry.[12]

Finally, Clinton's political economy rested on an assumption that the United States had to be at the heart of a regionalized world economy. Though Clinton was building here on an agenda sketched out by Bush, he pursued this particular objective with much greater determination and purpose. He was certainly more forthright in public debate in explaining why achieving this goal was so critical for the United States. It would, he asserted, ensure continued US leadership of the world economic system; it would guarantee that the various actors in the international economy played by US rules; and it would facilitate the movement towards a more open world economy on which future US prosperity and influence depended.[13]

Economists in the White House

Many of Clinton's key appointments gave a clear indication of the sorts of policies he might be pursuing. There was, of course, the usual sprinkling of lawyers and Wall Street financiers, including the powerful Robert Rubin. But many of his more interesting appointees came from the field of international economics, and a number were specialists in precisely those areas – trade access and competitiveness – that were to dominate the foreign economic policy agenda after 1992.

Perhaps the most commented-on, and criticized, of Clinton's early appointments was Laura D'Andrea Tyson, whose 1992 study *Who's Bashing Whom? Trade Conflict in High-Technology Industries* had already created an international stir. Tyson, who became Chair of the Council of Economic Advisers, never claimed that the main cause of US trade problems was unfair trading practices by other countries in general, and Japan in particular. Rather, US problems, she insisted, were the logical consequence of 'flawed domestic choices'. She did claim, however (and this certainly had policy implications), that 'traditional approaches to trade and domestic policy' which had 'served the nation well when American companies had an unrivalled technological lead' were now 'no longer adequate'. Indeed, it seemed as if in a number of key sectors including aircraft, telecommunications, electronics and supercomputers other economies were doing rather well, and were doing so in large part because they were playing by a different set of economic rules. The United States thus had to take decisive action, and devise what Tyson called new 'macroeconomic, trade and industrial policies' to promote America's high-technology industries.[14]

This call for what amounted to managed trade and an industrial policy made Tyson's views unpopular among more conservative economists. They were even more upset by her somewhat sceptical attitude towards the efficacy of free markets. The market, she insisted, could not reverse America's economic fortunes. Indeed, the main conclusion of her influential study was that the United States simply could not 'afford the soothing but irrelevant position that market forces alone' could solve America's problems. A more interventionist approach would be necessary.[15]

Tyson's focus on high-technology trade conflict with Japan was partially mirrored in the acclaimed work of influential trade official Jeffrey E. Garten.[16] In *A Cold Peace: America, Japan, Germany, and the Struggle for Supremacy* Garten concentrated on the new economic challenges facing the United States.[17] Though more popular in presentation and having as much to say about Germany as Japan, Garten's book agreed with Tyson that the threat facing the United States was now quite different from what it had been before. According to Garten, the country was confronted with important allies who were seriously challenging American economic hegemony; and all this in a context where the old rules about trade were breaking down. In this new era, America, he accepted, had been impelled to adopt a 'policy of managed trade'. But this did not appear to concern him so much as what he saw as the growing potential for 'cumulative economic tensions' between 'the big three' centres of power in the modern world economy. And without advocating an outright trade war against either Germany or Japan – most of his policy proposals were in fact designed to prevent such an outcome – he believed that the United States had to prepare itself for the economic battles ahead. In the new world order where economics was power (and American power by this definition was under challenge) the United States had to view trade issues in clear 'strategic terms'. In Garten's view, it was entirely reasonable to pursue a more 'aggressive' and self-interested 'nationalist' line in economic matters. Indeed, only by doing so could the country's 'national economic strength' be significantly enhanced.[18]

The idea of economics as security was also the central theme in Theodore Moran's 1993 study *American Economic Policy and National Security*.[19] Moran, who worked as senior adviser to the Policy Planning Staff during Clinton's first year, was possibly one of the most sombre analysts of the American economic scene.[20] The United States, he noted, faced at least three overlapping but 'conceptually distinct threats': a fundamental and cumulative economic decline relative to the other major industrial states; a loss of crucial economic and technological capabilities within the United States itself; and a growing dependence on other countries for vital goods. On these issues at least he was at one with Tyson. But unlike Tyson, Moran focused most of his analytic attention on proposals designed to bring about 'fundamental changes in American behaviour', rather than advocating what he termed 'neo-mercantilist policies' designed to shore up high-tech sectors or increase US trade access. He warned in fact against such policies, arguing that if the United States concentrated on getting short-term results instead of 'rebalancing America's mix of savings, consumption and investment', this could easily lead to a 'deterioration of the United States' international position'.

Finally, in this pantheon of economic influentials, one should include Clinton's close friend, Secretary of Labor Robert Reich. Reich, who had previously taught business and public policy at Harvard, was the author of several books on political economy in which the dominant theme had been American economic decline and the main argument that new policies were required to reverse it.[21] Though by no means a consistent thinker, his influence on the Clinton administration should not be underestimated. One idea of his in particular – globalization – played a crucial role in helping shape Clinton's economic outlook.

According to Reich, the nation-state as an economic unit had lost a good deal of its meaning; there was effectively no such thing as a distinct or separate American economy. As he put it in a famous debate with Tyson, in the modern world market, 'us' no longer existed. The administration had some doubts about this proposition, but it did accept some of the implications of Reich's thesis. First, it agreed that if America was, as Reich argued, a 'region' of a wider 'global economy', then it was quite impossible for the United States to escape from it. Isolationism was therefore economically inconceivable. It was also prepared to accept the equally Reichian notion that, in the new global economy, inequality within nations was bound to increase. It was thus one of the tasks of government to address the social consequences of globalization and by so doing maintain an American sense of community. Finally, in this new order, where companies had 'no particular connection to any single nation', the duty of the state was not just to protect the weak, but also to help retrain those who were the victims of economic progress. If globalization was inevitable, as Reich insisted it was, then it was imperative that the Clinton administration worked out ways of ensuring that all Americans could partake of its benefits. This not only made good sociological sense (after all, no country wanted a large and potentially dangerous unskilled underclass inhabiting its cities), it also made economic sense insofar as it would guarantee America a better-educated, and over the long term, a more productive workforce.[22]

Clinton and his critics

Viewed by their many critics as being both economic nationalists as well as 'big government liberals', the incoming Clinton team were undoubtedly the most economically focused ever to have come to office in the post-war period. Their concentration on creating more high-paid jobs inevitably made them popular with organized labour. However, they also received a fair amount of backing from US business, especially from those in high-technology industries or with major interests overseas. As one of Clinton's more vehement critics was forced to admit, by the time he took over from Bush Snr Clinton had more 'support from the business community than any Democrat since Johnson'.[23] Nor was this so surprising. With his tough-minded approach to public spending and his laser-like focus on getting the economy moving (within two years of becoming president employment had started to rise and those long-standing deficits had begun to fade away), Clinton soon became Wall Street's favourite.

Meanwhile, Clinton's assertive economic policies, designed to make the US more competitive abroad, soon translated into policy. In his first month in office, for example, he threatened to block US sales to the government of European telecommunications and power-generated equipment, charging that the European Community had conducted a 'buy-Europe' policy against American products. In January 1993 the United States ruled that Japan and 18 other countries had been dumping steel products on the American market – a move condemned by the UK Department of Trade and Industry as 'outrageous harassment'. Additional moves were then contemplated against Europe and Japan, with the US demanding 'results' from the latter while threatening the former with various sanctions if it did not open up its market to US goods and services. Naturally enough, Europe and Japan responded in kind, and by mid-1993 there was a fear in some quarters that the situation was fast getting out of hand.[24]

These concerns were mirrored in (and in part exacerbated by) a withering barrage of press criticism directed against Clinton's trade policies. In early 1993, for instance, *The New York Times* complained of a 'growing tension in trade relations' caused, in its view, by the President's 'new and more confrontational approach'. *The Wall Street Journal* (no friend of the Democrats) then accused the administration of caring 'less about principle than about making a political deal'. *The Economist*, not surprisingly, was even more scathing. Washington's approach, it asserted, was 'at best incompetent and at worst a step down the slippery path towards protectionism'. One noted British admirer of the United States (though not of Clinton) actually went so far as to suggest that the White House had been taken over by 'economic delinquents'. Writing in the *Financial Times*, Michael Prowse roundly condemned an administration that professed multilateralism in theory but in practice acted as 'judge and jury' on the world in general and the Japanese in particular. Prowse concluded that the United States was now being run by people who believed that the country was involved in some sort of 'race with Japan and the European Union' to determine who would be economically supreme in the 21st century. And he added, more in sorrow than in anger, that Clinton intended to 'take the gold'.[25]

The many charges levelled at Clinton reflected a combination of factors, including free-market opposition to a government summit which promised to play a more active role in economic affairs, a deep and abiding dislike by many of 'managed trade' and, among his several foreign critics, a belief that Clinton was an old-fashioned economic imperialist who hoped (in the words of one journalist) to 'beat the world into economic submission'.[26] The most celebrated critique of Clinton's foreign economic policy, however, was penned by MIT economist Paul Krugman. In what many regarded as a seminal article published in *Foreign Affairs* in early 1994, Krugman took the administration to task not merely for attempting to gain comparable access to foreign markets, but for even being concerned with the question of competitiveness. The 'idea that a country's economic fortunes' were largely determined by its success on world markets was a 'hypothesis, not a necessary truth', according to Krugman. Thus the whole Clinton agenda was based on a false theoretical assumption. In Krugman's view, moreover, the commitment to competitiveness was 'not only wrong but dangerous' and could easily skew domestic policies and threaten the very stability of the whole international economic system. A halt had to be called, therefore, to this new 'obsession': an obsession which in his opinion could easily lead to a 'wasteful spending of government money', 'bad public policy on a spectrum of important issues', and possibly 'protectionism and trade wars'.[27]

From NAFTA to the Uruguay round

Clinton's various critics were extremely vocal. But in one area at least they had to concede that he was extraordinarily successful during 1993: namely in the promotion of the cause of world trade expansion. Indeed, in a series of really quite bold moves, Clinton pushed forward on at least three economic fronts during his first year in office. This led to the signing of the North American Free Trade Agreement (NAFTA) in November. In the same month Clinton then met with other leaders from the Pacific Rim in an attempt to breathe new life into Asia-Pacific Economic Cooperation (APEC). And after seven years' negotiation in the Uruguay Round, the General Agreement on Tariffs and Trade (GATT) was signed in Brussels in December. Taken together, the two agreements and the APEC summit constituted one of the great watersheds of the Clinton presidency; but it all began with NAFTA.[28]

NAFTA

NAFTA had many goals, not just the more obvious ones of increasing the volume of world trade and improving US access to the critical Mexican market (Mexico being America's fastest-growing major export market, its second largest market for manufactured goods, and its third largest for agricultural products). Another main objective, clearly, was to institutionalize and, it was hoped, accelerate Mexico's continued transition towards a more open liberal market economy. This, it was reasoned, would promote political stability, which in turn would encourage a large inflow of new, as well as a return of old, capital that had fled the country in the early 1980s. And, if things went according to plan, the new Mexico would act as a beacon and an inspiration for other Latin American countries, encouraging them to continue down the road to free-market capitalism, so destroying their left-wing, nationalist proclivities once and for all.

Having successfully negotiated NAFTA through Congress (going against a large section of his own party to do so) Clinton was now in a strong position to press ahead with the much larger GATT agreement. Between the NAFTA vote and the GATT signing, however, came APEC.

APEC

Though nowhere near as significant as NAFTA in the short term, it was hoped that APEC would one day evolve into something much more important. As Mickey Kantor noted, though most people had probably never heard of APEC before 1993 – it had held its first meeting in Australia in November 1989 – he wagered that this would change in the next few years. As it matured and developed it would, he argued, play several key roles, acting as a 'forum for consultations on trade policy' and as a vehicle through which the United States could encourage the expansion of trade and investment. As the fastest growing area in the world economy, and the number one export destination for American products, the United States could hardly ignore the Asia-Pacific. But it still needed an organization through which it could try to guide the region's destiny; and APEC was the chosen medium for this.[29]

In itself APEC had little immediate impact on the US trade position. But it did signal an American commitment to the wider cause of multilateralism in an area that was not only vital economically but undergoing critical political change. APEC also sent a warning shot across European bows, letting them know, in effect, that the United States had important economic interests in other parts of the world and that if Europe did not sign up to the forthcoming GATT there might be serious repercussions. One unnamed French Foreign Ministry official was clearly less than impressed by this American attempt to bully Europe by appearing to tilt towards Asia. 'The thinly veiled US threats about having Asia as an alternative to Europe are absurd,' he argued. 'It's almost as if France said it no longer cared about the United States because most of our trade was with other European

Community countries.' Not surprisingly, US officials had a more positive attitude towards a summit which they felt had helped clear away some of the considerable obstacles still standing in the way of a final GATT agreement.[30]

GATT

The GATT deal in December 1993 was the result of many factors, both objective, in terms of the beneficial impact the agreement would have on world trade, and subjective, in the form of Peter Sutherland (the Director General of GATT) who played a vital part in negotiations during the last six months. But an equally critical role was played by Mickey Kantor ,US trade representative, and Sir Leon Brittan, the European Union's trade commissioner. Sir Leon managed to convince the Americans that the fractious and hydra-headed EU could actually deliver an agreement, while Kantor applied sufficient pressure on the Europeans to make them move ahead. Certainly, without their combined contribution GATT might not have been signed.[31]

The GATT agreement had its winners and losers. It also involved a good degree of compromise on the American side. According to most seasoned commentators, in fact, it was Europe and not the United States that gained most from the deal. Naturally, a number of questions remained unresolved, including the contentious issue of workers' rights and labour standards. But GATT was still a great achievement for the Clinton administration and its much-criticized tough approach to trade. It was also likely to lead to a massive increase in world trade over the next ten years: between $230 billion and $274 billion according to one estimate, and $745 billion according to the GATT Secretariat.[32] Finally, its success brought the developing nations (those which held the greatest growth potential for US companies) more completely into the traditional trading system. As Garten, a one-time sceptic about GATT, pointed out, although this meant that the new emerging markets would have 'enhanced obligations', it also implied that they would now 'have a fair shot at access to the industrialised country markets' as well. This was good news for them, for the world economy, and above all for the United States.[33]

Transforming government

The Clinton administration's support for GATT and the cause of 'open regionalism' was part of a broader strategy to establish a more dynamic global economy, within which it was hoped US companies would be able to compete successfully. But they could only compete, it was argued, if they developed a more intimate relationship with government. To give meaning to this new partnership, important reforms were necessary in the way in which government itself operated. In September 1993 the Trade Promotion Coordinating Committee, chaired by Ron Brown of the Commerce Department, published its key study, *Toward a National Export Strategy*, which was designed to have a big impact on the way in which government functioned.[34] Viewed by the administration itself as establishing a framework 'for an unprecedented strengthening' of America's 'export promotion efforts' (and by others as a new name for old-style neomercantilism), the document stood at the heart of the Clinton administration's approach to international economic affairs. Though not as original as its authors claimed, it certainly impelled those working for government to think and act far more 'economically' than they had done before. Consequently, US embassy staff up to ambassadorial level were given enhanced business support. A new economics-oriented curriculum for Foreign Service Officer training was introduced. Even those working in the 'caring' foreign policy sectors, such as aid and development, were urged to calculate precisely how their work helped to advance US economic interests. Indeed, the whole atmosphere in Washington changed during 1993 as government started to get more closely involved in the business of helping American business succeed.

But it was within the newly enhanced Commerce Department itself that this metamorphosis was most visible. What Brown called this 'enormous untapped potential' went through a renaissance under his leadership, effectively being transformed from an organizational backwater to an important policy player. Working on the assumption that exports not only had been but would continue to be the most significant element in the expansion of America's GDP (having accounted for 55 per cent economic growth between 1987 and 1993 while creating more and better jobs), the department laid out what amounted to a blueprint for improving government support for US exporters in an age of increased competition.

Briefly, the new export strategy called on all those involved in export promotion to identify 'client groups' more effectively and focus in a more determined way on 'meeting customer needs'. In order to 'improve service' to potential customers, however, it was vital to use the resources of both the private sector and local government more effectively, and to reduce or eliminate 'government-imposed impediments to exports'. This involved quite important changes, including the elimination of most preexisting export controls (except where these were deemed to be in the national interest). Significantly, in this area, the Commerce Department recommended a speedy liberalization of export controls on critical, normally high-value items, especially 'computers and telecommunication products'.

Taken together, these changes, it was hoped, would create a more streamlined governmental machine designed for an age in which economic success or failure in world markets would determine America's future. Brown himself was in no doubt about the significance of these various reforms.

Indeed, at the end of his first year in office, he thought they represented his 'proudest achievement'.[35]

Transforming research

To make America competitive it was vital not only to develop a coherent national export strategy but to implement economic reforms at home; and one of the most critical reforms contemplated by the Clinton administration (apart from deficit reduction) was in the area of federal support for research and development (R&D). Not only would a new type of partnership have to be established between the government and industrial research, but the government itself would have to rethink what sort of research it would support in a post-Cold War era. After all, what was the point of investing vast amounts of money in defence-related research (even as late as 1992 defence still consumed 60 per cent of government support for R&D) while spending on defence itself was declining as a percentage of GNP? This was seen not only as unnecessary but as an inefficient use of scarce resources that would be much better deployed enhancing the country's economic status in the world.

Clinton thus set out to change the balance in federal support between non-military and military R&D, and in 1992 announced that within six years there would be parity of esteem between the two sectors. This would involve cuts in military R&D accompanied by a gradual but measurable increase in spending on civilian R&D by 30 per cent over five years. But simply altering the balance was not enough: unless the right industries were targeted, the new partnership between the state and the private sector would lose all credibility. Thus a number of prototype projects were launched, one of the first being a $1.3 billion research grant to the big three car-makers in September 1993 to develop a vehicle that would be environmentally friendly (Gore's 'green car'). This was followed in the next year by other grants to industry: $1 billion to develop a high-performance computer and $2 billion for materials research. Another $2.3 billion was set aside in 1994 to encourage education in science, maths, engineering and technological subjects. The administration also announced a $1 billion package in April 1994 to fund the development and manufacture of flat panel displays as used in the increasingly lucrative portable computer market. The eventual goal here was to establish four large-scale manufacturing sites in the US with a view to supplying about one sixth of world demand.[36]

Nevertheless, a number of questions remained unanswered about this particular aspect of the administration's policy to enhance American economic power. One, clearly, was how far it would actually be able to go in reducing government spending on research for defence – a sector which had many vocal supporters in Congress. Equally, it was uncertain whether a Republican-controlled Congress would be prepared to support expensive research on non-military R&D to the degree necessary to achieve results. Finally, there were many who believed that even if Clinton could alter the whole research agenda and overcome congressional opposition, it would be quite foolish to waste money on a strategy that could never work. Thus many barriers remained to be overcome before scientific and technological research in the US could be fully 'Clintonized'.[37]

'Big emerging markets'

The Clinton administration's proposed programme of gradually switching government R&D away from the military clearly could not produce quick results. It focused, therefore, on those policies which could; and one policy it pursued with great purpose was to target what it called the big emerging markets, or BEMs. Ten such had been identified by the end of 1992. Significantly, five of these were in Asia (Indonesia, India, South Korea, China – including Taiwan – and Hong Kong), and three (Mexico, Brazil and Argentina) in Latin America. The others were Poland, Turkey and South Africa. Though these were not seen as alternatives to more traditional and much larger markets such as Canada, Japan or Western Europe, they were all regarded as critical areas of growth into the 21st century. Commerce Department planners, for example, estimated that by the year 2000 US trade with these ten countries could easily exceed that with Europe and Japan combined. The CIA also stressed the importance of the BEMs, and in one report calculated that between 1994 and 2010 they would account for something like 44 per cent of non-US growth in world imports.

Having identified its target countries, the United States set out to woo the BEMs with great determination. Revealing the same energy it had shown in Saudi Arabia in February 1994 (when after intense lobbying it had won a $6 billion order for American planes), Washington seemed prepared to use all means necessary to maximize market share.[38] One example of this more assertive US strategy was furnished by its trade activities in Brazil. Looking on Brazil's economic potential as being huge over the longer term, the ever-active Commerce Department, under Ron Brown's guidance, consciously set out to extend its economic ties to the largest nation in Latin America. In June 1994 Brown led a high-profile American trade mission to Brazil, accompanied as usual by a large number of executives from some of the biggest US corporations. In Sao Paolo, he also opened a new $2 million American commerce centre, noting in the ceremonial speech that the city had 'as many consumers as the whole of Argentina put together'. He also drew his audience's attention to the 'vital and growing importance' of US trade, with Latin America as a whole. And if current trends continued, the continent, he argued, would one day overtake Europe as the main trading partner of the United States. In negotiations with the Brazilian government, Brown then deployed his not inconsiderable bargaining skills in helping the United States to win a major surveillance project (SIVAM: System for Vigilance over the Amazon), consisting of a mixed satellite/aircraft/radar system that would allow Brazilians to spot environmental degradation in the Amazon basin, to be more effective in drug interdiction, and that would serve other land use planning purposes.[39]

Another significant American foray was into Indonesia, like Brazil a huge and important country with a long-standing security relationship with the United States. Here both Clinton and Brown played an active part in winning orders for American firms, most notably during and just after the APEC summit in November 1994. Clinton was quite forthright and while preaching the virtues of Pacific cooperation to his neighbours, announced (without any hint of irony) that the US was engaged in cut-throat economic competition with its overseas rivals. He also emphasized that his administration, 'in contrast to previous' ones, would be 'unashamedly active in helping' American business abroad. No quarter would be expected and none given. As if to underline the seriousness of American intentions, Ron Brown (fresh from economic triumphs in Malaysia and the Philippines, where he had just acquired $650 million worth of business for US companies) signed a number of contracts and memoranda with Indonesia valued at over $40 billion. The biggest winner of all was the American oil giant, Exxon Corporation Exploration. As a result of US government efforts on its behalf, it signed a basic agreement valued at nearly $35 billion with Indonesia's state-owned oil company, Pertamina.[40]

US successes in Indonesia were in part the result of a new credit facility offered by the Clinton administration. Involving government-to-government concessional financing linked to the purchase of donor country exports, the so-called Tied Aid credit offer was specifically designed to counter foreign competition by levelling the financial playing-field for US exporters. This same facility proved equally effective in India, and within two years of Ron Brown taking over the US had signed several deals with Delhi using this particular economic vehicle. Moreover, having identified India as one of the biggest of the new BEMs, the administration vigorously supported American firms to the tune of $300 million per annum. Ron Brown also led a large US trade delegation to India in January 1995. He began his economic tour with what one observer later described as an 'inspired piece of theatre'. This involved a visit to the site of Mahatma Gandhi's cremation on the birthday of the Indian leader's most celebrated American disciple, Martin Luther King. By the time Brown flew home, it looked as if he had won at least $7 billion of Indian business. Contained within this overall package was an order to supply seven out of the eight big 'fast-track' power generation projects destined to be constructed in India. It also included a deal involving the telecommunications company US West – the first privately operated corporation allowed to invest in the still backward (but potentially huge) Indian telecommunications market. More business looked likely to follow, and the Commerce Department was predicting $20 billion of new American investment by the year 2000 plus a rise in US exports to $5–6 billion annually – double the 1994 level.[41]

Finally, there was perhaps the biggest 'emerging market' of them all: China. As we show in the next chapter, Clinton made great play during his presidential campaign of attacking Bush Snr for having 'coddled' the Chinese dictatorship. Yet, once in office he virtually reversed course and by 1994 had de-linked human rights from the award of Most Favoured Nation status to China, arguing that while China had not made significant progress on many of the more sensitive political issues, a tough human rights policy was hampering the ability of the US to pursue other interests, including gaining access to the potentially huge China market. Backed by the majority of US corporations but opposed by a number of labour unions who feared that any deal with low-wage China would lead to a loss of jobs at home, Clinton was in little doubt that trading with China and pulling it into the global economy was the only way to go. There were perhaps wider geopolitical reasons for doing so. But as the American writer Thomas Friedman so pithily put it, 'in the end economic interests won the day. It wasn't really even close [...]'.[42]

Conclusion

In its first few years in office the Clinton administration demonstrated a real determination to reverse what many of its more influential members saw as the nation's economic decline and go on to win what some of them also conceived of as the struggle for economic supremacy in the late 20th century. But in spite of Clinton's energetic, indeed aggressive, pursuit of US economic interests, there were still a number of problems with his strategy.

The first was that being energetic alone did not necessarily get rid of trade imbalances. Indeed, in spite of the continuing growth in US exports (in 1994 they expanded by over 10 per cent), the United States still continued to carry a huge trade deficit of $166 billion. According to some economists this was neither particularly significant nor a reason for gloom. Nevertheless, so long as the deficit persisted, there were bound to be those calling for ever tougher action to deal with it; and that carried within it the seeds of future conflicts with other nations.

Second, there was within the Clinton administration an unmistakeable tendency to use the issue of competitiveness almost as a substitute for dealing with the country's own economic problems. Here one could detect a certain tension, in fact, between those who recognized that the solution to US economic ills lay at home and others who focused the greater part of their efforts on confronting and beating competitors abroad. However, because the latter could promise results, they inevitably became the dominant voice inside the administration. Again, this did not bode well for America's economic relations with its various competitors.

This brings us then to the third major problem with his approach – a somewhat uncritical attitude towards globalization. The new global economy may well have lifted all boats, but as one of his advisers, Robert Reich, pointed out at the time, there would be just as many American losers as winners under conditions of unfettered free trade. Furthermore, even if Clinton proclaimed the virtues of global cooperation, many of the policies he pursued were very much designed with America in mind. This not only contained within it the seeds of future disagreements with other states; it also had the potential for weakening the bonds holding the major democracies together. The United States, after all, could hardly practise dollar diplomacy one day and then expect cooperation from its allies the next.

Finally, the US obsession with competitiveness posed an even larger question about its broader mission in the world. If America's primary purpose was to win the economic race, then how could this be reconciled with its historic goal of promoting democracy? No doubt Clinton hoped, and certainly argued, that as nations became more closely integrated into the world market, democracy would inevitably follow. Indeed, as we shall see in the following chapter, Clinton and some of those around him genuinely did think that promoting democracy would advance America's economic interests. But as shall be demonstrated, the relationship between Clinton's economic agenda, which we have discussed in this chapter, and his desire to spread the cause of freedom, which we will examine in more detail in the next, were never easy bedfellows. How uneasy, we shall now proceed to discuss.

2

The Wilsonian Moment?
Promoting Democracy[1]

At the end of the two great wars that did so much to define America's position within the international system, American leaders talked in grandiloquent terms about a future world order based on international law, justice for all and liberal values.[2] Just how seriously American policy makers took their own rhetoric has, of course, been the subject of a good deal of comment, and while supporters feel that US efforts to make the world a more enlightened place should be taken at face value, others have dismissed such pronouncements as so much rhetorical hot air. It was perhaps George Kennan, the 'father of containment', who more than anybody else, articulated the most persuasive critique of what he termed this 'diplomacy of dilettantism'.[3] In a far-reaching series of lectures delivered in the intellectual home of realism at the University of Chicago, Kennan did not pull his punches when it came to attacking those American leaders of the past – Woodrow Wilson most notably – who had always been inclined (he believed) to substitute hard thinking about the balance of power with idealistic statements about how the world ought to be, rather than how it was. In principle, there was nothing wrong with democracy as such or even promoting it. However, if the US defined this as its main goal, then this could easily lead to overreach at best, or at worst, conflict with those states which did not share American values. As one of Kennan's latter-day admirers put it, an American foreign policy 'motivated largely by liberal ideals' would very soon land the United States 'in trouble'.[4]

With the end of the Cold War, one might have predicted that this somewhat overheated debate would have died out. But this was not to be. Indeed, the apparent urge in some quarters to find a new post-Cold War 'mission' for the United States led to renewed speculation that America was once again succumbing to the old temptation of wanting to refashion the international system in its own liberal democratic image. George Bush Snr was more or less immune to this particular temptation.[5] The same, it was argued, could not be said of his successor, William Jefferson Clinton. Guided by his own liberal instincts, buoyed up by electoral victory over the Republicans in 1992, and keen to develop a 'doctrine' of his own in a world without a clear point of ideological opposition, Clinton, some feared, soon gave in to those calling for a new foreign policy based on liberal principles rather than considerations of power. As one of Clinton's many critics pointed out, while liberalism embodied a legitimate, 'enduring and uniquely American approach to foreign policy', as a tradition it had proven to be less than useful when it came to dealing with the 'real' world of autocratic enemies and friends, powerful economic competitors and limited American resources.[6]

In this chapter, I explore the many facets of democracy promotion as a grand strategy during the Clinton presidency. I begin by examining in some detail the fairly concrete reasons why his administration opted for the strategy of 'democratic enlargement' in the first place.[7] After that, I ask and try to answer the question: was the Clinton administration ever as idealistically committed to the promotion of democracy as its critics suggested? This brings us to a third issue: the complex relationship between democracy promotion and Clinton's stated goal of aggressively pursuing America's economic goals (a subject which we explored in Chapter 1). This is followed by an exploration of 'Wilsonianism' and trying to understand who the 'real' Woodrow Wilson actually was.[8] Finally, I want to take up an issue raised in the critically important volume by Michael Hunt on the relationship between ideology and US foreign policy.[9] In a major reinterpretation of American diplomatic history, Hunt suggests that the outlook of policy makers has been shaped less by a desire to advance democracy than by other, rather less idealistic, notions. Indeed, according to Hunt, it was not political freedom in general that has inspired the United States from the late 19th century onwards, but a fear of instability combined with a belief until the late 1960s at least in the natural hierarchy of races. Hunt may or may not be right, but his challenging argument forces us to confront the age-old issue of the extent to which America has ever had a singular mission to promote democracy. It also raises the equally important problem of what America actually 'exports' to the rest of the world. Democracy may indeed be part of the overall package, but as all presidents, including Clinton, have discovered, the United States is bound to promote more than just its highest political ideals.[10]

Clinton and the politics of promoting democracy

Bill Clinton was both the first elected post-Cold War president and the first 'new' Democrat to occupy the White House. More concerned with domestic issues than with international affairs, his most pressing task, as he perceived it, was to build on and extend his base of support at home and the most obvious means of achieving this was by focusing like the proverbial laser beam on the one issue which almost certainly won him power in 1992: the belief that he could more effectively manage the American economy than Bush Snr.[11] This in turn connected to another important consideration: a belief that if Bush lost in 1992 it was not because he was incompetent, but rather, was more interested in foreign policy than he ever was in domestic affairs. This not only convinced the new Clinton team that it had to approach international affairs with great care. It also made it very wary of being sucked into other people's conflicts in faraway places. Always sensitive to public opinion, and determined not to sacrifice his presidency on the altar of foreign wars, Clinton's foreign policy inclinations were from the outset extraordinarily cautious, even minimalist.[12]

This not illogical response by the Clinton administration to the world did not of course mean it had no foreign policy at all. Nor is to imply that Clinton himself was uninterested in international politics. Indeed, he made a number of attempts to articulate a vision for the world in his campaign to become president, notably in his Georgetown speech of December 1991. Nonetheless, his concentrated focus on the home front did leave him open to the charge of being indifferent to international affairs and unwilling to forge an overarching vision to guide the United States through the uncharted waters created by the end of the Cold War and the collapse of the Soviet Union.

It was this, in part, that led to what Douglas Brinkley has rather tellingly referred to as the 'Kennan sweepstakes',[13] a bureaucratically driven exercise organized in late 1993 to come up with a notion or phrase that would most accurately encapsulate the foreign policy design of the Clinton presidency. Fearful of rhetorical overkill, but concerned to show a degree of serious thinking about America's role in the world, the term ultimately decided on was 'democratic enlargement'. The phrase appeared to have many political advantages. It was conceptually simple; it pointed to the self-evident fact that with the end of the Cold War the possibilities of expanding the zone of political freedom had grown enormously; and, unlike all the self-proclaimed competitor phrases like 'clash of civilizations', it had a positive rather than a negative sound to it. It also had an end goal in mind, though one so distant that it would be almost impossible to know whether the policy was really succeeding. For an administration keen to keep negative foreign policy news off the airwaves and the front pages of the major newspapers, this was not an unimportant consideration.[14]

The point at which the notion of 'enlargement' became official policy is not entirely clear. The consensus would seem to be, however, that after some period of discussion – though much less than one would have expected – it was finally adopted in the autumn of 1993. It was certainly alluded to by the apparently less than enthusiastic Secretary of State, Warren Christopher, in a speech he made at Columbia University on 20 September 1993. It was then made the centrepiece of a far more important address made at the School of Advanced International Studies by Anthony Lake, Clinton's national security adviser. Two days later, Secretary of State Madeleine Albright referred to it in a speech at the Naval War College. And finally, in a keynote statement to the United Nations on 27 September, the president himself talked quite openly about America's 'overriding purpose' to 'expand and strengthen the world's community of market-based democracies'. Presumably having had three of his most important foreign policy advisers float the idea to largely academic gatherings, Clinton decided it was time to give the idea of enlargement the official seal of approval.[15]

The launch of any big foreign policy idea is of necessity a potentially problematic exercise. Other more pressing issues, like the cost of housing and interest rates, are likely to be of greater concern to the average American. Moreover, unless the idea in question can capture the public imagination or play on popular fears, it is likely to be greeted with indifference rather than enthusiasm – particularly so in a country whose people were not known for their interest in the outside world. No doubt for all these reasons the idea of 'enlargement' turned out to be what one observer has called a public relations dud, with few, it seems, taking more than 'a passing interest' in the possibility, as Lake put it, of strengthening and extending the 'community of core major market democracies'.[16] Even those who did take the trouble to decode its meaning could not detect anything especially original about it. Republicans in particular – though apparently not House Speaker Newt Gingrich – viewed the whole idea as little more than window dressing designed to hide the fact that the emperor was conceptually naked when it came to foreign policy. Certainly, the general consensus seemed to be that a great opportunity had been lost, and that, instead of permitting the US to make the necessary transition from containment to something more appropriate for the post-Cold War world, the whole exercise had led only to confusion.[17] Clinton and his foreign policy team may have done a lot of hard thinking but there was very little, it seemed, to show for it all. Lake in particular came in for some especially tough comment, and the conclusion seemed to be that, although he was a decent human being, he was no Henry Kissinger or even a Zbigniew Brzezinski. Concepts, it seemed, did not become him. He was, to use the title of a slashing review of the man who had set out to win the 'Kennan sweepstakes', Lake Inferior.[18]

Promoting democracy promotion

If the idea of 'enlargement' did not fire the imagination of the American people, it did even less perhaps to quieten Clinton's political enemies.[19] Even the more moderate figures within the foreign policy establishment had their doubts. This was perhaps to be expected. For a generation hand-reared on the truths of realism and the doctrine of power politics, the idea that a change in the form of other countries' governments would enhance US security must have sounded a little odd, especially coming from someone so inexperienced in the ways of the world as Bill Clinton.[20] The response by the White House to these various criticisms, however, was not to sound the retreat but to mount a fairly muscular defence of the policy. Refusing to see the world in simple binary terms in which there were fine moral principles on one side and the real world on the other, and convinced in its own mind that democracy promotion was not just some idealistic add-on but something that would actually enhance world order, the administration thus decided to soldier on – partly because it would have been politically damaging to have abandoned the policy, but more obviously because it felt there were good reasons to do so. The question was: why?

One small part of the answer lay in the American experience and the widely shared belief that the United States was not just a successful democracy but a shining example for others to follow.[21] Clinton, in fact, was quite adamant that the character of a nation's foreign policy had to reflect its core values, and there was nothing more important in the American value system, he believed, than the principle of democracy. This, in the words of the title of a famous study by the historian Daniel Boorstin, was an essential part of the American genius.[22] But this was not all. While theorists of a more realist persuasion might try to build neat conceptual walls between the international system and domestic politics, Clinton refused to do so. In his view, there was a close, almost intimate, connection between the two spheres. They were, as he pointed out, two sides of the same coin. As he made clear in an early speech defining US strategy in the post-Cold War era, in the new world where so much had changed it was absolutely vital 'to tear down the wall in our thinking between domestic and foreign policy'. This was necessary if America wanted to compete economically, and it was essential too if it wished to promote a more stable international system.[23]

This argument was allied with another, equally important idea: the notion that democracy had become the political gold standard of the late 20th century. Strobe Talbott, the Russian specialist and deputy secretary of state, put the case particularly forcefully to a largely British audience in a speech delivered at Oxford University in October 1994. The world had altered beyond recognition over the past 25 years, he noted, with dictatorships from Latin America to the old Soviet bloc finally succumbing to the attractive pull of democracy. This had not only changed the lives of millions of people, but had also forced those who once believed otherwise to accept the self-evident truth that democracy was 'the best form of political organization'.[24] The facts – for once – spoke for themselves. As official US figures showed, in 1972 there had been 44 democracies in the world: 21 years later there were 107,[25] leaving very few outside the democratic fold.[26] Moreover, those that remained would never be regarded as wholly legitimate in a world where, according to Huntington, democracy had become the norm.[27] Hence, why oppose the inevitable?[28] Why stand against the tide of history? Indeed, why not ride the democratic wave and give it a nudge in the right direction? This not only made intellectual sense. From an American perspective it made foreign policy sense as well.

The assumption that democracy represented the wave of the future also became connected in the administration's mind with a theory made popular by political theorists like Michael Doyle and Bruce Russett: namely, that for a variety of structural and cultural reasons, democracies in general tended not to go to war with each other.[29] Possibly no other idea emanating from the academic community exercised as much influence as this one on the Clinton White House. To be sure, the more general relationship between war and political forms was, as Warren Christopher conceded, a complex one; and he agreed that it would be far too simple to conclude that democracies were 'incapable of aggression' or that war was 'always caused by dictatorship'.[30] Nevertheless, there was very strong evidence to support the more specific argument that democracies behaved peacefully toward each other. Clinton certainly seemed to believe so, and as early as December 1991 noted that it should matter to the United States 'how others govern themselves'; for, as he pointed out, using words once confined to the classroom, 'democracies don't go to war with each other'.[31] Talbott later went even further. In his view, the proposition was not just a self-evident truth or a 'bromide', but represented a fundamental law of politics. Indeed, in his opinion, it was 'as close as we're ever likely' to get 'in political science to an empirical truth'.[32]

Finally, the administration backed the idea of enlargement because it was convinced that democracy more generally contributed to global stability and security, especially in those countries that were in transition from communism to capitalism.[33] Here, it argued, democracy was absolutely essential if nations like Ukraine and Russia were to become normal members of the international community.[34] The same political rule also applied to the old 'Third World' where democracy, it was felt, might even help alleviate suffering and poverty. Talbott, in fact, believed there was a close relationship between democratic forms and food supply, and cited the famous economist Amartya Sen to the effect that famines did not occur where democracy flourished.[35] Clinton added a few more advantages to the ever-lengthening list, and noted, in a significant speech made before his election to the White House, that democracies did not sponsor terrorist acts; they were reliable trading partners; they protected the global environment; and they abided by international law. They were also likely to be more friendly towards the United States. Here he cited the examples of France and the UK. They had once been rivals of the US, and they possessed nuclear weapons. But precisely because they were members of the larger democratic club nobody seriously saw either as a threat. Hence, even though they had the capacity to destroy the United States, Americans did not fear 'annihilation at their hands', not because they did not possess the means, but because they shared the same political values. The existence of democracy in other countries, therefore, was not merely reassuring but of vital importance to American security. As Clinton noted, 'how others govern themselves' was not a matter about which the United States could be indifferent.[36]

Clinton: the pragmatic crusader

The administration's strong defence of democracy promotion as a policy objective was certainly robust. Yet, at the same time, Clinton and his various aides were extremely careful not to oversell the policy. It would not engage in what Clinton more than once referred to as 'reckless crusades'.[37] Clinton made it abundantly clear that he would not be doing so in an important, but rarely cited, speech he made on the campaign trail in 1992. Speaking to an enthusiastic student audience at the University of Wisconsin, Clinton was at his rhetorical best as he denounced Bush's poor record on democracy promotion. Bush, he claimed, was too much of a realist and as a result tended 'to coddle dictators' rather than support liberal values abroad. But he then went on to stress that, if he were elected to the White House, he would not be upsetting established US relations with important autocratic allies either. China in particular had nothing to fear from a Clinton administration. 'I will say again, I do not want to isolate China', he emphasized. Nor, it seems, did he want to alienate other countries of equally dubious political character. America, he accepted, had a special destiny. But this did not mean it could, or would, force its ideals on other people. 'Our actions' abroad, he agreed, had always to be 'tempered with prudence and common-sense'. After all, he continued, there were 'some countries and some cultures' that were 'many steps away from democratic institutions' and it would be foolish to think they could adopt democratic forms overnight. Moreover, though the United States under his leadership would do more than its predecessor to support the cause of democracy with tax dollars – for instance, by establishing a 'democracy corps' and reinforcing the work of 'the bipartisan National Endowment for Democracy' – it would not act rashly or without due consideration to America's other obligations. As he pointed out, there would be times 'when other security needs or economic interests' would compromise America's 'commitment to democracy and human rights'. Democracy promotion, he thus suggested, was not a moral duty that would override all other goals, but one objective among a host of others that would help guarantee America's place in a complex international system.[38]

Lake was equally clear on this point, and in a little-noted part of a much-cited speech, was insistent that the strategy of enlargement was bound to be hedged in by what he defined as a 'host of caveats'. We have to be 'patient', he warned; 'our strategy must be pragmatic', he went on. 'Our interests in democracy and markets do not stand alone [...] other American interests at times will require us to befriend and even defend non-democratic states for mutually beneficial reasons'.[39] Talbott made much the same argument. In a powerful defence of the administration's policy of democracy promotion, he attacked the critics – isolationists and realists alike – for failing to understand why it was in America's interest to support democracy in certain countries. But he was equally careful to distinguish between a policy driven by ideals alone and one – Clinton's – guided by enlightened self-interest. He was equally keen to point out that 'for the United States, the attractions and advantages of supporting democracy abroad must be balanced against other strategic interests'; and, he added significantly, 'against the difficulty of sponsoring transitions that will inevitably entail a degree of disruption, if not instability'. 'Support for democracy', he concluded, was 'not an absolute imperative'.[40]

These indications of a clear willingness to compromise did not go entirely unnoticed, especially by those in the corporate sector who perhaps had most to lose if the United States attempted to sacrifice its economic relations with influential authoritarian regimes on the altar of democratic principle. But the more business leaders heard from Clinton about the supreme importance of America's role in an increasingly globalized economy, the less they tended to worry about his unalloyed commitment to democracy promotion. As we showed in the previous chapter, his many speeches on the importance of American economic power in the world, his repeated references to the need to compete and win in the global marketplace, and his upgrading of economics at all levels of the foreign policy bureaucracy could only have reassured them that there was little to fear from this most pro-business of Democratic administrations. Clinton himself certainly did not give the impression of someone willing to exchange US economic influence for some distant prospect of democratization in countries such as China or Saudi Arabia. As he stressed in one of his most important interventions outlining US foreign policy, under his leadership the main aim would be to promote American economic power and 'make trade a priority element of American security'. Naturally enough, he would support democracy and human rights where it was feasible to, but never to the same degree or with the same seriousness as he would back American business efforts in the international economy.[41]

Clinton's stress on the importance of economics in US foreign policy was married to an equally strong attachment to the tools of traditional statecraft. Indeed, in spite of appearances, Clinton was in many ways a most orthodox president when it came to defining American interests; time and again he reiterated the simple but important point that what had worked before and brought the United States victory in two world wars and the Cold War – namely, strong alliances and an even stronger military – would not be abandoned in his time. Anthony Lake made much the same point in two key speeches made in 1994. Designed in large part to reassure the 'realists' that the Clinton administration was not about to unlearn the lessons of the past, Lake went out of his way to stress the centrality of 'military force' in world politics in general and American diplomacy in particular. He also made it clear that while it was in America's interest to enlarge 'the community of democracies', democracy promotion could not be made to bear all, or even most of, the weight of US national security. The world was simply too ruthless a place to abandon the traditional tools of international diplomacy. Democracy promotion was obviously important, he conceded; and a democratic world was more likely to be prosperous and peaceful than one which was not. But in the last analysis, he noted with Achesonian *gravitas*, there was no substitute for power. Power without diplomacy, he accepted, was 'dangerous'. However, 'diplomacy disconnected from power usually fails'. America would continue to negotiate from a position of strength.[42]

But perhaps the most significant indication of the administration's pragmatic approach was the manner in which it assessed the role of previous American presidents – including Woodrow Wilson, the personification of the idealistic strain in American foreign policy in the 20th century. Wilson, it was readily accepted, was a great Democratic president. But there were others too, and while Clinton himself paid homage to Wilson, he seemed to have more time for more traditional occupants of the White House like Harry S. Truman and John F. Kennedy, leaders whose policies were as hard-headed as they were sometimes ruthless, and whose commitment to democracy promotion never overrode their more general desire to balance the power of the Soviet Union. Moreover, though Wilson had much to recommend him, he also had his weaknesses the Clinton team noted. Hence, it would be foolish to slavishly follow his example. Lake made this argument in a key statement which revealed the administration's attitude towards democracy promotion as much as, if not more than, its attitude toward Wilson himself. Wilson, he agreed, 'had it right' when he argued that 'principles matter and that power unhinged from principle will leave us rudderless and adrift'. Wilson was also correct to insist that what happened 'within nations' was 'fundamental' to what happened 'among them'. In this sense, he was an especially important president whose 'core beliefs' about 'the value of spreading democracy to other nations' remained 'more relevant than ever'. But he was not without his faults and the most obvious one was a tendency to employ 'lofty rhetoric' which suggested the US would be engaged on a mission impossible 'to make the world safe for democracy'. The consequence of this, unfortunately, was to create the impression that the nation would be playing 'too global a role', something that frightened the American people back into the very isolationism Wilson was seeking to combat. Equally misguided was his reliance on and ill-founded 'confidence in the power of morality' to reshape the international order after 1919. Though commendable at one level, this approach left America and the world without the means to deter aggression and safeguard the peace. The results were catastrophic; and while it would be unfair to blame Wilson for what happened thereafter, his vain attempt to build a new world order on idealism alone contributed, albeit indirectly, to the several crises that followed. And it was only when the US had learned the lessons of its past mistakes that it could play a meaningful international role.

The implications of Lake's foray into history were obvious. The Clinton administration would be building on the legacy of Wilson, but it would be just as readily be drawing its real inspiration from those who were 'present at creation' of a new world order after the end of the Second World War, and who in Lake's opinion constructed a stable world that was neither naively liberal in the Wilsonian sense nor relentlessly realist in the conservative sense. As Lake observed, 'Today it is the spirit of the post-World War II generation that we need to recapture in forging a coalition of the centre'. This would draw on Wilson, albeit selectively, but it would also learn from realism as well. Only in this way could the US forge a foreign policy for a 'rapidly changing world' without overcommitting American resources or raising false expectations.[43]

Towards a political economy of democracy promotion

The Clinton administration's careful efforts to plot a course in foreign policy that it quite consciously regarded, and referred to as being, 'neither rigidly Wilsonian nor classically realist'[44] in character was often lost on opponents from both left and right: the former because they could see no difference between Clinton's grand strategy and those of his various predecessors, and the latter because, apparently, they could see too many. But what critics also seemed to pass over in silence was the administration's rather interesting attempt to relate the politics of democracy promotion to the economics of the global market. Yet Talbott made a very direct connection between the two. In 'an increasingly interdependent world', he noted in the context of a more general effort to spell out the national interest reasons for promoting democracy, Americans had a 'growing stake in how other countries govern or misgovern themselves'. This had not always been true, but 'a combination' of factors 'technological, commercial' as well as 'political' were 'shortening distances, opening borders, and connecting far-flung cultures and economies'. This had its upside, but it also posed new dangers as narcotics, criminals, terrorists, even viruses, moved more quickly across borders. To control this required cooperation; this in turn presupposed democracy; and 'the larger and more close-knit the community of nations that choose democratic forms of government' the less risk there was from these various threats. Moreover, in a world where the market was now the only serious economic option in the international system, the US had greater reason than ever for strengthening democracy in other countries: the two went hand in hand. Supporting political pluralism, therefore, was not just the right thing to do – though Talbott cautioned there would be circumstances where the US would not be able to get its way – but, more importantly, the economically smart thing to do as well.[45]

The belief that there was a symbiotic and positive relationship between market forms and political democracy was not, of course, shared by all commentators. The influential French policy maker Jacques Attali, for example, saw little relationship at all, and took the American administration to task for its lack of historical perspective and myopic belief that the market and democracy were logically or even empirically related. 'Contrary to popular belief,' he argued, 'the market economy and democracy – the twin pillars of Western civilization – are more likely to undermine than support one another.'[46] A similar point was made by the conservative American scholar, Irwin Stelzer. The 'relationship', he believed, was 'ambiguous'. However, 'democracy', he concluded, was 'no guarantor of prosperity, nor its absence a guarantor of poverty'. The 'linkages between economic and political structures' were in fact immensely complex, and simply to assume that the market and democracy were necessary partners was quite naive.[47] A number of realists took the same line. The market, they argued, could quite easily function in the absence of political freedom – note the case of China. Democratic reform, on the other hand, need not lead to a flourishing capitalist economy – witness the example of post-communist Russia.[48]

Yet in spite of what many saw as irrefutable evidence to the contrary, the Clinton administration persisted in believing that there was a positive, rather than an ambiguous or even non-existent, connection between capitalism and democracy. In many ways, the idea seemed to run like a thread through its thinking, influencing its rhetoric and helping to define its attitude towards the outside world – to such a degree that the strategy of enlargement came to be viewed not just as a stand-alone political objective but as an integrated part of the administration's larger effort to help the United States compete more effectively in the global economy. This is why Clinton found the idea so appealing. As has been pointed out, 'what Clinton liked best about Lake's enlargement policy was the way it was inextricably linked to economic renewal with its emphasis on making sure the United States remained the number one exporter'. Vice-President Al Gore was equally enthusiastic. A firm advocate of the classical liberal view that the expansion of trade and the spread of political freedom were the twin foundations of world order,

Gore, it seems, felt that commerce, democracy and peace formed part of a single whole.[49]

But it was more than just market access that interested Clinton and his foreign policy advisers. In some larger sense they really did think that over time democracy could not function without the market, or the market without democracy. Competition at the ballot box and in the marketplace were in this sense twins, with democracy being the necessary political accompaniment of free enterprise, and free enterprise the only secure foundation on which to construct and sustain democracy. It was no accident that Clinton and his advisers persistently coupled the two words together and employed the term 'market democracy' to more fully describe the policy of enlargement. They simply could not conceive of one without the other, or the strategy succeeding where either was absent. The question was: why? There were several parts to the answer.

To some degree it reflected the administration's rather heroic interpretation of the American experience. Here, democratic forms and market economics had always existed together, and the assumption was that if the two had coexisted happily in the US, there was no reason to believe they would not do so elsewhere, especially if the United States itself intervened to support and sustain nascent market democracies in other countries. This viewpoint was in turn bolstered by the administration's understanding of the end of the Cold War. There were, it was true, many causes of what led to the end of the Cold War in 1989, but the most critical, it was argued, was not the Reagan military build-up – a line championed by the Republicans – or simply that the Soviet economy was inefficient, but the attractiveness of Western institutions overall. But, as Talbott pointed out, the West did not win the Cold War because of the market alone, but because of the market and democracy together.[50] Lake agreed, adding that those who wanted to build a better world could not do so without introducing both forms. Democracy was essential if you wanted 'justice', and capitalism if you wished to generate the wealth and 'material goods necessary for individuals to thrive'. And while the two may have performed entirely different functions without which 'civilized societies' were bound to 'perish', neither could really exist without the other.[51]

The connection also seemed to make a good deal of sense for another, more practical, reason relating to the issue of economic restructuring in those countries where previously there had been forms of planning and social protection. How were these often painful changes to be introduced without generating deep resentment and political upheaval? The answer, it was suggested, was through the ballot box. It had, after all, worked in Poland after 1989. Here, the people voted for a government prepared to take the tough market measures that would have provoked political opposition under the old system, and there was no reason to expect that the same strategy would not work elsewhere. As Warren Christopher conceded, democracy had many advantages over the alternatives, but one was that it permitted countries to take harsh economic decisions. He noted, 'in nations undergoing economic transformation, market reformers who enjoy popular legitimacy are more likely to win popular support for tough economic measures' than those who do not.[52] Another official made much the same point. Democracy, he noted, helped new reforming elites in many ways, but in particular it allowed them to 'modernize their economies, ameliorate social conditions and integrate with the outside world' by legitimizing 'painful but necessary economic choices'.[53] Moreover, once these market democracies had undergone reform and been more fully integrated into the world economy, they were also more likely to be reliable trading partners.[54]

Finally, the Clinton administration saw a more general relationship between democracy and the market. Warren Christopher put it thus. The market, he argued, was not a self-regulating economic system but one that required a framework within which to operate – and the most appropriate framework, he believed, was a democratic one in which the rule of law operated. This was not because of any moral imperative; rather it was because mature market economies demanded stability, order and certainty – and democracy was more likely to provide these than any other system. The market also needed well-defined regulations that could govern contract, protect property and facilitate competition; and again, the best guarantee of all these things was a democratic polity with clearly defined rules. From this perspective, the rule of law under democracy was essential not only to protect 'political rights but also the essential elements of free market economies'.[55] Moreover, as markets evolved, they generated changes that were bound to threaten the integrity of even the most carefully constructed authoritarian regime. Again, this was not because the market was moral, but rather because it was dynamic and, in its own way, revolutionary too. Thus, as it developed, it spawned new social groups, including a more active middle class who placed increased demands on the political system. It also generated a need for a much higher level of information; this also was likely to promote change in a progressive direction. Even more corrosive of traditional political forms was the very dynamics of globalization, which impelled all countries to operate by the same standards; and if the dominant standards being set were those defined by the West, then this was bound to lead, over time, to liberalization. Naturally, the pace of change would vary from country to country. Moreover, there was no guaranteeing that the film of history would always run in the same pluralist direction, as the events of Tiananmen Square proved only too graphically. However, according to the Clinton team there was no escaping the longer-term logic of capitalism. In the end, even the most repressive regime would have to become more open as its economy adapted and became more integrated into the world market.

Will the real Woodrow Wilson please stand up?

The concept of enlargement, therefore, was not rooted just in a larger political theory about the world at large, but in a developed political economy about the relationship between democracy and democracy promotion on the one hand, and the market and global capitalism on the other. However, sitting like Banquo at this particular feast was (as we have already indicated) the ever-present historical figure of Woodrow Wilson, someone who according to critic and admirer alike – not to mention the Clinton administration – was the quintessential moral president in foreign affairs. Indeed, in the great contemporary debate about America's democratic mission, the name of Woodrow Wilson figures very prominently, and for good reason. More than anyone else, he remains the president most readily associated with the idea of democracy promotion. And while realists and liberals might disagree about nearly everything else, both seem to accept at face value the claim that Wilson was a true enlightenment figure whose ultimate goal was to make the world a more democratic place. The only difference is that whereas realists such as Kennan and Kissinger criticized him for having such a vision, liberals have not.

This of necessity leads to the obvious question: to what extent was, or is, this portrait an accurate one? Certainly, the view of Wilson as a rather simple-minded liberal idealist is not shared by all historians of the period. In fact, whereas most contemporary commentators see Wilson as someone slightly out of touch with international realities, one of his biographers actually views him as having been driven by a higher realism. This view has been upheld by more recent scholarship which portrays Wilson as a rather astute war-time leader who managed to maximize US negotiating leverage at the post-war conference table.[56] Levin paints an equally complicated, less soft-focused picture of a Wilson motivated not so much by idealism but by a more fundamental desire to make the word safe for capitalism in the immediate aftermath of the First World War, a view also endorsed by Lloyd Gardner.[57] Link even argues that he was inspired less by political idealism than by Christianity.[58] Nor do all historians subscribe to the view that Wilson underestimated the role of power. According to one historian of the Wilson presidency, nothing could be further from the truth. In fact, 'no other American president before or since used force more than' Woodrow Wilson. As Calhoun has observed, 'within four years, from 1914 to 1918, Wilson resorted to force twice in Mexico, in Haiti, in the Dominican Republic, in World War I, northern Russia and Siberia'.[59] This hardly conveys the impression of a staunch moral idealist and consistent advocate of the peaceful resolution of international disputes.

The search for the 'real' Woodrow Wilson should also take account of his hierarchical world-view.[60] Wilson may well have been a democrat in the formal sense, but there was always something distinctly elitist about his political vision. At heart a Burkean who worried more about threats to the established order than about representation, Wilson had little faith in the people, or even, it seems, in elections. According to one commentator, 'Wilson greatly downplayed the role of elections as the proper touchstone of democracy'. In Wilson's view 'democracy was not an electoral process as much as a meritocracy' in which the best and the brightest would rule on behalf of the ignorant masses.[61] This fear of *vox populi* partly reflected a fairly profound hostility to all things French, including Rousseau and the French Revolution; but it was also shaped by his own attitude towards the Founding Fathers. Though sometimes referred to as a Jeffersonian Democrat, Wilson had far more in common with the patrician views of Alexander Hamilton and James Madison – neither of whom could remotely be regarded as being Democrats – than he did with the populist Jefferson. This did not bother Wilson, however. Good government, he believed, was always preferable to majoritarian democracy, and the form of government which worked best, in his view, was one composed of what Wilson regarded as those 'of highest and steadiest political habits'.[62]

If Wilson had a restricted concept of democracy – he once argued that American democracy had nothing in common with 'radical thought and a restless spirit' – he had forthright views about race. A Virginian by birth who was more than a little sympathetic to the plight of the South and white southerners – he once objected to black suffrage on the grounds that what he viewed as the 'negro mind' was 'dark, ignorant, uneducated and incompetent to form an enlightened opinion' – he always tended to look at the world through the prism of colour. He certainly saw nations in terms of a racial hierarchy and in 1917 informed his Secretary of State, Robert Lansing, that 'white civilization and its dominion over the world rested largely on our ability to keep this country intact'. This is one of the reasons, among others, that he later opposed Japan's efforts at the Paris peace talks to have a clause about racial equality attached to the Covenant of the League of Nations. Wilson's motives in opposing the Japanese move were far from straightforward. In part it 'demonstrated his determination to maintain Anglo-American control' of the international agenda. But it also reflected his own racial prejudice. As Ambrosius has pointed out, 'sharing rather than challenging the racial attitude of white supremacy, the president chose to alienate the Japanese by rejecting their amendment'.[63]

Ironically, Wilson was also less than enthusiastic about the idea of self-determination. As Lynch has noted, there is no reference to the idea in any of his writings or speeches before 1914; and when he did advocate it later, he did so with the greatest of reservations. It is true that he opposed certain forms of imperial control in Europe, and was in the end forced to accept the dissolution of the Austro-Hungarian Empire.[64] But earlier he had actually argued for the union of the Austro-Hungarian peoples;[65] moreover, when the United States did enter the First World War, there is no evidence it did so in order to stimulate the dissolution Austria-Hungary. We should also not forget that Wilson did nothing for the Irish or the Chinese at Versailles; that 20 years earlier he had endorsed the brutal American takeover of the Philippines; and that he was not in favour of independence for all peoples, especially if they were brown or black. Furthermore, in spite of his suspicions of the British, he was something of an admirer of the British Empire and the British constitutional system. He even uttered more than a passing word of praise for pre-First World War Germany with its efficient and orderly bureaucracy. As Oren has shown, Wilson admired rather than attacked Germany under the Kaiser on the grounds that it embodied the highest form of administrative rationality. Indeed, the German system, he felt, was a 'shining model' that American reformers would be well advised to emulate.[66]

Finally, though Wilson may well have employed certain grand phrases like 'self-determination' and 'democracy', he did so not out of some mystical faith in reason but because he thought these broad objectives would help advance American power at a time when the world was threatened by hunger, chaos and a new ideology in the shape of Bolshevism. A new form of politics was thus essential, in his view, to build what he hoped would one day become a more viable international order. This was no simple-minded crusade for its own sake. Nor was it mere idealism. Rather, it was a recognition that the old order had collapsed and that unless the United States put itself at the vanguard of building a new one, then a great opportunity would be lost. It was also the only way in which Wilson could ever hope to mobilize a reluctant American public after the war. Dry talk of a clearly defined American national interest was all very fine in theory, but unless the notion of interest could be married to the ideal of democracy there was little chance of building a foreign policy consensus and breaking the political back of isolationism. Wilson, at least, seemed to understand this, even if his later realist critics did not.

Of course, to make these various observations is not to dismiss Wilson as an historic figure, but rather to challenge those who later either idealized or denigrated his role. Wilson was neither a fool nor a saint, and to portray him as if he was one or the other only serves to distort his place in history. In fact, the more one examines Wilson's ideas over time, the more one is drawn to the conclusion that there never was something so clear and unambiguous as 'Wilsonianism'. As one writer has noted, 'Wilson's connection with the doctrines ascribed to his name' remains 'tenuous at best'.[67] In fact, it was only after his death that the term acquired meaning. Unfortunately, the meaning it acquired – either as inspiration to those who hoped the League of Nations would save the world from war or as synonym for foreign policy utopianism – inevitably tended to simplify the record. The best example of this, of course, was Carr's highly influential work on the inter-war crisis.[68] Carr did not spare what he saw as the hapless Wilson, 'the most perfect modern example of the intellectual in politics'.[69] However, in his rush to judgement, Carr ignored the real Wilson and paints instead a caricature of some faintly risible figure rooted in the 19th century with no understanding of the ways of the world. The fact that Wilson might have been less naive than Carr believed, or more aware of power realities, was ignored in the English historian's scorching but highly effective attack.

Conclusion: but what to promote?

This brings us to our last question which is not whether the United States should or should not engage in democracy promotion, but rather, what is it exactly that America promotes? Thus far, the debate surrounding this issue has been unnecessarily polarized between two positions rather well defined by one of the doyens of American realism: Henry Kissinger. Kissinger summed up the dilemma for Americans in the following way. The United States had a choice he believed, either to promote its political values or simply to act as a democratic example for others to follow. As a seasoned diplomat with a distinctly *realpolitik* (some even called it a 'European') approach to world affairs, Kissinger himself was in no doubt which of those two options he preferred, observing that in the real world of competing states that it was simply bad politics and even worse diplomacy to try and export liberal ideas to countries that did not want them and were only likely to be alienated from the United States if it tried to do so. Liberals would no doubt claim that this was being far too passive, defeatist even. Nonetheless, his argument is one worth taking seriously if only because it draws our attention to a simple truth: that America is always exporting or projecting a narrative about itself even when it is not consciously trying to do so. This of course would suggest that the success or failure of the US in promoting democracy may in the end depend less on the amount of time or money it invests in backing the cause of liberty abroad and more on the ability of America to fulfil its promise as a nation. Clinton, one suspects, understood this only too clearly, which may in large part explain why he repeated what almost became his mantra: that American influence in the world after the Cold War would depend just as much, if not more, on what it could deliver at home to the American people as much as consciously trying to promote democracy to every corner of the globe.[70]

3

Failed Crusade? The United States and Post-Communist Russia[1]

As we showed in Chapters 1 and 2, Clinton concentrated his not inconsiderable talents on first making sure America could compete effectively in the emerging global economy and then attempting to square the circle (not always successfully) by linking this to a defined strategy of enlarging the number of democracies in the world. Clinton was liberal enough to know that his main task was to strengthen a liberal order from which America benefited; but he was realist enough too to understand that a post-Cold War order without the Soviet Union offered up huge opportunities that would afford the US a lengthy breathing space within which it would be able to consolidate its own hegemony, strengthen its position within the family of advanced liberal democracies, and where feasible, extend market capitalism to those countries attempting to make the transition out of planning and economic autarchy. Taken together, these formed what we might call the 'core' of America's strategic mission in the 1990s.[2] Getting Russia right however was central to all this.[3] If the US could facilitate the transition to a more Western-style political economy (as was beginning to happen in Central and Eastern Europe) then according to Clinton the future looked bright indeed. If, however, reform in Russia failed, the United States would face a very insecure future with the strong possibility, according to one very senior official, of 'a renewed nuclear threat, higher defence budgets, spreading instability, the loss of new markets and a devastating setback for the worldwide democratic movement'.[4] Engaging with reform therefore was not just in Russia's interest, but in America's too.

The discussion which follows attempts to chart the history of the US–Russia relationship through the 1990s. The argument advanced is a simple one: that in spite of various American interventions, facilitating an American-style transition in Russia proved to be an almost impossible task. Whether this was because of a failure on Washington's part to grant Russia the respect it felt it deserved, the decision to enlarge NATO, or the complex legacy left behind by the old Soviet Union followed by its headlong economic collapse after 1991, will no doubt be debated for many years to come. Whatever the reason, or reasons, what American Sovietologist, Stephen Cohen, once termed America's 'crusade' to remake Russia clearly 'failed'. This may not have led to anything resembling a new Cold War as some (including Cohen) claimed. Nor did the Russia that finally emerged at the end of the 1990s represent the same kind of threat once posed by the USSR. On the other hand, ten years of engaging with Russia delivered neither what reformers in Russia had hoped for nor what the US had striven to create: a 'normal' liberal democracy and a successful market capitalism.

In what follows, we shall look at the evolution of the relationship between the collapse of the USSR and the rise of Putin. I go into some detail, in part to show what actually happened year by year – a fascinating tale in its own right – but also to point to something that can easily get lost sight of by those who believe, naively, that the US or the West 'lost' Russia. As I try and show, Russia was not lost by the West. Rather, Russia found its own way after a decade of humiliation and setbacks – unfortunately for the West this 'way' was charted by Vladimir Putin. To make good on this claim, I begin by examining some of the early problems facing the relationship before going on to look at the US response to the first of many crises: the one that erupted in 1993 following the Duma elections which indicated very strong support for those opposed to reform. We will then look at the unfolding of events and the ways in which US policy toward Russia after 1994 became increasingly politicized by Clinton's enemies back in the US itself. This will take us to yet another crisis: the 1998 financial meltdown. Finally, we will analyze the emergence of Putin and how his coming to power affected Washington's understanding of what was happening in Russia and whether it brought to an end any hope that it was still possible for Washington to engage Moscow in serious dialogue.

Early problems: 1992–94

Having defined Russia as America's number one security problem, Clinton made great play after 1992 of the need to build what his key adviser on Russian affairs, Strobe Talbott, liked to term a new 'strategic partnership with Russian reform'. Indeed, for a period, it appeared that the only country in the world in which Clinton appeared to have any serious interest was in fact Russia. Nevertheless, his energetic approach towards Russia could not hide the fact that his strategy contained a number of obvious problems. These began to manifest themselves at the time of the 'aid to Russia' campaign in the early summer of 1993, continued during the late autumn as the United States began to toy with the idea of extending security guarantees to the countries of East-Central Europe, and reached a critical point when the December elections to the Russian Duma produced what the US openly admitted was the wrong result. Certainly, by the beginning of 1994 it was already beginning to look as if Clinton's idea of an alliance with a reforming Russia had run its course, and that either an alternative strategy would have to be devised or a modification would have to be made to his original policy.

The first and most obvious problem with US policy was that it made unwarranted assumptions about both Russia and what needed to be done to Russia to make it into a 'normal' country. Assuming that there had been a genuine revolution in 1991, which had cleared the way for a relatively rapid forced march towards the market, policy makers were somewhat surprised to discover that the obstacles still standing in the way of reform were immense.[5] Nor did the United States seem ready to match its strong rhetorical endorsement of the market with concrete economic support for the reform process itself. Having encouraged (some would even say, pushed) Russia down the path of painful economic restructuring, neither Congress nor the American people were prepared to extend very much material aid. There would be no 'Marshall Plan' for Russia.

The second problem with US strategy was less economic than political. Although American officials spoke in warm terms of their support for post-Soviet reform in general, in reality the main thrust of American policy was always directed towards Russia. Naturally, Washington tried to reassure the other republics, arguing that backing for Russia did not imply indifference to, or neglect of, the other new independent states. Warren Christopher, the US secretary of state, indeed insisted that the United States was totally committed to the integrity of the different republics and would assist in their integration into the world community. Yet there was little disguising the fact that in its essentials US policy was taken to mean, and certainly was perceived as being, a 'Russia first' policy. This had a number of negative consequences. The most important perhaps was to fuel non-Russian suspicion of American motives. To most non-Russians, in fact, it now looked as if the United States either favoured some partial reconstruction of the Union, or was prepared to turn a blind eye to Russian activities in its 'near abroad'. The other consequence, according to critics, was to encourage greater aggression by Russia itself. Working on the not illogical assumption that Washington had few serious objections to it throwing its weight around, Moscow started to assert itself. In some cases the consequences were merely unfortunate; in Chechnya, however, they turned out to be horrendous.

The final problem was to be found within Russia itself. Here the situation showed no sign of real improvement after 1992. For a president elected on the promise that he would push Russia more rapidly along the capitalist road, Clinton had little to show for his efforts during his first term in office. One need not blame Clinton personally, but while he continued to talk up the reforms Russia seemed to lurch from one near-fatal crisis to another. Yeltsin managed to negotiate his way through the first of these in April 1993, when he won his referendum. He then navigated the next crisis in October of the same year, but only after having bombed and then closed down the Russian parliament. The third crisis, however, proved far more difficult to resolve, not merely because the December elections in 1993 revealed strong opposition to economic change, but more significantly because those hostile to the market now had a genuine democratic mandate. This was a disaster of the first order that was bound to have serious consequences back in the United States.

Crisis and response

Perhaps one indicator of the seriousness with which the Clinton administration viewed the situation in Russia was its half-hearted public attempts to play down the significance of the December elections and the 'rise' of the Russian ultra-nationalist Vladimir Zhirinovsky. The official line at first was to make light of the anti-reform vote, more or less dismissing it as a 'protest' against short-term problems that would evaporate once things improved. This exercise in damage limitation could not hide the administration's concern, however. According to one source, the White House was 'startled and shaken' by the outcome. Al Gore, it is reliably reported, was 'dazed and speechless' when the results came in. Indeed, so confused was he that he and others attempted to place at least some of the blame on Western economic policies. In Talbott's famous or (infamous) phrase, there had been too much imposed 'shock' and not enough 'therapy' in Russia. Hence it was necessary, or so he implied, both to slow down the reforms and to take account of their negative social consequences.[6]

Once the dust had settled the White House set about picking its way through what looked like the debris of a failed policy. Some modifications would clearly have to be made to the original strategy. However, both Talbott and Clinton were determined to soldier on. The administration was not about to abandon Russia. Nor as one analyst suggested at the time, was it going to move Russia from being 'the most highly favoured of nations beyond the old iron curtain to being only in the second rank'. Clinton himself made this perfectly clear on his visit to Russia in early January 1994. During this, he went out of his way to reassure Russians of America's continuing support and friendship. He also played to Russian *amour propre* by talking (somewhat over enthusiastically) of the nation's 'greatness' and US recognition of its special place in world affairs. A few days later Talbott followed up on these remarks in an important statement to the House Committee on Foreign Affairs. He accepted that Russia was passing through its 'time of troubles' and that 'reformers in Russia were worried and demoralized'. But this was no reason for America to jump ship. In fact, precisely because there was what he called a 'titanic struggle' going on in Russia, in which the United States had a 'huge stake', it was more important than ever to remain engaged. Moreover, according to Talbott, the situation was more 'mixed' than the pessimists claimed. The democratic process was up and running. Over one quarter of the labour force was now employed in the private sector. In the 'near abroad'[7] there had been progress, although there were some problems still left to resolve. On the security front, too, things were getting better, with Ukraine just having decided to transfer all its nuclear weapons to Russia, and the United States and Russia having agreed to 'detarget' each other. It was not all doom and gloom, therefore.

Naturally, Talbott accepted that things could still go badly wrong. The 'next two and a half years – between now and the elections scheduled for mid-1996 – would be critical'. But Russia had not yet passed beyond the point of no return. There was still everything to play for. What the United States should not do, he warned, was base its policy today on 'worst-case assumptions about what tomorrow may bring'. This would not only be foolish, but could lead the United Sates to 'fall into the trap of the self-fulfilling prophecy'. America had to remain patient and steady, therefore, and continue to work for the integration of Russia rather than begin planning for its containment. The advantages of doing so were self-evident, for 'a Russia integrated rather than contained', he argued, would 'mean fewer tax dollars spent on defence; a reduced threat from weapons of mass destruction; new markets for US products; and a powerful, reliable partner for diplomacy as well as commerce in the twenty-first century'. There was still a world to be won.[8]

Towards a new realism?

If one result of the December 'wake-up call' was to cause initial confusion followed by a resolute White House defence of its original strategy, the other was to open a floodgate out of which poured a tide of criticism. A good deal of this, clearly, had as much to do with Republican frustrations and right-wing dislike of Clinton as it did with the administration's policy on Russia. Yet it would be wrong to conclude that all Clinton's critics were motivated only by political animus. There were genuine questions that needed an answer – first, about how to deal with a Russia in which communists and nationalists were now in a majority in the new parliament; second, about a Russia that was showing an alarming tendency to reassert its prerogatives in the near abroad; and finally, a Russia in which the reformist Yeltsin only seemed able to hold on to power by stealing the rhetorical clothes of his anti-reformist enemies. To many, indeed, it looked in early 1994 as if Clinton's 'love affair' with Yeltsin and his fear of 'losing Russia' was now standing in the way of a more balanced American approach to post-Soviet problems.⁹

In good Cold War fashion the debate over Russia reached a critical point following the disclosure that a senior CIA official had been working for Moscow for several years, apparently with deadly consequences. As one of Clinton's more vocal opponents noted in late February, 'Americans really did not need a major spy scandal to tell them that the honeymoon with Russia was over. But the arrest of the CIA's Aldrich Ames makes the point with some finality.' With this discovery (coinciding as it did with a particularly tough statement by Yeltsin on Russian foreign policy) the attacks against Clinton intensified. The Republicans' chief spokesperson on foreign affairs, Richard Lugar, declared that the United States had 'to get over the idea' that it was involved in a 'partnership' with Moscow. 'This is a tough rivalry,' he insisted. Much the same point was made at Talbott's confirmation hearings for the post of deputy secretary of state in February 1994. Here the Republicans launched a bitter attack on what one senator called a policy that endangered 'our national interests'. The Republicans also used the occasion to criticize Clinton's foreign policy more generally. 'If Ambassador Talbott is confirmed by the Senate,' argued Senator D'Amato, 'another wrong signal will be sent: that the people who carry out our foreign policy offer nothing but inexperience and naiveté.'¹⁰

The case against Clinton was certainly a powerful one, which logically led some of his more articulate critics – Zbigniew Brzezinski most obviously – to some fairly radical conclusions. Brzezinski was no passive observer of the foreign policy scene, and since the collapse of the USSR had been indulging in what one observer called 'a bit of freelance foreign policy', the primary goal of which was to cultivate links with the non-Russian states of the former Soviet Union, to which he thought 'the American government should have been paying more attention'. Believing that Talbott's 'romantic fascination with Russia' (Russophilia, even) was getting in the way of clear strategic thinking, Brzezinski called for a number of changes to US policy. Most importantly, he argued that the countries of Eastern and Central Europe should be invited to join NATO sooner rather than later. This was critical. Furthermore, in his view, the United States should set as its main objective 'the consolidation of geopolitical pluralism' within the space once occupied by the old Soviet Union. Only in this way could countries like Ukraine be assured and America achieve a more balanced relationship with the new Europe as a whole. Indeed, according to Brzezinski, the creation of a belt of independent states around Russia, closely allied to the West, would not only serve America's interest but would help Russia as well; for only when its periphery was secured – and when Moscow was no longer tempted to play a spoiling role there – could it become both stable and democratic itself.¹¹

The net result of all this was to bring about an adjustment in US policy. This expressed itself in at least four ways. The first was at the level of public presentation. Hitherto, the Clinton team had talked quite boldly and optimistically about an alliance with Russia and Russian reform. Now this line was modified to include a recognition that, on certain international issues at least, there were bound to be serious divergences between the two countries. As Defense Secretary William Perry pointed out in March 1994, 'even with the best outcome imaginable in Russia, the new Russia' would have different interests from America's. Nor should the United States be particularly concerned about this, for as Perry pointed out (picking his countries carefully), 'even with allies like France and Japan, we have rivalry and competition alongside our partnership,' and so it will be with Russia.[12]

The second change in policy was in the US attitude towards the other new republics. Sensitive to the charge that it had tilted too far towards Moscow and Yeltsin, Washington now began to make a much greater effort in building stronger relations with countries other than Russia. This not only pleased a number of countries in the former USSR, but Brzezinski too, who saw this as exactly the sort of initiative the Clinton administration should have taken much earlier. Whether the White House saw it this way is much less clear, but there was no mistaking the shift in policy. This expressed itself in many ways – both symbolic and practical. Thus, during a scheduled visit by the new Ukrainian president to Washington in March 1994 (the first ever undertaken) Clinton reaffirmed 'American support' for Ukrainian independence. Four months later Clinton met with the three leaders of the Baltic republics. Other meetings were held during the course of the year. At the same time, the United States issued a series of warnings to Moscow that good relations between Russia and the United States assumed – indeed, presupposed – better relations with its neighbours.

Third, these various moves were accompanied by perhaps the biggest change of all in US policy: in its attitude towards NATO and NATO expansion. Accepting now that there could be no halfway house for the countries of Central and Eastern Europe, it decided during the course of 1994 that it was time to extend the privileges of full NATO membership to Poland, the Czech Republic and Hungary. Having initially been persuaded by Talbott back in 1992 that this was not the way to go after the events in Russia (indeed a promise it seems had been made to Moscow that NATO would not be expanded eastwards), the United States felt it had no alternative but to do so. Though in part a move designed to assuage critics both at home and abroad (and to find a new mission for NATO in a post-Soviet world) clearly underlying the move was a growing recognition that Russia's future could not be guaranteed. Once spoken of as only a theoretical possibility, by late 1994 the likelihood of the reform process in Russia going into reverse seemed far less unlikely. Thus there was good reason for the US to hedge its bets and secure the peace in Europe now by guarding against a resurgent Russia in the future.

The final shift in US policy was less dramatic but still significant. Since being elected, President Clinton had not only promised a review of US military objectives but important cuts in the US military budget as well – and three months before the December elections in Russia he made good on both promises with the publication of his defence review, suitably titled the *Bottom-Up Review*. Though hardly a radical document, it provoked a wave of criticism from conservatives in particular, who attacked it, in effect, for undermining American national security by failing to spend enough on the military. For a while, Clinton was able to fend off his opponents. However, as events in Russia unfolded it became increasingly difficult for him to do so. The result was to make him far more 'cautious' on defence matters. With Russia's future as yet undecided and the Republicans attacking him for being weak, it would have taken a much bolder American president than Clinton to have now argued the case for large cuts in American military spending.

Partnership in crisis again: 1994–98

While the United States took what it regarded as sensible measures to guard against any future eventuality, it still did not accept that the situation in Russia was hopeless. As Talbott reminded the Senate in early 1994, though the United States would be acting cautiously, it had no intention of planning for the worse. Nor did it have any intention of cutting the Russians off from those all-too-important IMF loans. For a short while, things did begin to stabilize, leading some commentators to talk somewhat prematurely about Russia's 'economic success story'.[13] But the underlying trends were far from reassuring. In December 1994, Yeltsin formally came out against NATO expansion. In the same month, Moscow launched its ill-fated 'invasion' of Chechnya. In early 1995, Russia then sold two light-water nuclear reactors to Iran. In December, the Russian communists did particularly well in elections to the State Duma. And in the race for the Russian presidency in June of the following year, Yeltsin only just managed to win.

Worse was yet to come, as the situation continued to deteriorate in Russia.[14] Indeed, nearly all of the main indicators pointed to further economic decline and possible political instability too. One rather obvious sign of the times was Yeltsin's somewhat startling decision in March 1998 to sack his entire government; 'good theatre but poor politics,' opined one Western source.[15] Another was a stark warning then delivered by the new Russian Prime Minister Sergei Kiriyenko, who claimed Russia was now living on what he called the 'never-never'. He did not mince his words. Russia's foreign debt, he noted, stood at about $140 billion, workers were not getting paid, and capital continued to leave the country at a far more rapid rate than it was coming in. Meanwhile, living standards for all but the wealthy few continued to decline. Russia, he warned, was staring into the abyss. Extremely dangerous days lay ahead.[16]

How dangerous became only too clear when in August Russia's financial system effectively collapsed, in the process wiping out rouble savings overnight. Furthermore, coming when it did (in the midst of a wider global financial crisis) the very real fear was that meltdown in Russia could easily spark a worldwide recession. As *The Wall Street Journal* pointed out, although the international weight of the Russian economy was small, accounting for only 1 per cent of the world's GDP, any move to default on its large foreign debt could easily precipitate similar actions elsewhere. Equally, if Russia took steps to prevent foreigners from getting their money out, then other 'at risk' countries might be tempted to do the same. As the newspaper speculated, 'already Malaysia has imposed rigid controls' and there was a genuine worry that if Russia did the same, then others would follow suit.[17]

The impact of these momentous events precipitated yet another 'great debate' within the United States. One guru of doom was Martin Malia, the American historian who had earlier predicted the failure of perestroika. 'The only certainty in Russia's present crisis,' he argued, 'is that it marks the end of an era – the Yeltsin years.' In his view, it also marked the 'end of a theory', the one advanced by Francis Fukuyama in the late 1980s, which suggested 'that market democracy had triumphed as a universal ideal'.[18] George Friedman was even more pessimistic. Indeed, whereas Malia had simply noted the failure of the liberal Western model in Russia, Friedman predicted its replacement by a new form of Stalinism combining economic and geopolitical 'anti-Westernism'. And there was nothing the West could do about it. 'The new Stalinism' could 'not be stopped', he asserted. This left the United States with only one option: to abandon a strategy that assumed that reform was possible and adopt a new policy that assumed it was not.[19]

Confronted with the crisis, US officials charged with Russian policy clearly had an uphill task, one that was made all the more difficult by yet another change of government in Russia itself. Though rather less alarming in composition than some commentators assumed at the time – one stressed that Yevgeny Primakov, the new Russian prime minister, 'was a former KGB agent, a friend of dictators in Iraq and Serbia, and an enemy of the West'[20] – the new team could hardly be described as reformist. Furthermore, while Primakov himself talked reassuringly about his commitment to the international community and his opposition to strident nationalism, his selection of economic advisers seemed to point backwards to the pre-Yeltsin years rather than forward to the market. As one seasoned observer noted, his choice 'sent strong signals that his approach will be a throwback to another era when economists tried to introduce some free market ideas within a

Soviet system'. The return of this cast of Soviet characters according to the American journalist, Celestine Bohlen, was 'eerie, even alarming'.[21]

American disquiet at the direction now being taken by Russia was expressed most forcefully by Madeleine Albright, since 1997 the American secretary of state. In her first comprehensive review of United States–Russia relations since Primakov was confirmed as prime minister in September, Mrs Albright was in no mood to pour American oil onto Russia's troubled waters. Washington, she declared was 'deeply concerned' about the direction in which Russia seemed to be moving. Of particular concern was the apparent shift in economic policy. While praising Primakov as a foreign policy pragmatist, she was highly critical of the new government's economic proposals, which included – among other things – plans to print new money, index wages, impose price and capital controls and restore state management of 'parts of the economy'. This was not the way to go. Indeed, she made it abundantly clear that Washington's 'initial reaction to some of the directions' was not 'positive' at all; moreover, if Moscow continued along this particular road, it would raise a major question mark about the future of the US–Russia relationship. Though the United States was keen to maintain the partnership and 'help Russians help themselves', if the new leadership in Moscow took the country down the path of statism rather than free enterprise, America's ability to support Russia in any way would 'go from being very, very difficult to being absolutely impossible'.[22]

The view that Russia had reached a crossroad was stated with equal force by Strobe Talbott – the original architect of American policy towards Russia. Talbott did his best to defend his original creation. The partnership, he argued, had been a useful one, and in a short space of time had done much to draw Russia out of its traditional isolation. Russia, moreover, was now playing an increasingly responsible role in a number of major international institutions such as the G8, the Council of Europe and the United Nations. As he observed, Russia had 'gone from being a spoiler to a joiner'. But there was no hiding the fact that the reform process in Russia had reached an impasse to such an extent, he argued, that Western terms like *reform* and the *market* had gone from 'being part of the vocabulary of triumph and hope, to being, in the ears of many Russians, almost four-letter words'. The situation was thus dire and could get a good deal worse. Nothing could be ruled out. Hence, even though democracy had struck some roots in Russia, it was in Talbott's opinion 'too early' to 'proclaim Russian democratisation' to be irreversible; and the 'longer the economic meltdown continued, and the more serious it becomes, the harder it would be for Russia to sustain and consolidate the various institutions and habits of what we call political normalcy'. Furthermore, though Russia had gone a long way to 'joining the European mainstream', there was a very real danger that it could take the wrong turn in the future. This would depend on many factors, but the most critical in his view was Russian economic policy. If the country decided to persist with painful reform, then it had a chance of rejoining the international community. If, on the other hand, it began to assert its own economic identity and distance itself from the West, the most likely result would be 'heightened tensions over security and diplomatic issues'. Russia had changed a good deal since the collapse of the USSR in 1991. But if it formally and finally abandoned Western-style economic reform, then there was a very real chance that the film of history could run backwards.[23]

Finally: the Putin 'problem'

The emergence of Vladimir Putin seemed to confirm all of America's worst fears about the unfolding events in Russia. A former member of the KGB who had come to power on the back of a brutally conducted war in Chechnya hardly looked like democracy's chosen emissary in post-communist Russia. Even so, policy makers in Washington were more than willing (or so it appeared from their public statements) to give Putin the benefit of the doubt. His smooth accession to power – with Yeltsin's warm words of endorsement ringing in his ears – as well as his early promises that there would be no great change in Russia's relations with the West, did much to reassure US officials. As Albright noted in December 1999, the United States had been especially pleased 'by the way in which the transition' had taken place. Washington had been equally reassured by promises made by Putin that there would be 'no shift in terms' of Russian 'foreign policy'. This was also confirmed in conversations with Foreign Minister Igor Ivanov with whom she had secured 'agreement on a whole host of issues'. Together, these would ensure that Russia and the United States would be able to continue to work 'together around the world'. It was all very 'encouraging,' she concluded.

The implication that Putin was a man with whom the United States could do business was expressed with equal force by the influential US Ambassador to NATO, Alexander Vershbow. In the context of a wide-sweeping speech in the first month of the new century, Vershbow provided a sober, but balanced assessment of the state of US–Russia relations. There was, it was true, much to be concerned about. The rule of law had not been established, Russia did not yet have 'an effective judicial system', and there had been a worrying growth of Russian chauvinism over the past year. But it was essential to maintain a sense of balance. Putin obviously presented a challenge. On the other hand, statements made by him since December were decidedly reassuring. His commitment to the market (something he had talked about at some length in his important 'Millennium Document'), his willingness to abide by the constitutional process, and his stated desire to remain engaged with the West while encouraging further trade and investment had all been most welcome. There was no reason to be downhearted, therefore 'a return to the competitive relationship of the Cold War' was not on the cards.

The view expressed by Vershbow, 'that there were too many areas of common interest for Russia and NATO not to work together', was one also endorsed by the Director of the CIA in a statement to the Senate Foreign Relations Committee two months later. Though careful not to engage in idle speculation about Russia's future over the long term – though he did predict that 'Acting President Putin' would win the 26 March election – Director Tenet pointed to what he saw as some positive signs. The most obvious, perhaps, was Putin's 'voiced support for finalizing the START II agreement and moving toward further arm cuts in START III – though the Russians, he added, would 'want US reaffirmation of the 1972 ABM Treaty in return for Start endorsements'. Putin and 'many Russian officials' had also expressed 'a desire to integrate more deeply Russia into the world economy'. Finally, 'with regard to its nuclear weapons, Moscow' appeared 'to be maintaining adequate security and control'. This did not mean there were no areas for US concern. As he pointed out, there were several issues that would test US-Russian relations in the coming months and years. That said, the prognosis was far from bleak. The proverbial glass still remained half-full.

US efforts to put what many saw (and some criticized) as an unnecessarily positive gloss on the turn of events in Russia, did not mean that policy makers were insensitive to the problems that lay ahead. Indeed, for every upbeat statement made by officials there were equally significant downbeat evaluations made as well. This lent US policy a somewhat incoherent tone at the beginning of the new millennium. At least five issues continued to cause concern among American policy makers.

The first was the situation in Chechnya. Here Washington was careful to balance between a felt need to protest the human consequences of Russia military actions, but without breaking with Moscow itself or challenging the integrity of Russia as a nation. In reality there was little or nothing America could do anyway – other than criticize Russia's scorched earth policy from afar while all the time warning Moscow that the only consequence of its actions would be to lead to an ever-lengthening list of Russian casualties and a loss of goodwill abroad. Whether this would do much to deter a ruthless nationalist like Putin (who had cleverly exploited the war for his own political purposes) was far from certain. As Vershbow rather wearily admitted, 'sad to say, it is hard to be optimistic that Russia will heed our calls for an end to an indiscriminate use of force.' Politically, it had no reason to do so. As another official observed, while the first Chechen war from 1994 to 1996 'ended in significant measure because it was so unpopular,' the 'current war' appeared to have 'broad popular support'. This is what made it so intractable and less likely to conclude in the political settlement favoured by Washington.

If the brutal war in Chechnya hung like a Damocles sword over US–Russia relations, so too did the figure of Putin himself. Efficient and young though he undoubtedly was, he was nonetheless a long-serving member of the security services who surrounded himself with advisers drawn from a similar background – key figures like Sergei Ivanov (head of the Security Council), Nikolai Patrushev (head of the Federal Security Service or FSB) and Viktor Cherkesov (the FSB's first deputy director). This 'KGB-ization' of Russian politics at the highest level raised at least two critical questions for US policy makers. The first concerned the future of Russian democracy and whether Putin could he trusted to protect basic human rights. There were severe doubts about this, expressed not only by Americans but even more significantly by civil rights campaigners in Russia itself, who feared that Putin's elevation represented a new stage in Russian history or what Yelena Bonner (Andrei Sakharov's widow) characterized as 'modernized Stalinism'. Others were equally wary of Putin's ready manipulation of enemy images as a way of consolidating his position at home. Thus while his initial pronouncements to Western visitors sounded reassuring, when he spoke to other more Russian audiences, he sent out quite different signals. It did not go unnoticed in Washington that in December 1999 he declared that 'several years ago' – in the immediate aftermath of the collapse of the USSR – 'we fell prey to an illusion that we have no enemies'. Nor was it especially reassuring to hear the future president of Russia refer regularly to some of his political competitors at home not as legitimate opponents but as traitors to the country.

A third American worry was more precisely economic. Having confidently predicted in the early 1990s that a regimen of privatization and market reforms would in due course transform Russia, nearly ten years on US officials were sounding decidedly less confident. Even the most upbeat of Americans could not ignore the fact that the form of 'crony capitalism' that had emerged in Russia with its huge concentrations of economic power in a few hands, did not correspond to their preferred model of a market economy. Moreover, though an economic meltdown had been avoided after the great financial crash of 1998 (in part because of a rise in the price of oil and partly because of an improvement in the trade balance caused by devaluation and a sharp downturn in Western imports) the situation for the majority of Russians remained grim. The US response to this was not to deny the statistical evidence but to argue – somewhat unconvincingly – that it would take many more years than originally anticipated to reform the Russian economic system. As Under Secretary of State Tom Pickering noted in a keynote speech a few days before Putin's election, the long view was needed when assessing Russia's economic future. Meanwhile, the outlook was far from rosy. Nor was there much expectation among US policy makers that Putin would improve things very much; indeed, the consensus seemed to be that the same powerful oligarchs who had supported Yeltsin, but limited the scope of economic reform, would also continue to shape Putin's options.

If the oligarchs of the Yeltsin years looked set to play a key role in the Putin era, then so too were those in and around the Kremlin who suspected NATO and opposed the expansion of NATO into East-Central Europe. Naturally enough, American policy makers hoped they might be able to convince the Russians that NATO and Russia, to use Vershbow's words, could be 'partners' rather than 'protagonists'. Indeed, Vershbow set out an eight-point plan of action: concrete measures that NATO and Russia could be working towards 'over the long term'. These included discussing respective military strategies, working together 'to prevent further proliferation', cooperative efforts in 'the area of theatre missile defence against rogue states' and sorting out 'ways to improve the capacity of their military forces to operate together in peace support operations'. But Vershbow was not naive and no doubt realized that Putin's own nationalist inclinations and stated objections to NATO expansion in the past meant that relations between the organization and Russia would remain difficult.

A final American worry concerned Putin's oft-repeated assertion that his ultimate objective was to rebuild Russian power after nearly a decade of neglect and decline. Talbott addressed this issue in some detail in a speech delivered at Oxford University. According to Talbott, there was one consistent theme in Putin's speeches and writings: 'a desire to see Russia regain its strength, its sense of national pride and purpose'. Talbott conceded that this was not an illegitimate objective; on the contrary, it was 'not only understandable' but 'indispensable' if Russia was going to prosper. There were two dangers, however. One was that Putin might decide to rebuild Russia's strength at the expense of his immediate neighbours in the former USSR; the other was that he could easily come to define Russian security in zero-sum terms. This would not only fail to bring Russia the security it craved; according to Talbott, it was bound to generate a negative reaction in an already suspicious West as well. Putin, he went on, thus had to choose between two concepts of security: today's or yesterday's – and how he chose could easily determine US–Russia relations in the new millennium.[24]

Putin's emergence to the front rank of Russian politics at the turn of the 21st century thus posed several difficult questions for American policy makers, ones to which they readily admitted there was no easy answer. In many ways the only thing that could be done in the near term, it was reasoned, was simply to wait and see. As Madeleine Albright noted, 'there's little to be gained by trying to make final judgment at this point – because we don't really know the answer, because we're going to have to deal with what Putin does, not with what he thinks.' And what he did was more likely to be determined by events within Russia rather than by new initiatives coming out of Washington.

The United States thus appeared to be locked into a policy that promised little, but to which there appeared to be no realistic alternative. But perhaps it was not all gloom and doom, and policy makers could at least console themselves with the fact that even if Russian reform had failed, Russia itself was in such disarray that it simply did not appear to have the capacity to challenge the West. As the Czech leader and former dissident, Václav Havel, rather cynically pointed out, chaos in Russia might be bad for Russians, but for other countries it could easily turn out to be a good thing. As he put it, 'Better an ill Russia than a healthy Soviet Union.' Furthermore, while Putin espoused a strong Russian nationalism on coming into office, the dominant line in Moscow (as opposed to the noisiest) seemed to be that there was no longer any point in confrontation with the capitalist world. It was just not in the country's interest.[25] Finally, while most Russians agreed that Western-style capitalism was not feasible in Russia, few (including Russia's remaining communists) advocated a return to a Soviet-style system. This might have been small comfort to US policy makers as they gazed backwards at their original vision, but it did imply that some form of working relationship might be possible in the future. This was not exactly what American policy makers had planned for back in 1992. It certainly represented a lower-level goal than the one the White House had in mind when they set out to remake Russia in the wake of the Soviet Union's collapse. But in an imperfect and increasingly unstable world it was perhaps the best they could hope for.

PART II

Bush Jnr: Empire in an Age of Terror

When Clinton left office he was replaced by a very different kind of politician in the shape of George W. Bush, a conservative of limited intellect but from a very powerful Republican dynasty whose rise to the White House – via a Supreme Court decision following a long dispute as to what really happened in Florida during the 2000 election – was bizarre by any standards. As a Brookings report was later moved to observe, 'no work of fiction could have plausibly captured' the many 'twists and turns' which finally led to Bush becoming president. Nor of course could anybody have anticipated what happened a few months later when on September 11 four planes acting as flying bombs not only killed close to three thousand people but completely changed the direction of US foreign policy. Though initially inclined to view the world in classically realist terms in which states were the primary actors, with the attack launched by a non-state actor espousing an ideology inspired by a particular reading of Islam, everything changed. It also allowed those around Bush (known in popular parlance as 'neo-cons') to articulate a decidedly expansive – even 'imperial' – strategy to deal with what they believed was the profound crisis facing the Middle East. America, they insisted had been a long liberal 'holiday from history', and if nothing else 9/11 was a stark reminder that the world was a very hostile place harbouring all sorts of very dangerous people and states. Certainly, sitting back and waiting was no longer an option. As the late Donald Rumsfeld put it, using an American footballing analogy, in a world of unknown unknowns 'the best, and in some cases the only, defence is a good offence'. To see how this offensive translated into action, I focus in the two chapters which follow on the links between 9/11 and the Iraq War and explain how the Bush team exploited the crisis occasioned by the 'Fall of the Towers' in order to pursue a more 'imperial' foreign policy, and why this strategy was more likely to end in failure than success.

4

American Power after the Towers[1]

When Clinton departed the White House, America – and indeed the vast majority of Americans – had never felt so secure. Tragically, not only did this secure world collapse on 9/11, but so too did a number of cosy assumptions, one of the most influential being that under conditions of globalization the propensity for international conflict would more likely diminish than increase.[2] As the terrorist attacks on New York and Washington revealed only too graphically, American-style globalization not only appeared to have as many determined enemies as well-meaning friends, but enemies of a quite novel character. What it also revealed – again to the discomfort of those who assumed the world was becoming a safer place – was that the worst sometimes happens. But even the most imaginative of right-wing conspiracy theorists could not have predicted that a group financed by the multi-millionaire son of one of the richest Saudi families could have carried out an attack which devastated two apparently indestructible buildings in the heart of New York, nearly destroyed the Pentagon and then go on to make a series of ghoulish videos boasting of the fact to loyal followers around the world. It was all too unreal for words.[3]

The president whose responsibility it was to respond to all this was, of course, the inexperienced George W. Bush. Less than hugely popular when he entered the White House, within a few short weeks of the attack he had moved from being what many regarded as the questionable winner of a contested presidential election into becoming America's commander-in-chief leading a nation in a war against a dangerous foe. If nothing else, this bolstered his position in the eyes of the American public. But something else changed too: America's willingness to deploy all that hard power it had been storing away in its locker for so many years. Indeed, as America flexed its muscles and launched its deadly response to the initial attack, one pundit was even moved to observe that it was no longer useful to describe the US as a mere 'superpower' but rather a veritable 'behemoth' strutting its stuff 'on the planetary stage'.[4] Even that old guru of US decline, Paul Kennedy, had to recant on past intellectual misdemeanours. The US, he confessed after the

Taliban had been vanquished, was now the 'only player' left on the field of world politics. The eagle, whose wings he thought had once been clipped, was now flying higher than ever.[5] But it was Mrs Thatcher, not Kennedy, who made the point with the greatest force, and in a moment of rare poetic inspiration even quoted Milton to describe the United States in its new muscular form. 'Methinks, I see in my mind a noble and puissant nation rousing herself like a strong man after sleep, and shaking her invincible locks.' Go ahead America, she continued in a slightly less literary vein, make the world a safer place.[6]

But as the history of conflicts has shown, it is sometimes a lot easier to wage a war than to know when to bring it to an end. No doubt if the immediate defeat of the Taliban had led to some kind of closure then the world just might have returned to something resembling normality. But this is not what happened. Indeed, 9/11 not only transformed the United States – effectively putting the country on a war footing – but American foreign policy too. As a result, America moved from being a relatively cautious nation dealing with threats only after they had manifested themselves, to becoming an altogether more assertive power which was now compelled to confront threats even before they had struck. Pre-emption was now the name of the game, not containment. If anything, to some in the Bush administration the attack only confirmed what many of them had been thinking for some time: that in an uncertain world composed of many aggressive enemies the only way of maintaining and sustaining a stable order was not through multilateral agreement, international treaties or international law (Clinton's chosen instruments) but through the threat or the use of force. From this perspective the danger now, according to some critics, was not that the US would suddenly decide to pack its bags and return to base, but do precisely the opposite and go forth to 'slay the dragons' lest the dragons come back to slay you.

Crisis and response

There were of course many reasons why 9/11 had such a profound impact on US foreign policy, not the least of which was the scale of the attack and who did the attacking. Not since the British had burned down the White House in 1814 had the US homeland been subject to a direct attack. The British however were a known quantity engaged in what might be described as a 'normal' war using the normal means employed by normal states. The same could not be said of America's religiously inspired terrorists whose rage was not just directed against the foreign policy of what bin Laden called the 'Great Satan'; rather, they were against what America was as a type of secular, liberal society. That would have been disturbing enough. But it was also what the attack implied about the world beyond US borders that proved equally unsettling. Americans may have felt good about themselves before 9/11. Unfortunately, a large number of individuals in the world clearly did not feel so well disposed towards them. Indeed, it was evident that in spite of all the hyperbole about the 'Americanization' of the world in an age of globalization, there were people 'out there' who not only did not share the American world-view but actually hated what the US represented. Perhaps few were prepared to openly applaud what happened. In fact, if one survey taken at the time was to be believed, then the most sensitive group of all – Muslims in Islamic countries – actually felt a great deal of sympathy for the US immediately following the attack itself.[7] Nonetheless, there were more than a few who appeared to take quiet satisfaction in seeing the hegemon hit where it hurt most in those quintessential symbols of American power: the Twin Towers and the Pentagon.[8] Osama bin Laden and his associates had chosen their targets well.

The immediate costs of September 11 were without doubt huge. Yet every crisis, as President Bush was to remind the American people on several occasions thereafter, represented an opportunity as well as a challenge. Thus how the United States responded to this particular challenge was going to be crucial. Few doubted that the US would take military action. However, hardly anybody could have anticipated the speed with which it acted and the resolve it showed. In the process, the Taliban were forced to retreat (though were never destroyed), allies who had hitherto been critical of Bush quickly signed up to his war on terror, the US acquired a set of new bases in countries within the former Soviet Union,[9] and for a very short while the US even seemed to get closer to Iran and Russia. It was all very heady stuff. Some even saw the attack as representing a tipping point moment in American history, and in much the same way that the struggle against communism had led to a major change in the way the United States viewed the world – more or less as a massive canvas on which an epic competition between two ways of life was being played out – the war against this new global enemy had a very similar impact on US thinking. Little wonder that certain analysts began to talk of the war against terror as being 'Cold War II'. Others even suggested that America was at the start of an entirely new epoch. The post-Cold War order, they argued, had come to an end after only ten short years.[10]

America at war

As the American writer on strategy Fred Iklé once observed, all wars come to an end.[11] The intervention in Afghanistan, however, led to something quite different; rather than coming to a conclusion, it turned out to be the first act in a drama which appeared to have no end. As Bush himself admitted, the defeat of the Taliban and their allies was merely the opening shot in what was bound to be a long hard struggle against an enemy whose aim was nothing less than the destruction of Western civilization itself. Moreover, if America was in it for the long term, then it would require the means necessary to conduct operations. Taking advantage of a quiescent Congress and a traumatized nation, Bush went on to announce the biggest military increase in US defence expenditure in over 20 years. Indeed, so huge was the new programme that some, including the president himself, hoped it would kick-start an ailing American economy.[12] Rarely in recent American history had a peacetime leader been quite so explicit in making the connection – but he did, and in the process increased defence spending by eye-watering amounts. As a result 'base' spending overall rose from $287 billion in 2001 to $513 billion by 2009. Furthermore, if one added the 'base budget' to 'emergency' war spending caused by the war in Afghanistan, the final amount spent was $700 billion, far more than Medicare outlays, which totalled $452 billion in 2010 and $486 billion in 2011.[13]

Finally, in terms of measuring the United States' response to September 11 we have to take account of the impact it had on the US itself.[14] One thing soon became clear: the country would never be the same again. Aside from the creation of a new cabinet post whose purpose was to deal with the problem of homeland security, the Bush administration acted speedily in an attempt to reassure the American people that no such attacks would take place again. This was not easy. Too little would achieve nothing; too much might raise questions about the state of civil liberties in the country. Bush, though, was in no doubt where his priorities lay; within a month of the attack, Congress had already passed the aptly named USA Patriotic Act, which gave the government significant new powers in dealing with the terrorist threat. This was followed a month later by an executive order signed by President Bush himself (without consulting Congress), which made it legal to try alien terrorists in military tribunal courts with no criminal law or evidential rules of protection.[15]

Such measures initially proved remarkably popular in a country which, having recovered from the initial shock of September 11, was now experiencing a wave of nationalism whose most visible expressions were the mass flying of the American flag and what to outsiders seemed like the almost perpetual singing of the American national anthem – understandable acts of catharsis perhaps, but not without their political consequences. Certainly the 'new patriotism' not only helped bolster the Bush presidency (not to mention the position of Bush himself) but also served to unite the country. It also helped prepare the ground for what was to follow. After all, if the US was to take action against Iraq, Iran or even North Korea – the three countries specifically described by Bush as constituting an 'axis of evil' in his State of the Union Address in January 2002 – then it would need the backing of the American people. The so-called Vietnam Syndrome might not have been overcome completely as a result of what was now happening. Nonetheless, September 11 did a great deal (for the moment at least) to make Americans a good deal less reluctant to support US military action abroad. Whether or not the same Americans would continue to support such action over the longer term remained to be seen.

The future

As we have shown, 9/11 represented a crucial watershed moment, of which one of the consequences was to make it much easier for America to project its power around the world; another was to narrow the range of political discourse at home where even asking questions about the conduct of the war started to look decidedly suspect. Even American liberals – who were especially vocal in their criticism of Bush before September 11 – could see no alternative (for the moment) but to go along with what was happening.[16]

But what about the future after 9/11, and what lessons were there for the US to draw from all this? Perhaps the first lesson (largely ignored) was that devastating though the initial attack had been, the group which launched it using an 'ungoverned space' as its base of operations failed in the end to attract any serious international support. Indeed, while many Muslims and Arabs might have had little liking for the United States – and even less perhaps for the 'war on terror' – they had even less for the Taliban who harboured a network of international terrorists, whose activities gave Islam a bad name and whose political rage was just as likely to be directed against other regimes in the Muslim world as it was against the West.

This in turn raised another issue about the wider US response. Attacking and destroying the regime in Afghanistan turned out to be a relatively easy task; taking the war forward against 'rogue states' like Iraq, Iran and North Korea, which had no intention of attacking the United States, was likely to prove to be a much riskier undertaking. Yet against much advice from more cautious analysts – including many in the international relations profession – that was precisely what the Bush administration started to contemplate. Indeed, within a very short space of time the short-term war against the Taliban and its allies started to segue into something much wider – namely 'a war against regimes the US disliked', including of course Iraq.[17] Even the so-called moderates within the Bush team seemed to think this would be no bad thing. As US Secretary of State Colin Powell admitted, getting rid of Saddam Hussein 'would be in the best interests of the region, the best interests of the Iraqi people' and 'we are looking at a variety of options that would bring that about'.[18]

Finally, if 9/11 revealed anything about the United States it was its propensity to taking unilateral action when it felt the need to do so.[19] Historically, there had never been a time when the US – because of its identity, geography and Constitution – had not always reserved the right to act when it liked, how it liked and basically where it liked. Now, of course, the tendency to go it alone and indeed expand the original mission of going into Afghanistan was almost overwhelming – in part, because America was 'now in such a dominant position internationally that the normal restraints on state behaviour no longer' applied,[20] but also because the Bush team contained key players who believed that the best way of solving the world's problems was taking decisive action without seeking permission from either the UN (whose intentions it suspected) or from allies who had little to bring to the table militarily.[21] Nor should the charge of 'unilateralism' simply be laid at Bush's door. Indeed, even the Clinton administration had not been immune to the lure of going it alone. As Madeleine Albright once put it, 'we will behave multilaterally when we can, and unilaterally when we must'. However, some in the Bush administration appeared to have taken this to an altogether different level, especially those who worked closely with Secretary of Defense Donald Rumsfeld. As one member of the Rumsfeld team admitted, the secretary of defense and his team were 'firm believers in unilateral American military power'.[22] This might have upset those of its allies who may have felt sidelined.[23] But given the prevailing mood in America, there was little chance that this would make a great deal of difference to those in Washington who were determined to reshape the Middle East while putting everybody else on notice that America would no longer brook any opposition. If its friends were prepared to come along for the ride and lend their support, then all well and good; but if not, America would 'bowl alone'. Allies may have mattered, but they were not indispensable.

5

Empire, Imperialism and the Bush Doctrine[1]

Introduction

It is an empire without a consciousness of itself as such, constantly shocked that its good intentions arouse resentment abroad. But that does not make it any the less of an empire, with a conviction that it alone, in Herman Melville's words, bears 'the ark of liberties of the world'.[2]

If all history according to Marx has been the history of class struggle, then all international history, it could just as well be argued, has been the struggle between different kinds of empires.[3] Empires, however, were not just mere agents existing in static structures. They were living entities that thought, planned, and then tried to draw the appropriate lessons from the study of what had happened to others in the past. Thus, Rome learned much from the Greeks, the British in turn were inspired by the Romans, and the British liked to think that they were passing on their imperial knowledge to their Atlantic cousins at the end of the Second World War, remarking as they did so that like the sophisticated 'Greeks' of old, they were now transferring responsibility to those untutored but extraordinarily powerful 'Romans' who happened to be living besides the Potomac.

Nor were the Americans themselves unaware of the historical stage onto which they were now stepping. Certainly, one of the more important architects of the post-war order was quite clear in his own mind about the importance of empires in history. A great admirer of the British Empire himself, Dean Acheson talked in almost glowing terms of the indispensable economic and strategic role played by Britain in the previous century, the obvious conclusion being that what the British had done for the peace and prosperity of the world after Waterloo, the Americans would now do in an era turned upside down by war, revolution and the rise of a modern revolutionary state in the shape of the Soviet Union. His British peers could not have agreed more. Indeed, like Acheson, they took the long view, pragmatically concluding that if they had to pass on the imperial torch to anyone, far better it went to their white Anglo-Saxon allies across the Atlantic than to anybody else. Out of this imperial moment of decline and renewal was thus born that which came to be known more prosaically as the 'special relationship'.[4]

Central to this transition, of course, was a shift of power to the United States, whose massive economy, global reach, moral authority and military power meant that few at the time had much difficulty in thinking of it as a new kind of imperium.[5] Certainly, the idea of a *Pax Americana* sounded no more odd to Americans after the Second World War than did the idea of *Pax Britannica* to the British in the age of Victoria.[6] In fact, many Americans were so taken with their new-found imperial mission that they sometimes looked to others for guidance, and found it, significantly, in the work of Arnold Toynbee, the famous British scholar of world history. As has been observed, this 'tutor and mentor to a generation of British imperial administrators' had 'little difficulty reconciling himself to American imperialism'.[7] For a while he even enjoyed something of a cult-like status in the United States itself, largely because he provided the American foreign policy establishment with a general theory of history and how and why imperial orders rose, endured and finally faded away.[8] Even the emerging discipline of international relations seemed to recognise the need for a single imperial power willing 'to create and sustain order'.[9] Indeed, if no such power existed, or refused to face up to its responsibilities – as the United States had refused to after 1919 – then chaos was bound to be the result. The implications were obvious. The United States had to use its vast capabilities and project power so as to compel, or entice, others to do its bidding. Only in this way could it construct the kind of secure world that had been absent for so long.[10]

This leads us, then, to an interesting paradox: the deep resistance by many Americans of thinking of the United States in terms of empire.[11] Indeed, such has been (and largely remains) the reluctance to employ the notion, that those who were most inclined to break the taboo were those who probably had the least intellectual influence within the United States itself: namely critics on the left.[12] Marginalized during the early years of the Cold War their idea about America as empire made quite an impact during the 1960s and for a while even helped define the debate about the US role in the world. Indeed, according to the most influential of American radicals who had done so much to revive the discussion, empire had become a 'way of life' for the United States, a drug almost from which the country would one day have to wean itself. If it did not, then slowly but surely it would eat away at the core values of the republic, possibly even undermine its claim to be a democracy.[13]

This, however, was not a view shared by those of a rather different ideological persuasion. Indeed, according to a new cohort of conservative intellectuals who began writing in the 1990s, empires in general were broadly speaking a good thing, the United States was itself the most benevolent empire there had ever been, and it was high time that it denied being one. By any stretch of the imagination, this was a most extraordinary turnaround. After all, the previous century had witnessed the collapse of all empires, yet here now was a group (some even close to George W. Bush's inner circle) talking about the need for a new one, and all this in a country where 'one of the central themes' had always been that there was no such thing as an American empire.[14] As one rather astute analyst pointed out shortly after the 9/11 atrocity, 'a decade ago, certainly two', the very idea of empire would have caused 'righteous indignation' among most US observers. But not any longer, it seemed.[15] 'How recently we believed the age of empire was dead' wrote another pundit, but how popular the idea had now become, especially so among those who appeared to have a very clear and direct connection with key Bush policy makers.[16] Bush himself may have insisted that the US had no 'Empire to extend'.[17] But that was not what many in and around the White House were saying at the time.

In what follows, I ask and try to answer three big questions about the American empire. The first addresses why the debate re-emerged in the post-Cold War period. The second reflects in more general terms on what is actually meant by the term 'empire' and whether or not it should be applied to the United States. Finally, we look at Bush's imperial strategy and whether or not there was ever much chance of it succeeding. Some assumed that because of setbacks in Iraq the 'new' American empire was almost stillborn;[18] others took the view that the United States had so many assets that it could act with virtual impunity.[19] Both views are too one-sided – the first because it underestimates the staying power of the United States, and the second because there never has been, and never will be, an empire without limit.[20] Nor does imperialism come cheap. Indeed, the United States under Bush soon discovered just how expensive in terms of blood and treasure this 'new' American empire was turning out to be.[21]

Imperialism with American characteristics

Though many writers over time have talked in loose terms about the US as empire, the 'new' empire debate that started in the 1990s was the direct consequence of a very special moment in history following the collapse of the USSR, a period which saw the American position in the international system being massively enhanced: in part, because the military capabilities of others declined; in part, because those of America's remained relatively intact; and partly because the US faced no peer rivals worthy of the name. Moreover, as we saw in an earlier chapter, Clinton took economics extremely seriously and implemented a series of critical regenerative measures, which eliminated the deficit, boosted domestic productivity, and transformed the American state into an even more powerful agent of international economic competitiveness.[22] The results were impressive by any measure. The economy boomed. Profits soared. And America's position in world markets was enhanced. Clinton might not have been the most serious commander-in-chief in American military history.[23] Nevertheless, he did much to enhance the US position in an era of cut-throat competition where the real battles, it seemed, were not between ideologies or armies but companies and corporations. Not for nothing do his admirers now look back on the 1990s as being an especially heroic 'moment' in American history, one which left the nation in a more prosperous and secure position than it had been for years.[24]

Yet in spite of this, there were still some who felt the US could do much better, or more precisely, do far more to exploit all its various assets and turn them to even greater American advantage.[25] Strong believers in American exceptionalism and America's mission to change the world, their analysis was not without its own internal logic. At its core was a simple and none too original thesis about the international politics of power. This led its advocates to conclude that the United States was in such a dominant position that it really should start acting in a far more assertive way: America already had the power, so why not deploy it?[26] Indeed, why not seize the moment presented by this most favourable of conjunctures and push ahead with measures that would guarantee what amounted to a permanent American hegemony? As the influential writer on foreign affairs, Charles Krauthammer, put it, why play 'pygmy' when you could be doing 'Prometheus'?[27]

Even history was plundered in order to justify this more assertive approach. Two periods inspired the new imperialists most: the late 19th century when America moved from being an economically dynamic nation to becoming a major world power, and the Reagan years during which the United States had used its power to bring about regime change in the USSR. The former, they believed, had turned the US from being an inward-looking economic power into a force to be reckoned with in the wider international system. The latter had in the end led to the fall of the Soviet Union and the possibility of constructing yet another American century. The lesson to be drawn was obvious. America would have to be bold again. This of course explains why they were so hostile to Clinton's multilateral approach to foreign policy. His administration may have talked about the US as the 'indispensable' nation. But there was no consistency of purpose. Indeed, instead of using the power he had, he took the United States off on what his own CIA director later called an extended 'national beach party'.[28] The result, it was argued, was to undermine US credibility and make the world a potentially far more dangerous place.[29]

Long before the election of George W. Bush, therefore, the intellectual ground had already been prepared for a far more aggressive policy, the ultimate objective of which was to impose a new (or perhaps not so new) set of American rules on the world. This in turn would necessitate vastly increased levels of military spending, a more determined opposition to those who did not play by the rules of the game, and a liberation from the various constraints that had been imposed on the US by those treaty-addicted, Kantian-inclined Europeans.[30] Naturally, forging what amounted to a neo-imperial foreign policy for a post-communist world would be no easy task.[31] And not surprisingly, during its first few months in office, the newly elected Bush team ran into a barrage of international opposition to its policies.[32] This is why 9/11 was so important, not because it reduced criticism from abroad – though for a brief moment it did – but because it created an acute sense of crisis which made previously controversial policies now seem far more acceptable.[33] As many members of his inner circle were to admit, September 11 was a wake-up call. It certainly proved that unless decisive action was now taken things could easily get much worse. Moreover, if as it was now claimed, America was threatened (as it was) by a transnational and undeterrable enemy with hidden cells here and shadowy allies there who were prepared to use weapons of mass destruction to achieve their theological ends (which they were), then Washington quite literally had no alternative but to intervene robustly and ruthlessly abroad. The fact that this might cause resentment in other countries was unfortunate. But this was of much less concern to these particular Americans than achieving results.

Of course not everybody in the Bush administration believed they were engaged in a latter day form of imperialism, no more than all those who went to war in Iraq believed they were building an empire. As Bush himself pointed out on more than one occasion, other powers in history did imperialism, the US did liberation.[34] However, as one of the more articulate supporters of the idea of an American empire noted at the time (interestingly a Scotsman trained in history at Oxford) denying one was an empire in all but name was not just questionable on empirical grounds. It also ignored the rather obvious fact that all empires in the past have insisted that what they were doing was for somebody else's benefit. As Ferguson noted, 'President Bush's distinction between conquest and liberation would have been entirely familiar to the liberal imperialists of the early 1900s, who likewise saw Britain's far-flung legions as agents of emancipation'. Nor did it matter much if Americans like Bush said that the US did not 'do' empire and that therefore 'there cannot be such a thing as American imperialism'. As Ferguson observed, it was not just that American forces had intervened decisively in Afghanistan to remove those in power. That was imperial enough. It was rather that it saw the world and many of the states within it in need of reform and improvement by the only country that had the means and the desire to bring this about.[35]

Empire? Sure! Why not?[36]

Yet even if we accept this interpretation of the Bush strategy, this still does answer the more basic question about whether or not the United States should be regarded as an empire. In fact, even those who argue that the real issue was 'not whether the United States' had 'become an imperial power' but 'what sort of empire' it was likely to become,[37] still had to face the problem that the term empire when applied to the US was riddled with problems. As its many critics have argued, the notion (in the wrong hands) was just as likely to mislead as illuminate. The United States, after all, was not in possession of other people's territory. It championed the idea of liberty. And it lived in a world of independent states. Furthermore, as John Ikenberry has astutely pointed out, under conditions of globalization, where there was a complex web of international rules to which even the United States had to adjust its behaviour, what sense did it make to talk of an American empire?[38]

Let us deal first with the issue of territory. The point has been made so often before that it does not need too much elaboration here. But the argument runs thus. Most states ultimately become empires by annexing the territory of others. The motives are not important; the outcome however is. In the American case however there has been no such annexation. Ergo, the United States is not an empire. As one of the more intelligent sceptics has put it, 'there has to be some sort of direct rule over the dominion for a power to be classified as an empire'. It follows therefore that the United States cannot be an empire.[39]

This particular argument has been restated so often that few now seem willing to question its validity. But it is critical to do, for the rather obvious reason that it happens to be seriously misleading when we come to look at American history. After all, when the first new nation broke away from Britain, it constituted only 13, fairly insignificant states, on the edge of a huge continent which still happened to be occupied, owned or possessed by other people. Yet a century or so later, this vast space was now in the hands of the heirs of those original colonists. Indeed, those who now repeat the line that the US cannot be an empire because it has never acquired other people's land seem to forget the rather obvious, and no doubt deeply uncomfortable 'fact', that the nation we now call the United States of America only became this particular entity because it acquired a great deal of the territory by purchase in the case of France and Russia, through military conquest when it came to Spain and Mexico, by agreement with Britain (Oregon), and, most brutally of all, by a systematic process of ethnic cleansing in the case of those various 'Indian' nations who were nearly all eliminated in one of the largest land grabs in modern history.[40]

Even some Americans were aware that something more than just another nation was being built at the time. The Founding Fathers no less talked quite openly of building an 'Empire of Liberty' that would one day stretch from sea to shining sea.[41] Their successors talked more belligerently still of an American Manifest Destiny, and by the 1890s were practising a particular form of this in the Caribbean and the Pacific. Certainly, it is difficult to see how the United States acted any differently to their European counterparts when it took over Hawaii and then brutally conquered the Philippines, in the process killing nearly 30,000 insurgents. Nor were they averse to some good old fashioned imperial interventionism of their own in Central and Latin America. Indeed, if the United States was the exception to the imperial rule, as many claim, then how do we explain the Monroe Doctrine of 1823, its sending of those black ships under Commodore Perry to intimidate Japan, and Woodrow Wilson's use of military force on no less than ten occasions? If this was not an imperialism, it is difficult to think of what might be.[42]

Yet the more general question remains: why did the United States normally prefer to exercise control abroad through means other than the direct acquisition of territory? One part of the answer lies in the extraordinary resources of the American economy and its historically proven ability to shape the affairs of others using its vast material capabilities. This method of exercising control had at least two very advantages: control could be exercised indirectly and one did not have to bear the costs of running other people's countries. Moreover, as Michael Doyle has shown in his now much forgotten classic on the subject,[43] empires can assume many complex forms; and a study of the most developed would indicate that they have invariably combined different forms of rule, none more successfully than America's presumed predecessor, Great Britain. As the famous Gallagher and Robinson team have shown in their justly celebrated work, British imperialism entertained both formal annexation and informal domination, direct political rule and indirect economic control. The real issue for the British therefore was not the means they employed to secure the outcomes they wanted, but the outcomes themselves.[44] Thus if one could create a system overall that guaranteed the right results – which for Britain meant a stable space within which it could access crucial raw materials, find a market for its goods and deny access to competitors– then that would be perfectly fine. In fact, it was precisely this model of empire (underpinned by overwhelming military superiority) that the Americans had in mind when they contemplated the post-war world in 1945.[45]

Of course, nobody would be so foolish as to suggest that the United States achieved total control of the whole world in the post-war period. Empire, we should recall, is not the same thing as omnipotence. Nor did America always get its own way, even with its most dependent allies.[46] Nonetheless, it still managed to achieve a great deal. The results, moreover, were quite remarkable. Indeed, in a relatively short space of time, following what amounted to a 30-year crisis before most of the guns finally fell silent in 1945, it managed to build the basis for a new international order within which others (old enemies and traditional economic rivals alike) could successfully operate. It also achieved most of this under the most testing of political conditions with all sorts of enemies constantly trying to pull down what it was attempting to build. So successful was it, in fact, that after several years of costly stand-off, it even began to push its various ideological rivals back. Not for it therefore the Roman fate of being overrun by the Mongol Hordes or the British experience of lowering the flag in one costly dependency after another. On the contrary, by the beginning of the 1990s, the American empire faced neither disintegration, imperial overstretch nor even the balancing activities of other great powers, but rather a more open, seemingly less dangerous world in which nearly all the main actors (with the exception of a few 'rogue states') were now prepared to bandwagon and remain under its protective umbrella. Clearly, there was to be no 'fall' for this particular empire.

But this still leaves open the problem of how we can legitimately talk of an American empire when one of the United States' primary objectives in the 20th century has involved support for nationalist movements opposed to empire?[47] The objection is a perfectly reasonable one and obviously points to a very different kind of empire to those which have existed in the past. But there is a legitimate answer to this particular question: that if and when the US has supported the creation of new nations, it has always done so with great care (Wilson did not support self-determination for the 'less civilized' peoples of the world); nor has it done so out of pure idealism but because it realistically calculated that the break-up of other empires was likely to decrease the power of rivals while increasing its own weight in a reformed world system. As the great American historian William Appleman Williams noted many years ago, this moral purpose more often than not worked to its own particular advantage.[48] Others of a less radical persuasion have come to exactly the same conclusion, noting that if and when the United States did act 'ethically' it did so for largely self-interested reasons.[49] Imperialism, as has been noted, can sometimes wear a grimace and sometimes a smile, and in the American case nothing was more likely to bring a smile to its face than the thought that while it was acquiring friends by proclaiming the virtues of liberty, it was doing so at the expense of its European rivals.[50]

This brings us then to the issue of influence and the capacity of the United States to fashion outcomes to its own liking under contemporary conditions. The problem revolves as much around our understanding of what empires have managed to do in the past as it does about what we mean by influence in the modern world. As any historian of previous empires knows, no empire worth the name has ever been able to determine all outcomes at all times within its own *imperium*. All empires in other words have had their limits. Even the Roman, to take the most cited example, was based on the recognition that there were certain things it could and could not do, including by the way pushing the outer boundaries of its rule too far.[51] Britain too was well aware that if it wanted to maintain influence it had to make concessions here and compromises there in order not to provoke what some analysts would now refer to as 'blowback'. How otherwise could it have run India for the better part of 200 years with only 50,000 soldiers and a few thousand administrators? Much the same could be said about the way in which the United States has generally preferred to rule its empire. Thus like the British it has not always imposed its own form of government on other countries; it has often tolerated a good deal of difference; and it has been careful, though not always, not to undermine the authority of friendly local elites. In fact, the more formally independent dependent countries were, the more legitimate American hegemony was perceived to be. There was only one thing the United States asked in return: that those who were members of the club and wished to benefit from membership, had to behave like 'gentlemen'. A little unruliness here and some disagreement there was fine, so long as it was within accepted bounds. In fact, the argument could be made — and has been — that the United States was at its most influential abroad not when it shouted loudest or tried to impose its will on others, but when it permitted others a good deal of slack. It has been more secure still when it has been invited in by those whose fate ultimately lay in its hands. Indeed, in much the same way as the wiser Roman governors and the more successful of the British Viceroys conceded when concessions were necessary, so too did the great American empire builders of the post-war era. Far easier, they reasoned, to cut bargains and do deals with those over whom they ultimately had huge leverage rather than upset local sensitivities.[52]

Yet the sceptics still make a good point. Under modern conditions, it is extraordinarily difficult for any single state to exercise preponderant influence at all times, a point made with great force in one of the more interesting attempts attempt to theorise the notion of empire[53] and a liberal effort to rubbish it.[54] The argument is well made. In fact it is obvious: under conditions of globalization where money moves with extraordinary speed in an apparently borderless world, it is very difficult for any state, even one as powerful as the United States, to exercise complete control over all international relations. There is also the question of its own economic capabilities. However, one should not push the point too far. After all, the US economy by the beginning of the 21st century still accounted for nearly 30 per cent of world product, the dollar still remained the most important global currency, and Wall Street still represented the beating heart of the modern international financial system. Not only that: the biggest and most important corporations in the world were still located in the United States. Furthermore, as the better literature on globalization indicates, the world economic system is not completely out of control: governments still have a key role to play. Indeed, the enormous resources at the American government's disposal not only gives it a very large role in shaping the material environment within which we all happen to live but also provides it with huge influence within those bodies whose purpose it is to manage the world capitalist system. America's control of these might not be complete, and the outcomes might not always be to its liking. But they get their way more often than not. As one insider rather bluntly put it in 2002, 'IMF programmes are typically dictated from Washington'.[55] Moreover, as Robert Wade has convincingly shown, by mere virtue of its ability to regulate the sources and supply routes of the vital energy and raw material needs of even its most successful economic competitors, the US quite literally holds the fate of the world in its hands.[56]

Finally, any assessment as to whether or not the United States is, or is not, an empire, has to address the problem of ideology and how American leaders view the US role in the world. The issue is a complex one as there are many strands to America's world outlook. Nonetheless, the United States does have an ideology of sorts, one that leads most members of its foreign policy elite to view the US as having a very special role to play by virtue of its unique history, its huge capabilities and accumulated experience of running the world since the Second World War. At times they may tire of performing this onerous task. Occasionally they falter. However, if it was ever suggested that they give up that role, they would no doubt throw up their hands in horror. Being number one does, after all, have its advantages. It also generates its own kind of imperial outlook in which other states are invariably regarded as problems to be managed, while the United States is perceived as having an indispensable role to perform. This is why the United States, like all great imperial powers in the past, is frequently accused of being 'unilateral'. The charge might be just; basically however it is irrelevant. Indeed, as Americans frequently argue (in much the same way as the British and the Romans might have argued before them) the responsibilities of leadership and the reality of power means that the strong have to do what they must – even if this is sometimes deemed to be unfair – while the weak are compelled to accept their fate.[57] So it was in the past; so it has been, and will no doubt continue to be with the United States of America.[58]

A failed empire?

The Iraq venture was doomed from the outset by the attempt made by American neo-conservatives to create what some of them styled a 'New American Empire'. This exaggerated American powers, made facile historical comparisons with previous Empires, and mis-identified the century we live in. So this early 21st attempt at Empire is failing.[59]

Recognizing the utility of the idea of empire however is one thing. Speculating about the future of empires is quite a different matter, especially in the American case there has been so much disagreement about whether or not it will go the way of all other great powers in the past — namely, downwards — or, unlike its imperial predecessors, remain dominant in the world.[60] This in turn connects to a more specific issue about the Bush strategy. Here, again, opinion is deeply divided between those who point to its many successes — getting rid of a tyrant in Iraq, pushing the terrorists onto the defensive while forcing a number of states that had once turned a blind eye to terror to do so no longer — and critics who note the negative impact it has had on human rights[61] and the way in which it has inflamed opinion throughout the Arab world. Moreover, far from the 'new' imperial strategy making the empire more secure (which was presumably the original aim of the new strategy), it has, if anything, made it a good deal weaker.

Why might this be so? One reason connects to the issue of power itself. Here we need to return to the much maligned Clinton to illustrate the point. Clinton may have had many flaws. However, the one thing he understood especially well was how to sell American power to others. Believing that the United States had to lead from the front by playing the triple role of progressive policeman, benign economic shepherd, and fair-minded umpire in the world's many trouble spots, he made it easy for most states to look on the United States in a rather favourable way.[62] Indeed, under conditions of globalization, by far and away the most effective way of making US power acceptable to others was by acting, or at least appearing to act, not just in America's interest, but in that of its major allies too. Bush, as we know, had no such vision, and egged on by his neoconservative advisers effectively abandoned what they saw as a policy of weakness. The net result might have freed the United States from formal constraint; unfortunately it did so at a price of transforming it from appearing to be benign into looking like an arrogant braggart.[63]

This leads us then to the more general question of legitimacy.[64] As liberals have always been keen to point out, there are some rather obvious reasons why the United States ought to be working with others, the most self-interested being that it helps validate its policies in the eyes of those who might otherwise be critics.[65] Thus one is cooperative not because it is the nice thing to be, but as Madeleine Albright once quipped, because it is the 'smart thing' to do. Acting assertively might get speedy results, but taking military action (especially when it came to Iraq) without widespread support even from key allies was bound to lead to a crisis. The result, as many analysts foresaw, was to be most damaging. Indeed, as several realists commented at the time, never had the United States gone into battle with so few allies actually prepared to back it enthusiastically; and never had such a war, according to another writer, generated so much global opposition in the process.[66] As a relatively friendly European later remarked, rarely in history had one nation mobilized so much hard power in such a short space of time, and never had it lost so much soft power in the process.[67]

Which brings us to the question of consensus and the American public, that vital 'second opinion' according to Grieco.[68] The United States, as we have earlier suggested, has always faced a very real dilemma of on the one hand pursuing an imperial strategy while on the other denying it was doing so. During the Cold War the circle was squared, in large part, by arguing that its own policies were not so much the result of some expansionary logic but a reasonable reaction forced on it by the aggressive policies of another power. In the same way, Bush sought to justify his actions by insisting that these were the necessary response to global terrorism, and in some very obvious way, they were. But this was never going to be an easy job. As one of the new right's few foreign admirers has noted, Americans suffer from several deficits, but the most serious by far is that concerning their attention.[69] After 9/11 the Bush team was able to exploit a state of emergency in order to mobilise support for a more active foreign policy. But it proved increasingly difficult to sustain this. Al-Qaeda might have been reactionary, dangerous and deadly; but it was hardly a powerful opponent. Moreover, its extremist ideology was unlikely to appeal to millions of people around the world. This meant that support for the 'war' against it was always going to be more difficult to sustain, especially when the US did not have the full support of important friends abroad.

There is, in addition, the very important problem of costs. Historically, there has always been a close relationship between empire and economics, with the more successful empires in history always being able to maintain a healthy domestic base, make a reasonable return on their overseas investment, and where feasible, transfer as much of the burden of their imperial rule to their various satellites. In all these various areas the United States had been massively successful since the end of the Second World War.[70] But not any longer, it seemed.[71] Never the favoured candidate of Wall Street and crucial sections of capital, Bush faced a raft of criticism from sections of the American economic establishment who sensed that the team in Washington were a group of economic irresponsibles who might have known a great deal about weapons systems and the revolution in military affairs, but seemed to understand very little at all about the modern capitalist economy.[72] Capitalists are the most pragmatic of people but several did start to wonder whether Bush was putting the US economy at risk.[73]

All roads in the end, though, led back to Iraq, that most visible military result of a policy designed in the 1990s, made possible by the election of the most right-wing president in over 20 years, and sold to the American people as the most effective way of fighting the kinds of terrorists who attacked them on September 11. Comparisons with Vietnam might be unfair. But that well known 'Syndrome' associated with that well known disaster in South East Asia in the 1960s had not yet gone away. Nor was it likely to.[74] Talking imperialism is one thing. Putting it into practice in a country where historic images of body bags and the like have burned a deep hole in the American imagination, is something else altogether. It would be ironic indeed, though by no means surprising, that in their rush to prove their 'manly' virtues in Iraq, the United States ended up undermining the case for other interventions in the future. It happened after Vietnam: there is no reason to think it could not happen again, if and when the Americans finally decide – as they probably will – to leave Baghdad.[75]

PART III

Obama: Towards a Post-American World?

For a president who saw as his role as healing the nation after eight very turbulent years, Obama turned out to be a most controversial president. Some claimed that he was not hard-nosed enough when it came to dealing with the 'real' world; progressives, on the other hand, felt he was far too cautious; meanwhile, conservatives on the right (including his ultimate successor, Donald Trump) accused him of being a dangerous liberal who was undermining US national security. Some of the more conspiratorially inclined even claimed that not only was Obama not an American – and thus ineligible to be president – but he may even have been a Muslim planning to undermine America from within. Clearly, a large part of the more lurid tales spread about the 44th president had to do with race and the fact that Obama was the first African-American in the White House. But there were also long-standing differences, both over domestic politics (many Republicans accused him of being a socialist) as well as foreign policy. Indeed, from day one he was attacked on almost every front from his willingness to engage with America's rivals to his determined efforts to push forward on climate change. Multilateralist by inclination but realist in outlook, his subtle diplomacy certainly made itself an easy target for those advocating simple solutions to deal with complex global problems. Obama, however, always remained optimistic when it came to the United States. He did not agree with the fashionable idea that America's best days were behind it. On the other hand, he did accept that the world was becoming less of an American playground and that the US would have to make the necessary adjustments to deal with the new situation. However, his first task, as we show in Chapter 6, was to pull the United States out of the deep economic recession it found itself in following the 2008 financial crisis before it could go then on to address America's many other global challenges. One of these, as we indicate in Chapter 7, was how to breathe life back into a transatlantic relationship which under Bush Jnr had suffered one setback after another. Chapter 8 then examines what over time would prove to be the biggest challenge of all facing the United States and the West: an increasingly close strategic partnership between Putin's Russia and Xi's China.

6

Navigating the Rapids

Introduction

As we have shown in previous chapters, both Clinton and Bush faced challenges of a quite different character: in Clinton's case these arose out of victory in the Cold War and in Bush's out of a devastating attack on the American homeland. Barack Obama's stunning electoral victory in 2008 came at yet another critical point in the post-Cold War history of the United States. Already five years into a costly and increasingly unpopular war of choice in the Middle East, the US was suddenly confronted with something it neither chose nor expected: a financial crash that quickly morphed into something far more threatening. Born out of a combination of economic hubris, cheap money, an overheated housing market and a lack of proper oversight by the rating agencies, all embedded into a complex financial system which the economics establishment had predicted would never fail, the situation confronting Obama when he assumed office was, in the words of one economic notable, probably as bad, if not 'actually worse' than that which had faced the United States back in the early 1930s.[1] Clearly, this was no mere blip but a profound crisis of the whole system, which was to bring Wall Street to its knees by the end of 2008 before going on to cause the worst global downturn since the end of the Second World War.

Moreover, what happened did not just have economic consequences. At home it changed the course of the election while internationally dealing a major body-blow to the oft-repeated claim that the American model of capitalism represented the wave of the future. As Roger Altman, a former Clinton official, observed in a much-cited piece published in *Foreign Affairs* just as Obama was settling into the White House, 'the financial and economic crash of 2008 [...] the worst in over 75 years', represented a 'major geopolitical setback' for the liberal world order as a whole, one which would not only have material impact on people's everyday lives but would also have major international repercussions as well by 'accelerating trends' that were already 'shifting the world's center of gravity away' from the United States and the West towards other rising powers in the world, China most obviously.[2]

Altman's sober assessment was one which Obama was bound to take very seriously. An avid student of world politics himself who had majored in international relations at Columbia University, Obama never seemed to buy into the then fashionable notion (fashionable even before the crash) that the United States was in decline.[3] On the other hand, he did not believe the US could, or would, be able to sit on top of the world for ever. Drawing intellectual inspiration from a number of popular writers who emphasized the important changes brought about by globalization,[4] he appeared to see the world less in terms of a 'zero-sum game' fought out between rising and falling powers – the classical realist view – and more in terms of an interconnected order in which all nations had a stake.[5] Nor he believed was there any necessary reason for the US to be especially concerned about the new world economic order in which (until 2008 at least) all boats appeared to be rising and from which big emerging economies like India and China could only benefit. Though radically inclined in his youth, by 2008 Obama had become a thoroughgoing centrist who even if he was not insensitive to the problems associated with open markets and free trade (at one point he was even wondering whether it had been wise to allow China into the World Trade Organization) nevertheless felt that every country could find a place within a global economic order in which the United States would continue play a vital but not 'top dog' role.[6]

If defining a strategy to deal with this 'post-American' world was one of the more long-term tasks facing the incoming team, then of more immediate concern was what to do about what Obama had much earlier called that 'dumb war' in Iraq.[7] Conceived by neoconservatives as a way of draining the ideological 'swamp' that was the Middle East under the cover of looking for weapons of mass destruction, by 2008 it was clear that public support for a war which had already led to over 4,000 US troop deaths was fast ebbing. Indeed, by October, two thirds of all Americans were now claiming they were opposed to an intervention which they had overwhelmingly backed in 2003, and to which, of course, Obama had always been opposed. This may not have been an especially popular stance for him to have taken a few years earlier; however, five years on, it was clearly working to his advantage. Certainly without Iraq, and what looked like his principled opposition to it, there was little chance he would have secured the Democratic nomination in the first place, let alone go on to win the White House just over a year later. It was by any measure a most remarkable achievement for a young African-American who had next to no foreign policy experience, who was never the favoured candidate of the Democratic Party establishment and in a country that was still overwhelmingly white and which had given Bush Jnr a second term in office only four years earlier.

In what follows we shall provide an overview of the way in which Obama attempted to address all the major challenges the US faced when he assumed office in 2008. In the first part therefore, we will look at the threat posed by the great financial meltdown, how his team tried to deal with it and with what longer term consequences. In the second section we will examine the changing distribution of power in the international system, and in particular at how Obama tried to deal with the rise of China. The third part will assess the difficult legacy left by Bush in the Middle East and the new crises which then arose during Obama's first term. We will then look at the foreign policy question to which there seemed to be no easy answer: what to do about post-communist Russia? Finally, in a brief concluding section we will try and assess how successful or unsuccessful Obama was in dealing with these multiple, overlapping problems.

Saving America

> On the morning of January 27, 2009, my first full day as secretary of the Treasury, I met with President Barack Obama in the Oval Office. The worst financial crisis since the Great Depression was still raging, and he wanted to put out the fire for good.[8]

Apparently Lenin once remarked that there are decades when nothing very much happens, and then along comes a moment in time when the world is quite literally turned upside down. 2008 was such a 'moment 'which in its own way followed another, equally remarkable 'moment' in US economic history which had seen nearly 30 years of low inflation growth, often referred to in the economics literature as the 'great moderation'. The great moderation was soon followed however by the great panic, and the great panic in turn by the great American downturn. At first, policy makers no doubt assumed, or at least hoped, that this was just another 'classical financial panic' which have been a regular feature in US economic history, and which could easily be offset by more intervention on the part of the Federal Reserve. But however much policy makers intervened (and they intervened a great deal from March onwards) nothing seemed to work. If anything the crisis only deepened, so much so that in a one month period alone 'starting in September' the government was compelled to nationalize the two 'mortgage giants' Fannie Mae and Freddie Mac, provide an $85 billion government rescue loan for the giant insurance company AIG and guarantee 'more than $3 trillion worth of market funds' to support the banking system. Yet even this could not prevent the 'venerable investment bank' Lehman Brothers from going under, and as we know now (though this was not anticipated at the time) once it collapsed, the markets went into an ever steeper dive.⁹ So too did the 'real' economy and in the fourth quarter of 2008 the economy contracted by over 8 per cent and 2 million jobs were shed with many more to come. It was by any measure a 'perilous time' made all the more dangerous by the fact that following the November election the US was now between one president who was at best a 'lame duck' and another who until January 2009 had no power. As a number of key policy makers later remarked, 'it's hard to overstate how chaotic and frightening' it all felt at the time.¹⁰

It was not just the economic crisis however that was causing policy makers a problem as Obama soon discovered. It was also the limited options they had before them. Indeed, whichever way they turned they ran into opposition. Thus if, or when, they moved to bail out the banks and the bankers on the grounds that they were just 'too big to fail' they were accused of rewarding the 'arsonists' who had caused the inferno in the first place. But if they did not, then there was every chance of the US falling over the edge into a 1930s style depression from which there might be no escape at all. Equally, if they decided (as they did with Fannie Mae and Freddie Mac) to take failing assets under government control – the economic equivalent in the US of breaking all ten commandments – they were accused of undermining the free enterprise system. Then there was the whole issue of 'moral hazard' and the view expressed by many that it was ethically wrong to save those financial institutions which had failed, especially if it was being done with hard earned taxpayer's money. Finally, of course there were the freewheeling followers of the libertarian school of economic thought – not uncommon in the United States – who basing their argument on the work of the great Austrian economist Joseph Schumpeter insisted that every now and then capitalism had to go through its own *Sturm und Drang* period to weed out the weak in order to allow the strong to become stronger. Theoretically of course this sounded all well and good. But when millions were being laid off and the markets in free fall, this was not an option open to politicians who wanted to retain any degree of support at home.

When Obama finally entered the White House, he thus confronted both an economic crisis which showed every sign of getting worse, as well as a policy conundrum. In fact, as he himself quickly found out, there were no easy fixes. Moreover, whatever he did, there would always be a price to be paid by somebody somewhere, and there was a very strong chance that this was more likely to be paid by the average citizen living metaphorically on 'Main Street' than the 'fat cat' financiers who ran 'Wall Street'.¹¹ It was no surprise therefore that even while the dust was settling and the economy began to show signs of life a year into his first term, populist movements began to spring up with the Tea Party on the right calling for less government (while accusing Obama of taking the nation down the un-

American path of socialism) and the 'Occupy Wall Street' movement on the left demanding social justice and that something be done about the vast inequalities in wealth which were just as great after the crash as they had been before. Indeed, if one result of the crash was to lead to a long-term fall in US GDP of about 4 per cent, a loss to the average American of something like $70,000 per person and a $2 trillion bill (more than twice the cost of the war in Afghanistan) another was to highlight some of the deeper problems facing the United States such as wage stagnation, declining levels of social mobility, and significantly, the fact that wealth and income disparities in America had been rising exponentially ever since the late 1980s.[12]

Obama's problems did not just lie at home, however. Sitting as America did at the heart of the international economy it was inevitable that what happened to the US could not but have a massive impact on the rest of the world. Indeed, the crisis not only damaged the American economic order, but had an equally significant impact on other countries, and indeed on America's standing in the world. As one of Obama's key advisers later confessed, as the crisis accelerated and spread far beyond America's own borders, this had a very great (and necessarily damaging) impact on perceptions of the United States.[13] Some regions and countries were especially hard hit including those in Central Europe, the less competitive economies in the Eurozone (Greece most visibly) as well as emerging economies whose combined GDP was about US$1.3 trillion lower in 2010 than might have been predicted a year before the crisis. Moreover, even if the world economy did not collapse – the system survived – there was no recouping what had been lost.[14] By any reasonable measure the damage wrought was enormous, with a loss to global output coming in at around US$10 trillion by 2014 (close to 15 per cent of global GDP) accompanied by a major loss of jobs (approximately 60 million) worldwide. Even the prosperous North Atlantic economies felt its impact, and according to one assessment, together experienced a cumulative gap of trillions of dollars between what output would have been had these economies followed the pre-crisis trend and actual production. Nor finally did 'rising' China escape the economic tidal wave with the best part of 20 million workers losing their jobs in just under 18 months.[15]

But perhaps the greatest damage done to the international economy was in terms of the blow it dealt to the once influential idea that globalization was by definition a good thing. Advanced with almost embarrassing gusto by Clinton in the 1990s and endorsed by the majority of mainstream economists as the solution to nearly everything from eliminating global poverty to allowing once less-developed countries to emerge, following 2008 it became increasingly difficult to say that it 'worked' or worked well, except of course in the ironic sense that problems generated in one country very quickly spread to all the others.[16] The British Prime Minister at the time,

Gordon Brown, stated the problem rather well in his book on 2008 which he significantly sub-titled the 'first crisis of globalization'.[17] Brown himself had always been one of the more avid supporters of open markets and free trade insisting that its benefits over 30 years clearly outweighed any problems it may have generated in its wake. But with the world now facing a major downturn and international living standards falling in the wake of 2008, it was perhaps inevitable that globalization itself would come under increasing scrutiny. As the managing director of the World Bank warned even before the crisis had taken off, 'globalization' could 'only be sustained if it created 'opportunities and benefits for all'. As the years rolled on following 2008 it seemed to many observers that the opportunities and benefits of which he spoke were fast disappearing to be superseded by austerity, decreasing employment opportunities and rising insecurity. The ground it seemed was being prepared for a backlash that was bound to come one day.[18]

Towards a post-American world?

> The crisis of 2008 [...] may well mean the end of a certain kind of global dominance for the United States.[19]

The issue of America's unique position in the wider international system has been a source of much intellectual speculation ever since the American publisher Henry Luce first coined the term the 'American Century' back in 1941 in perhaps one of the most influential articles in the history of journalism. Part call to action and part anticipation, his analysis of America's pre-eminent role in the world certainly seemed to provide an extraordinarily accurate prediction of what then went on to happen throughout most of the post-war period – and possibly even more so after the US had seen off its superpower rival in 1991 and began to enjoy its 'unipolar moment'. Even the turbulent Bush years did not entirely destroy a narrative, which took as its starting point the idea that a preponderance of American power was not only inevitable but was a functional necessity in a world where having a liberal hegemon delivering a package of public goods was the only sound basis on which order could be guaranteed.[20]

At what point this narrative came under more serious scrutiny is by no means clear. There was, of course, a whole flurry of books and articles in the 1970s and 1980s anticipating the slow but inexorable 'fall' of the United States as a great power. Indeed, one particular study on the subject by Paul Kennedy went on to become an international best seller, though almost as soon as the volume had been published the USSR went under, the US led a successful coalition against Iraq in 1992, and the much-hyped Japanese model failed, while the United States itself went on to experience one of the more sustained economic booms in its history. Yet the spectre of decline never quite went away. No doubt the long drawn-out agony that became Iraq played its part in undermining confidence, as did of course the crisis in 2008. But perhaps even more important were the shifts beginning to take place in the wider international system, largely as a result of economic changes brought about by globalization.

As we have already suggested, Obama's initial approach to dealing with these shifts was less to oppose them but rather seek a way to work with change in order to channel it along acceptable channels. Thus he took a fairly relaxed line to the BRICS organization (until he decided it didn't matter very much); as we shall see, he also tried reset relations with Russia; and perhaps most important of all, he made every effort to maintain a working relationship with China. Obama himself was not naive when it came to China and readily conceded that it posed a serious challenge to the liberal world order. On the other hand, it had become too big to contain and far too important to ignore; furthermore, on a whole range of big international questions from dealing with North Korea through climate change, and on to helping sustain growth in the world economy, China's involvement was essential.

However, as China continued its rise and became increasingly assertive – especially in the South and East China Seas – dealing with Beijing became more difficult. What made it all the more difficult was how China then reacted in strategic terms to the 2008 crisis. There were those on the Chinese side, including most of its economists, who were deeply concerned about what had happened, and who went on to point out that because the two economies were so intertwined what hurt one (America) was bound to hurt the other (China). Others in China, however, took a very different view. Nationalist in outlook and deeply suspicious of American intentions, they interpreted 2008 as either being a clear indication that America was either in decline or facing problems of such a magnitude that it had become (in the words of one well-known study of American foreign policy published many years earlier) a 'crippled giant'.[21] Distracted by its own problems at home, tied down as it was bound to be for some time in the Middle East, and viewed by many outside the US (even its allies) as a globally 'irresponsible' power with little interest in the impacts of its actions on others, the future according to this reading looked decidedly problematic for the United States and increasingly bright for a rising China.[22]

This, of course, did not prevent either China or the United States from trying to maintain what by later standards was a reasonably open dialogue. Obama, in fact, made a well-publicized trip to China in 2009, and the then-Chinese President Hu Jintao made an equally well-publicized trip to the United States in 2011. Yet, however much Obama continued to repeat the liberal mantra that China's emergence as a great power was not something to be feared, it was perfectly obvious that many in the United States took a less sanguine view, including influential realist scholar John Mearsheimer who had for years been warning that China's rise could never be peaceful.[23] Meanwhile, on the Chinese side the view remained what it had been for some time: that America's underlying, if not stated, policy was one of slowing down China's rise. Indeed, when in 2010 Obama's Secretary of State Hillary Clinton declared that the US was now 'returning to the Asia-Pacific' – a policy later recast as a 'strategic pivot' and then of 'rebalancing' – the Chinese saw this as living proof of US hostility. The fact that the speech was made in the same year (2010) when it was announced that China had finally overtaken Japan to become the second-largest economy in the world only reinforced the view in Beijing that even if there were areas where the two countries might continue to cooperate, the relationship was becoming increasingly competitive.[24]

Ever the optimist, Obama continued throughout his two terms to look for areas where China and the United States might work together, all the time fearing that if the relationship deteriorated to the point of no return, then this would not only hurt American business as it tried to climb out of the deep hole dug for it by the crash of 2008, but also have an impact on the stability of the important Asia-Pacific region. Nonetheless, the general direction of travel in the relationship was in the opposite direction to where Obama might have hoped it would be going when he assumed office. This in part flowed from the broader differences between the two systems. But it was also the result of a big shift in American public opinion, which had become decidedly hawkish on China; this in turn was the very direct consequence of an increasingly influential narrative that began to connect many of America's economic woes to China's economic rise.[25] Nor was the criticism only coming from Obama's enemies on the right. For example, the left-leaning Economic Policy Institute released a report in 2012 purporting to show that of the many millions of manufacturing jobs which had been lost since the start of the new century, 2.7 million of these were the result of the US–China trade deal signed in 2001. Wages of American workers, it also claimed, had been affected because of the competition, with a 'typical two-earner household' losing something close around $2,500 per annum as a result.[26] The same organization published another report in 2014, which calculated that job losses between 2001 and 2013 now stood at 3.2 million.[27] Just over a year later, a detailed study by four academics seemed to confirm this analysis. There was much to be said in favour of an open trading system, they agreed. The problem with trading with an economy as big as China was that its labour costs were so low. This not only led to large trade deficits with the United States. As China's share of world manufacturing exports increased from 2 per cent to 16 per cent between 2001 and 2012 – largely as result of the country's accession to the World Trade Organization in 2001 – wages and manufacturing jobs in the United Sates began to decline.[28]

Meanwhile, on the Republican right, China very quickly became a weapon of choice which was deployed with increasing regularity to attack Obama, either for not understanding the danger it posed to US interests or for continuing to believe that it could be turned into a 'responsible stakeholder' when all the evidence suggested otherwise. Moreover, the closer the United States came to the tipping point election of 2016, the more persistent the attacks on the Democrats became. 'The lack of common sense in this White House is beyond breath-taking,' claimed former Arkansas Governor Mike Huckabee in 2015. 'We need a different strategy to confront Chinese behavior – whether in the South China Sea or in cyberspace,' Carly Fiorina (the former Hewlett-Packard executive) insisted on Facebook. America is just being 'walked over by rivals and adversaries' including China, declared Senator Lindsey Graham while announcing his candidacy to lead the Republican Party into the next election.[29] No politician, however, was quite as scathing as Trump. A long-time critic of China, Trump took the debate to an altogether different level, linking his attack on the Democrats to their supposed love affair with globalization and trade deals, and then linking both with China's economic rise and therefore to the desperate plight in which American workers now found themselves.[30]

How far these attacks on the Democrats' record on China made much of a difference to the outcome of the election in 2016 is not at all clear. There is little doubt, however, that 'China bashing' played well to Trump's deeply conservative base. Moreover, fearing that they might be outflanked on the issue, the Democrats decided there was nothing to be lost and everything to be gained, politically, by drawing a clear red line between their own positions and those in the United States (including most obviously US corporations) who upheld the line that in spite of certain obstacles China remained a partner with whom they at least would continue to do business.[31] It is true that the Democrats never went as far as Trump in claiming that China had been economically 'raping' the United States, or that climate change was a Chinese trick designed to undermine US competitiveness! Nevertheless, their various comments on a range of issues from human rights to labour standards hardly suggested that the relationship in future was going to be an easy one. Moreover, while Clinton and Trump during the campaign clashed on almost everything, the one thing they seemed to agree on was that something needed to be done about China, and in particular 'that China had stolen millions of American jobs and must be made to give them back'.[32] Whether there was much chance of this ever happening was doubtful. However, what it did seem to point to was the enormous sea change that had taken place in the US–China relationship ever since Obama had declared only three years after becoming president that the US should 'welcome' rather than fear 'China's rise'.[33]

Beyond war: the Middle East

The American public had turned to the Democrats in 1976, after the end of the Vietnam War. The country chose the Democrats in 1992, after the end of the Cold War. In 2008, once again, voters handed to the Democrats the task of straightening out America's role in the world in the wake of the war in Iraq.[34]

In his run for the White House in 2008, one of Obama's big promises, if not his biggest, was to 'distance the United States from the neoconservative foreign policy legacy of his predecessor, George W. Bush, and usher in a new era of a global, interconnected world', in which the US would achieve its goals through deploying its power in a 'smart' fashion rather than through the blunt military instrument which he argued had been favoured by his predecessor.[35] Naturally enough, Obama did not eschew the use of military force altogether. On the other hand, after the devastating experience of Iraq (not to mention Afghanistan) he was insistent that 'military action had to be, first, limited to the defence of vital US interests and, second, carried out by a leaner, more flexible military force acting not unilaterally but multilaterally in cooperation with local allies'. Recognizing, as Obama seemed to, the need for a major foreign policy rethink – which some claimed added up to a distinctly new 'doctrine' – his approach to international security could best be summed up in the following ways: only engage militarily when it was absolutely necessary to do so (no more 'wars of choice'); curtail all unnecessary overseas commitments (including, most importantly, that undertaken in Iraq); engage with all powers (even possible rivals like Russia and China) if it lowered the costs of foreign policy; and finally, demonstrate to the world at large (and to the Middle East especially) that the United States could be part of the solution rather than being, as it appeared to be, the source of the problem.[36]

Engaging the Middle East was, of course, Obama's number one foreign policy priority. Here though, his larger goal was not to increase America's presence in the region but rather to create the conditions in which it would become a good deal less visible. The first thing he did, therefore, was to start planning for a major US troop withdrawal from Iraq. The second task was to work with his European allies and get Iran onside by engaging it on the nuclear question, and in this way (hopefully) bring the Islamic Republic in from the cold. The third part of the strategy was to continue to support Israel – military aid to the country went up substantially under Obama – but make a more serious effort to bring about peace between the Palestinians and the Israelis. Underpinning all this, in turn, was a determined effort to try and win the 'hearts and minds' of people in the region by demonstrating that the United States was neither hostile to Islam as a religion nor to Muslims as a category of people, something which Obama set out to do in his famous Cairo speech in the summer of 2009. Finally, though the United States would not be imposing its way of life on others, if political change was to come to the region, this would be something the US would embrace if it was in the American national interest to do so.[37]

Obama's diplomatic strategy certainly did not lack in ambition. Nor was it without its own logic. Indeed, if it could be made to work, it would not only help the US reduce the size of its footprint in a region where views of the US ranged from the deeply suspicious to the downright hostile; it would also allow it to focus on other issues in other parts of the world, Asia most obviously. Applauded by some as introducing a large dose of realism into US thinking, but by others as signalling the beginning of the end of America's serious commitment to the region, the chances of Obama ever realizing his ambitions without upsetting someone or some interest group back in the US was always very low. Thus, by signing an agreement with Iran, he caused a furore in America among those who not only hated the Islamic republic but continued to see it as the main threat to the stability of the Middle East as a whole. It also caused a breach between Obama and the Israeli government, which could not but be deeply suspicious of this liberally inclined president in the White House who did not buy into Prime Minister Netanyahu's stated objective of constructing more and more Jewish settlements in the West Bank. Finally, though withdrawing from Iraq may have been politically popular back home, there was every chance that as US forces started to leave, Iran and its Shia allies in Baghdad would begin to act with greater aggression towards the Sunni minority and so drive them into the hands of Islamic State (ISIS). Moreover, once ISIS had emerged as serious threat in both Iraq and Syria, the only way it could be combated on the ground – as opposed to from the air – was by turning to other actors like Hezbollah and the Kurdish militia with whom the United States could hardly be said to be on friendly terms.[38]

Obama faced an even larger problem of what exactly the United States should do if real pressure from below started to bring about change in the region, as it began to with the onset of the Arab Spring in 2011. Hitherto, the US position had been a rather simple one: support the various authoritarian regimes that ruled the region for fear of what might follow if they were to go. Now, with street protests spreading across the Middle East demanding something the US was ostensibly in favour of – a free press, free speech, economic opportunity and the rule of law – the Obama administration now found itself caught between a political hard rock known as 'people power' and a hard place called 'instability'. Even his own team had different opinions on this, with those of a more realist persuasion urging the president to keep backing rulers like Hosni Mubarak in Egypt, and others who felt America had to come down on the side of the 'Arab street'. In the end the 'street' won (at least did in Egypt), and Mubarak was persuaded to go. However, none of this seemed to work to America's advantage. Indeed, not only did the end of the Mubarak era horrify America's traditional allies across the region, his going only threw up new challenges when he was replaced by the Muslim Brotherhood who could hardly be described as ideological moderates or being well disposed towards the United States.[39]

Nor were there any easy or straightforward policy choices in any of the other Arab countries. In some cases, for example, Obama decided to stick with the status quo. Thus, in Bahrain the US simply stood by and watched without demur as Saudi and Emirati forces imposed order following a Shia uprising in 2011. In the Yemen, it even provided 'logistical and intelligence support' for an air campaign aimed at defeating the Houthis, an Iran-backed insurgency, a policy which one of his key advisers later confessed did not cover the Obama administration 'in glory'.[40] However, in Libya, far from opting for 'order', under pressure from his European allies and the interventionists in his own administration, he decided to support military action against Gaddafi with results that could hardly be described as optimal as the country sank into chaos and very quickly turned into a failed state. Syria, of course, proved even more of headache. Here the US was strong on rhetoric but weak when it came to doing anything to get rid of Assad; and in the absence of any decisive action Russia stepped into the vacuum and helped (with support from Iran) to save the regime from what looked like its inevitable fate at the beginning of the upheavals there.

Given all these various setbacks it is very easy to argue, as many have done, that Obama's whole approach to the Middle East failed miserably. Indeed, according to critics, the net result of his actions – or inaction – was to leave behind a number of alienated allies and a region that was probably no less anti-American than when he had taken over from Bush in 2009. Even his keynote nuclear deal, they insisted, did nothing to change the drivers of Iran's foreign policy. Experts in arms control may have found much to praise in a deal which they claimed held Iran's nuclear programme in check. However, this is not how it played out in Washington where his bold new policy towards Tehran found itself under siege from those on the Republican right – Trump most vocally – who were prepared to use any argument or device to prove to the American people that a wholly new approach to the Middle East was essential.

Putin's Russia

> America's way of dealing with Russia was always to change it. Bill Clinton wanted to help Russia change. Dick Cheney wanted to change Russia by destroying it, and Obama – well you know what happened.[41]

Vladimir Putin was born in 1952 (the year before Stalin died); he attended a not very distinguished university, then successfully applied to join the KGB, from which perspective he observed three developments that went on to shape his later political outlook. One was the reforms undertaken by Gorbachev, which culminated disastrously, in Putin's view, in the end of East Germany where he was then serving. The second was the collapse of the USSR two years later, an event which he later went on to characterize as 'the greatest geopolitical tragedy of the 20th century'. And the third was the economic implosion of post-communist Russia in the 1990s accompanied by its reduced international status, which allowed the United States to regard it less as it once did – as a threat to be taken seriously – and more as a country which could almost be disregarded. Russia's first post-communist leader Boris Yeltsin even seemed to personify Russia's fall from grace. More often than not inebriated, corruptible and corrupt, and too easily bamboozled by his American counterpart Bill Clinton, Yeltsin seemed to represent everything that had gone wrong in Russia since the middle of the 1980s.

It is often said that Putin came into office with a clear goal of contesting the Western-led liberal order. This may have been his deeper purpose. But as we argued in Chapter 3, initially at least, he did not appear to be seeking confrontation with the United States or the West. He was, we should recall, the first foreign leader to send President Bush a note of condolence in solidarity following the attacks of 9/11. He also supported the NATO intervention in Afghanistan, and in 2001 was even suggesting Russia might become a member of a reformed version of the same organization. In addition, he encouraged foreign direct investment, talked glowingly of a new European security architecture, and did nothing to discourage Russians from either travelling to, working or studying in the West. Nor it seemed was he opposed to Western-led institutions like the European Union, and until 2014 at least appeared keen to see Russia become a member of the G8. Sceptics may now argue that this was all a front and that he was never 'pro-Western'.[42] They may also point out that in the eight years after having taken over Russia in 2000, he had not only transformed the country by allowing his friends in the KGB to make it over in their own image, but demonstrated an unrelenting hostility to the West in general and the United States in particular. Thus, why bother trying to 'reset' the relationship, as Obama then went on to do?

The answer to this lies in part with the ascent of Dmitry Medvedev to the Russian presidency in 2008, and in part with Obama's broader understanding of the world. Ever the pragmatist when it came to international relations (interestingly, he was a great admirer of Bush Snr's 'realist' approach to world affairs), Obama appeared to take the view that it behove the leader of the free world to achieve the possible, rather than the impossible, and not allow the pursuit of a perfect world to become the enemy of one within which all powers might be able to find a place. Fearing a return to a Cold War that he thought was avoidable, meant that every effort should be made to find ways of working with Russia rather than accepting its hostility as 'a matter of fact'. This in turn involved looking for areas of common concern where Russia and the United States might work together. Obama even travelled to Moscow in 2009 where officials there proved to be more than willing to work with the US in facilitating supplies into Afghanistan. Meanwhile, the US started discussing the possibility of Russia joining the World Trade Organization. Nor did the minor 'thaw' conclude there. Indeed, the two countries set up a series of working groups (19 in all), to work together on a range of issues from security to trade and scientific exchanges. June 2010 then saw the US and Russia at the UN Security Council approving a resolution directed against Iran. At the same time, the then-Russian President Medvedev visited Silicon valley in northern California before travelling on to Washington to discuss a further expansion in trade relations.[43]

By the end of 2010, therefore, US officials had good reason to feel satisfied, even more so by 2011 when the two states signed a major arms control agreement. Indeed, if Obama's original vision was to work with all international actors (even the most difficult) to achieve concrete foreign policy outcomes following years where there appeared to have been very few, then his 'reset' strategy appeared to be working rather well. This may not have satisfied those in the West who had for some time been announcing the onset of a 'new' Cold War caused in their view by Putin's increasingly authoritarian policies at home, his brutal interventions in Chechnya, and last but by no means least, by Russia's intervention in Georgia in 2008.[44] However, for an American public grown tired of confronting the world and beginning to turn inwards following the economic crisis of 2008, Obama's policy of trying to work alongside post-communist Russia appeared to be one with which they could, for the time being, live.

The downward spiral in the relationship which followed Obama's initial efforts was the consequence of at least two unforeseen events, both resulting from developments in the Arab world. One was the collapse of Libya and America's role in bringing about regime change there, much to Russia's displeasure; the other was the ongoing conflict in Syria and Russia's decisive intervention to support its old Ba'athist ally. But another factor probably played into this as well: namely, Putin's formal return as president following a period when Medvedev had ostensibly been at the helm. Whether or not there was ever a real difference between Medvedev and Putin when it came to relations with the West is a moot point. Nor is at all clear even when he was president whether Medvedev was actually in charge. Nonetheless, it did appear that he was willing to engage with the Americans in a way that Putin appeared to find more difficult. Either way, as soon as Putin took over the presidential helm (again) the 'relationship dynamics' changed for the worse.[45]

Inevitably, the crisis in the relationship soon inserted itself into the US political discourse back home. Indeed, during the race for the White House in 2012 Obama's opponent, Mitt Romney, attacked Obama not only for not taking the Russian threat seriously but for failing to identify it as being either 'a' or possibly even 'the' 'number 1 geopolitical foe' to world peace. Forced onto the defensive, Obama's rather weak riposte was that there were many threats in the world of which Russia was only one; moreover, under his 'reset' policy there had been some important gains for the US. But it was clear that the political mood was shifting. Never the American public's most favoured nation, following the 2012 presidential race, which of course Obama won by a clear margin (Obama received 51.1 per cent of the popular vote to Romney's 47.2 per cent), attitudes towards Russia began to move from being a 'majority favourable' towards becoming decisively 'unfavourable'.[46]

Clearly, the most immediate reason for this was the crisis in Ukraine beginning in 2013 and concluding with the Russian annexation of Crimea and the unleashing of a war in eastern Ukraine. Meanwhile, as the relationship went into freefall as a result, the intelligence community started warning the Obama team that Russia was 'ramping up its intelligence operations and building disinformation networks it could use to disrupt the US political system'.[47] Russia's official line against the West also shifted from being merely suspicious to being profoundly hostile. By 2015, even the Russian public began to view the Western world in broadly negative terms.[48] Nor did the unfolding war of words and actions stop there as Putin deployed all his skills as a former KGB-man to present his actions as being a defensive response to Western subversion. Putin himself even developed something close to a credible narrative justifying his actions. As he repeated to any Western journalist who cared to listen, Russian interests had been ignored time and again since 1989: first in the 1990s when the US enlarged NATO (in spite of a promise to Gorbachev that it would not do so); then again in 2013 when the EU had tried to pull Ukraine into the Western fold by getting the government in Kiev to sign an association agreement.[49] Nor was this particular construction one that everybody in the West rejected. A number of former officials – as well as a few international relations scholars[50] – agreed that by acting in the way it had by enlarging NATO the US had unnecessarily provoked a Russian reaction.

Faced with what looked like the implosion of its original strategy, the Obama administration was left with the rather unenviable task of responding as forcefully as possible to increased hostility from a Russia it had earlier attempted to woo. Obama himself even went on the ideological offensive, criticizing Putin at a G7 meeting (from which Russia had been suspended indefinitely in 2014) and asking whether he wished 'to wreck his country's economy and continue Russia's isolation' for the sake of recreating 'the glories of the Soviet empire'.[51] Putin, however, was in no mood to be given lectures, let alone retreat. With China providing him with diplomatic cover, oil and gas revenues still pouring in, and a vast sovereign wealth fund there to cushion the Russian economy from any Western sanctions, Putin was well aware that he could ride out the storm. Indeed, far from retreating he went on the offensive by interfering in the 2016 US presidential elections in an effort to 'damage the Clinton campaign, boost Trump's chances and sow distrust in American democracy'.[52] The jury may still be out as to the impact all this had on the final result. But there's no doubting who Moscow wanted to win, and when Trump won (albeit by the narrowest of margins) the whoops of delight coming out of the Russian parliament could almost be heard all the way to Washington. However, irony or of ironies: even as the results were pouring in, Obama himself was blamed by his political opponents – including Trump, no less – for having known that all this skulduggery was going on but doing nothing to stop it while he was still president!

Conclusion

It is in the nature of American presidential politics that when a president finally leaves office, pundits and historians gather round to determine whether he (so far there has never been a she) should be judged 'great, near great, average, below average or a failure'. According to whom one consulted, Obama came close to fitting into any one of these five categories! Certainly when he left office, his own personal ratings were reasonably high.[53] Supporters would also point to his very real achievements at home – notably in health care reform, and to the fact that he did a great deal to push the whole issue of nuclear weapons and the danger posed by what he termed 'nuclear terrorism' right to the top of the global agenda.[54] Moreover, though often overlooked by those who claim he did not confront China energetically enough, it was in fact under Obama that the United States pushed for the Trans Pacific Partnership (TPP) as a way of both extending US economic reach and challenging China in the Asia-Pacific region.[55]

His conservative critics have never been quite so charitable. Indeed, having done all in their power to undermine him from day one, they found very little – indeed, nothing at all – to say that could be construed as being positive about Obama. Not only was he dangerously naive when it came to Iran and directionless when it came to the Middle East, they claimed. He also stood back and watched as America's great power rivals ran amok from Syria to the South China Sea.[56] From this reading, Obama was about as bad any leader of the free world could be. Even those who could not be construed as Trump supporters found little positive to say about Obama's foreign policy. He had, it is true, done a great deal on the economic front, and according to Steve Walt at least, was right to negotiate a nuclear deal with Iran. On the other hand, he should have done more (or, more precisely, much less) and gone a good deal further in reducing US commitments around the world.[57]

Of course, it might have helped the Democratic cause if those whom one might have expected to have been in the Obama camp had not had their doubts too. But even among progressives and liberals there were those who still found much to criticize about the Obama presidency. Not energetic enough when it came to promoting human rights, initially promising but then failing to close down Guantanamo, and being far too timid when it came to reforming the US economy after 2008, Obama, they claimed, talked a good game but at the end of the day delivered a good deal less. He may well have helped restore America's image abroad by taking climate change seriously and engaging the rest of the world.[58] Yet over his two terms, US foreign policy did not change in its fundamentals. More problematic still, many ordinary Americans were still left wondering why none of those who had brought America to its knees in 2008 had gone to jail, why their own lives seemed to be as hard as ever, and why manufacturing jobs were still being lost to US competitors abroad. Whether or not his successor had an answer to any of these questions was doubtful. But by focusing on those issues that preoccupied many ordinary American citizens, Trump seemed to have found the key which finally helped him unlock the door to the White House in November 2016.[59]

7

Stresses across the Atlantic[1]

In historical terms, the relationship between the US and Europe constituted one of the most intimate in modern times. Indeed, if the US began life as a distinctly European project, Europe's very own 'Thirty Years' War' between 1914 and 1945 brought about a major role reversal. This left the Western powers on the continent less masters of their own house and more dependent on an all-powerful, liberal, hegemon situated 3,000 miles away across the Atlantic. There was no inevitability about any of this. But as one of the more perspicacious international relations theorists noted as early as 1920, if one global war had already tilted the balance of power towards the US another – which he thought was inevitable – would almost certainly finish the job completely. Trotsky did not live to see one of his more brilliant (and this time more accurate) forecasts come true. Nor can we be sure that he would have been altogether happy with this prospect, given the role the US went on to play after the Second World War.[2] But as the dust began to settle after 1945, one thing must have been patently clear to all: the continent that in 1900 could claim the title of 'world hegemon' was hegemonic no more. To all intents and purposes, 'the European age was at last over'.[3]

Inevitably, the international system after 1945 was the very entity of that which had existed before, no more so than in terms of America's relationship with Western Europe. In strictly formal terms, the US and its European allies formed part of a voluntary alliance entered into by self-determining, equal, sovereign states. In effect, the relationship was to be shaped by two realities: a massive imbalance in power and strategic dependency by the Europeans on their American protectors from across the ocean. This was not something that brought much joy to the hearts of all Europeans; even less did it please those who for a short time after the Second World War believed it would be possible to build a third European pole between the superpowers. But the brute facts of the matter meant that the Europeans had little choice but to invite the Americans to become their benign imperial protectors.[4] Even that strategic and political irritant known as de Gaulle accepted that France remained part of something defined as 'the West'. Integration into the military command structure of NATO may have been a step too far for the army general. But in the larger international system it was perfectly clear that its protestations of independence notwithstanding, France was locked into a world underwritten by American power even if many people in France were by no means sold on America itself.[5]

If the Cold War was the cement which held the Europeans and Americans together through turbulent times, it followed that when it came to an end it was bound to have an enormous impact on the relationship. However, in what follows we will not be discussing the relationship as a whole, but instead focus on two of the critical challenges that confronted it in the new century.

The first was the attack of 9/11. The question I ask here is not what caused the attack or what its consequences were – we have tried to answer that already – but rather did the 'war on terror' which followed helped fill the strategic gap left by the end of the Cold War and thus help strengthen the transatlantic relationship? My answer is straightforward: it did not. Indeed, if anything, the war on terror – unlike the Cold War – probably did more to divide the West than unite it.[6]

The second challenge arose out of the election of Obama in 2008. At one level, Obama (as we have seen in the previous chapter) seemed like a breath of fresh air following the dark days of Bush Jnr. However, in spite of the Obama 'bounce', the relationship once again faced yet another challenge. This time, though, the cause of this was not the foreign policy of a particular kind of conservative administration but the belief in Europe that Obama was 'tilting' away from a continent which, in his view, represented the past, and towards a rising Asia, which embodied the future. As one critic of the Obama tilt noted at the time, it wasn't that Obama was against 'us' (meaning Europe). He just isn't that 'into us' any longer. Recognizing that Europe was 'no longer the cockpit of world affairs' he started 'reorienting' America 'to face up to the rise of the Far East'. Nor was this just a short-term move; rather, it was 'the most important strategic shift since the Cold War'.[7]

The 'war on terror' as a new Cold War?[8]

As we have argued earlier in this volume, 9/11 constituted a critical turning point in US foreign policy. Indeed, if 1989 represented the formal closure on one era, then so too did the attacks on the US on September 11, and as the dust began to clear from the streets of downtown Manhattan, a raft of born-again, neoconservative pundits emerged from under the rumble to declare the bloody end to a decade of 'drift and lethargy'. Each crisis in history produces its own particular version of the immediate past, and so it did once again in the days and months immediately following 9/11 when official after official declared the post-Cold War era had ended and an entirely new phase in the history of US foreign policy had begun. Still, every crisis is also an opportunity and 9/11 represented such a moment. The tragedy was real. But there was no doubting that it had the potential to be exploited. As Condoleezza Rice, a senior member of the Bush foreign policy team, declared a few months after the attack, the United States was on 'the cusp of a new era' in which all the great powers could now unite to fight the common threat of terrorism.[9]

There has been a vast body of literature describing the response by the Bush administration to the attack on the Twin Towers and the Pentagon. But what has often been left out of the discussion is how much the Bush administration, faced with what it quite legitimately regarded as a novel situation, constantly returned to history in order to make sense of the new world it was now facing. No doubt because it was the first attack on the American homeland since the beginning of the 19th century, something (though not much) was made of the war between Britain and the US when the former had the temerity to burn down the White House. Much more though was made of Pearl Harbour, a surprise attack if ever there was one, carrying the important message that when ruthless men did unspeakable things to the US they had better beware the consequences.[10] But it was the Cold War, more than any other historical experience, that was compelled to do most of the heavy lifting, so much so that in a relatively short space of time a number of pundits began to talk of the 'war on terror' as representing something akin to a new Cold War: some because it was the conflict they remembered best, a few because most of Bush's key advisers were old Cold War warriors themselves, and a good number because national security was now back at the top of the policy agenda. For all these reasons, and no doubt a few more, it was not at all unreasonable for writers to think of this new and uncertain present in terms of a known past.

Within the Bush team, however, the purpose of such analogical thinking was less to reflect seriously about the past, and more to establish frameworks within which it could legitimize policy decisions. In the process, it did what all administrations had done since the end of the Second World War: derive the lessons it wanted to draw and ignore those that complicated the telling of a particular tale. That said, the tale it narrated had its own internal coherence. It began with the end of the Cold War itself. Here the Bush administration made the not insignificant point that even if the defeat of Soviet communism represented a massive victory for the US, it had had the unfortunate consequence of leaving the US without a purpose. As one well-known American historian close to the Bush White House pointed out at the time, the US might have won the Cold War but, in the process, had become a great power lacking a grand strategy.[11] Now, at a stroke, the vacuum had been filled by the challenge posed by global jihad – the perfect antidote to Western sloth and what some around Bush viewed as an America grown decadent and flabby in an era personified by Clinton. Some were more explicit still. Without a clear and present danger they proclaimed, America was more likely to decline than to lead. It might have possessed a preponderance of power, but there was very little the US seemed to be able to do with all this spare capacity. To all intents and purposes, the US had turned into a superpower – perhaps even an empire – without a mission. Now, because of 9/11, the US appeared to have been presented with one.[12]

If 9/11 provided what looked like a 'solution' to what some regarded as the US's strategic vacuum, the Cold War also offered the Bush White House a ready-made supply of easy arguments about what to do next. Naturally enough, Bush himself was highly selective in terms of what he chose to learn and from whom. However, the fact that he felt compelled to learn anything at all says a lot about the power of the past and the hold it had on a president of even his limited intellectual powers. Unsurprisingly, the Cold War president whom Bush clearly tried to learn from most was Ronald Reagan: Republican hero, enemy of the original evil empire (it was no coincidence, of course, that Bush himself later talked of an 'axis of evil') and the ultimate reason – at least according to many on the US right – as to why the Soviet Union had finally been consigned into the dustbin of history. Reagan seemed to be the perfect role model. Like Bush, he fervently believed in the promise of the US and its mission to save the world from evil. Like Reagan, Bush also assumed that one only did business with others from a clearly defined position of strength. Moreover, he entered office (much like Reagan) after what many saw as being a period of foreign policy drift (Reagan often talked of the 1970s as a 'decade of neglect'). There were also many around Reagan who were anything but realist in international outlook. Indeed, one of the more obvious similarities between these two very different presidents was that both sought to challenge the status quo: one by trying to move beyond containment and the other by questioning the US's traditional reliance on authoritarian regimes in the Middle East.

The Cold War warrior Reagan, and indeed the Cold War more generally, thus served as a significant point of reference for the Bush team in a period of heightened threat. Yet, as many inside the Bush administration readily conceded, having a clear threat was not without its advantages. It would remind Americans that the world remained a very dangerous place. It would permit a very rapid build-up of US military power. It would justify a more assertive foreign policy. And, as a bonus, it might even help revive that battered ideological edifice known colloquially as the 'West'. Islamic terrorism was not exactly the same thing as communism. But in its own way it might serve a similar purpose.[13] Indeed, when NATO invoked Article 5 a day after 9/11, insisting that the attack on the US had been an attack on all, it very much looked as if the West had never been so united.[14]

Still, even in the midst of all this solidarity, cracks began to appear; and as time went by, and the war against al-Qaeda segued into a wider war against those states that formed part of what Bush termed the 'axis of evil', relations began to fracture badly. Indeed, by 2003 and 2004, even some of the more sober voices in the foreign policy debate were arguing that this was by far the most serious crisis in the long history of the transatlantic relationship. A few even predicted divorce between the US and its European allies. Of course, this simplistic analysis obscured as much as it illuminated. After all, many European countries did in the end support the war against Iraq. Moreover, in the US itself there was a powerful current of academic opinion that attacked the Bush administration on the distinctly European grounds that Bush was fast destroying the legal and institutional foundations of international society by going to war without UN support. Still, there was no doubting the divide. Indeed, at least one influential American closely associated with the new Bush doctrine of pre-emption even penned what turned out to be an influential essay in 2002, discussing the underlying causes of the division. As Robert Kagan went on to explain, the divide was not about personalities or policies; rather, it was about the different kinds of international entities the US and Europe (the EU in particular) had become since the end of the Second World War. The US, he noted, was the only superpower with global reach, international responsibilities and a military capacity to match its commitments. Europe, on the other hand, was primarily concerned with making peace and building a new kind of Europe. In his own much-quoted words, Americans as result had become 'Martians' – willing and able to deploy hard power – and Europeans 'Venutians' – constitutionally incapable of using force when necessary to address serious international issues.[15]

The discussion about the sources of what was now assumed by many to be a profound breach in the transatlantic relationship continued unabated through most of the Bush presidency, with many Americans now accusing Europeans of being anti-American and many Europeans (notably on the left) attacking the US for its unilateralism and arrogance. But another, equally profound difference, began to emerge too. This, however, had less to do with power and more with the very different ways in which Europeans and Americans seemed to construct the threat itself. Terrorism, it was agreed, was a problem facing both continents. But when Bush began to talk of a global war against terror, critical European voices started to be raised. As Michael Howard pointed out in an early but highly influential critique, the idea of a 'war' on terror was a dubious one. Not only did it lend legitimacy to al-Qaeda; the notion was also strategically incoherent. No state or group of states could declare war on a method and nor should they try to do so.[16] Even the Bush team at times seemed unsure of how to frame the problem. Indeed, at one point his administration even replaced the notion of a global war against terror with the apparently less offensive idea of a 'long war'.[17] At one level, such rhetorical framing mattered not one jot. However, it did point to (at best) a lack of strategic clarity and (at worst) to a lack of confidence in what the US and its allies were supposed to be uniting against.

This in turn raised a second, more theoretical, issue about whether or not it was possible to sustain any kind of alliance against something as nebulous as terrorism. Here the way alliances had been forged in the past, and the way this new alliance was being put together bore serious comparison. As different writers have shown, alliances may be formed for many different reasons, but one of these has to do with the existence of a credible state threat. Herein lay a problem for the war on terror. As Barry Buzan has observed, 'while serious, the terrorist threat' simply lacked the 'depth of the Soviet/communist one' and the key reason it lacked such depth was that it had no tangible reference point in the shape of a well-defined state with serious power capabilities.[18] To complicate matters even further, there was a growing belief on one side of the Atlantic at least, that the Bush administration was manipulating tensions created by the security situation either to build a new US imperium or to further his own political ambitions. Scandals such as Abu Ghraib and Guantanamo did not help either. Indeed, it was not just the decision to go to war against Iraq that caused such consternation in Europe; it was also what looked to most Europeans as being Bush's abandonment of the core values closely associated in their minds with the idea, and indeed the ideal, of the West.[19]

This brings us, then, to the question of the ideological source of jihad. Here again, the global war on terror involving the wider Atlantic community faced significant, perhaps insurmountable, obstacles in creating anything like a consensus. There were at least three reasons why.

First, radical Islam, unlike communism, only had limited ideological appeal. Consequently it was much less likely to have the same uniting and mobilizing capacity. Second, most Muslims (unlike most communists during the Cold War) did and do not seek the overthrow of the various states in which they happened to be living. Indeed, as opinion polls in the West were to show, while Muslims in general may not approved of Western interventions in the Middle East, only a very small minority were prepared to translate that criticism into support for violence. Third, though Islam may be defined by some in the West as 'the problem', policy makers themselves understood that if jihad was to be successfully contained, the West had to seek some understanding with those states that were themselves Islamic in character. Even the US was forced by the logic of its war to seek alliances with at least two countries – Pakistan and Saudi Arabia – whose elites had either displayed some sympathy with the ideology, if not the actions of the terrorists, or had been willing to use them for their own political purposes.[20]

Finally, the war on terror was launched into an international system that was altogether more complex in character than the somewhat simpler world that had been left behind in 1989. As Fred Halliday reminded us some time ago, the great success of the Cold War in forging accord between potentially fractious and competitive states was not because the USSR was more powerful than the US, but because the US as the leader of the West was able to construct the world in such a way that other critical issues were seen as being secondary to it or could be folded into the larger East–West competition. This nesting of issues was to prove altogether more difficult in the first decade of the 21st century. Indeed, if polls were to be believed, until 2008 as many people in Europe (if not in the US) viewed global warming to be just as much a threat to world order as terrorism. Then, with the onset of the economic crisis in 2008, the focus shifted again, but not towards terrorism but instead towards the profound uncertainties facing ordinary people as they began to come to terms with the biggest material challenge to their lives since the end of the Second World War.[21]

A disappointing love affair: Obama and the Europeans

The failed attempt to construct a new foreign policy paradigm that would unite allies and mobilize support on both sides of the Atlantic led to what can only be described as a profound crisis in the relationship. Bush, to be fair, did make several attempts during his second term to repair the damage but to little or no avail. It would in the end require a very different kind of US leader to make good the damage.[22]

It is difficult to recall a time when the election of a new US president excited as much enthusiasm in Europe as did the election of Barack Obama in November 2008. Indeed, whereas Bush had found it increasingly difficult to visit Europe without a massive police presence to protect him from often violent anti-war activists, Obama on his many early visits across the Atlantic was greeted with quite extraordinary enthusiasm. Even in France, where anti-Americanism had become an integral part of French identity, Obama appeared to be able to do no wrong. In Germany, too, the mood swung back from sullen opposition to US foreign policy to a recognition that someone very different, espousing what many felt was an acceptable world-view, was now in charge. Nor did the rapprochement end there. Indeed, a year after his election, a new and influential book appeared suggesting that, far from being Martians and Venutians with competing world-views and different attitudes to the uses of power, Americans and Europeans were in fact remarkably similar in outlook. Some may have liked to stress how different the two were. But according to American sociologist, Peter Baldwin, they did so not because the differences were especially great but because they were, in fact, fairly minor. As it turned out Americans and Europeans were more like each other than anybody else, and much more like each other than some conservative Americans and certain leftish Europeans would ever dare to admit![23]

Obama's efforts in the early months of his administration to revitalize the transatlantic partnership both in word and in deed – Secretary of State Hillary Clinton argued in January 2009 that the US had no closer allies than the Europeans – could not, however, paper over the cracks. Even Obama himself, with his own very special kind of background – born in Hawaii, raised for a while in Indonesia with an African father and a white mother – never quite sounded like a 'natural' Atlanticist. Nor did his own world-view admit of too much sentimentality when it came to thinking about Europe. Though well aware of the important role Europe played in US grand strategy, the world more generally was fast changing and America could not (to use a colloquialism) put all of its eggs into one transatlantic basket. This did not mean falling out with the Europeans or even taking them for granted. Indeed, he managed to get on especially well with the German Chancellor, Angela Merkel. However, there was no denying that there was a marked shift in US thinking if not away from Europe so much as towards an Asia whose economies were growing much faster than Europe's, where two of the most populous countries in the world happened to be located, and where China was fast making its mark. It was perhaps an exaggeration to talk of Obama, as some began to, as the new 'Pacific president' sitting in the White House. This though was how things began to be seen across the Atlantic.

Nor did Obama do much to reassure America's old allies, most obviously the British who sensed that they were no longer as 'special' as they had once been; but even among NATO members more generally there was a feeling that Obama was not quite as impressed by their contribution to global security as they felt he should have been. In Libya, for example, he made it clear that it would be the European members of NATO, and not the United States, that would be leading from the front. Nor, it seems, were some of his officials impressed with the contribution the Europeans were making to NATO either. Thus Robert Gates, who served as secretary of defense under both Obama and his predecessor George W. Bush, warned in 2011 of an impending transatlantic divide 'between those willing and able to pay the price and bear the burden of commitments, and those who enjoy the benefits of NATO membership but don't want to share the risks and costs'. Likewise, then-Defense Secretary Leon Panetta later that year underlined the need for increased defence spending in Europe lest lack of investment 'hollow out this [NATO] alliance'.[24]

The sense that Europe was beginning to matter less to the US was also made clear in a widely publicized opinion poll published in the US two years into the Obama presidency. The results were very worrying for those concerned about the state of the transatlantic relationship. The problem was not just that Europeans were not doing enough militarily; it was that Europe as a whole was fast losing its privileged importance in the eyes of most Americans. Indeed, according to Pew, whereas 44 per cent of Americans in 2001 regarded Europe as being of the greatest importance to the US, 10 years on it was now Asia that was viewed as being more central. Moreover, within the state system as a whole, it was now China and not, say, more traditional allies such as the UK or Germany, that was increasingly seen as being more crucial to the US's long-term national interests.[25] Nor was this new interest in Asia and China confined to the American public. In the academic world, book after book and article after article began to be written about the supposed power transition now under way in Asia. Meanwhile, in the popular press the number one story was fast becoming China's rapid economic rise and what this was going to mean for the US: economic opportunity, strategic threat or, perhaps, even a combination of the two? Either way, there was no getting away from the fact that in the US, views about the world were changing, and changing in ways that were starting to generate some nervousness on the other side of the Atlantic.

But it was what American policy makers began to say and do that set alarm bells ringing, and possibly nothing set them ringing more loudly than when the administration began talking of a 'pivot' to Asia in what some were predicting would soon be a new Asian century. Secretary of State Hillary Clinton could not have been more explicit. The US, she argued, had been for too long preoccupied with threats arising from within the wider Middle East. Now it would be turning its attention more and more towards Asia – in part because it was in Asia where real growth was to be found, and in part because Asia was home to two of the world's rising superpowers – India and China. Clinton also made it clear that she was breaking from tradition and would now be making Asia her top priority. She even emphasized how many trips she had already made to Asia by late 2011 (seven in all) before going on to outline in some detail why America had always been, and presumably would always remain, an 'Asian power'. Clinton's bold vision certainly made for exciting reading. However, it had the presumably unintended consequence of upsetting two very distinct audiences: one in Beijing which saw all this talk about pivot (or later, rebalancing) as nothing less than a manifesto of containment directed against China; and the other in a Europe which felt that Europe was fast becoming invisible. Where, they asked, did Europe fit into this brand new order of rapidly shifting partnerships? It was not at all clear. Moreover, if the world was going to be defined by what transpired in Asia, as Clinton most clearly suggested, then what exactly was the purpose of the transatlantic relationship? No answers were provided but the implication was clear: in a new international order where alliances were, in her words, being updated to cope with the challenge posed by China, more established relationships would almost certainly become less important. The contours of a new world order beckoned.[26]

Conclusion

In this chapter I have looked at two moments in the history of the transatlantic relationship since the end of the Cold War: one that divided allies badly because one of those allies chose to respond to the crisis occasioned by 9/11 in ways that many Europeans were unable to accept; and another that led the same ally to conclude that in a world where economic power was shifting eastwards towards Asia, the transatlantic relationship was bound to become less significant. Of course, this did not mean the relationship was over or divorce was on the cards. There was too much at stake economically for this to happen.[27] Moreover, the two together shared a whole raft of common values. And for all its weaknesses and inadequacies, the NATO alliance continued to be the only serious multilateral, military alliance in the world – one from which the US, as much as the Europeans, still derived enormous benefit. Still, it would have been foolish to have ignored the warning signs by hiding behind the old transatlantic mantra that in a world of uncertainty the democratic West would for ever remain united. A less certain future faced the transatlantic relationship.

8

Axis of Opposition: China, Russia and the West[1]

Western assessments of the China-Russia relationship generally reach one of two conclusions: hyperventilation about a Beijing-Moscow alliance that aims to upend the existing international order or a blithe dismissal of a temporary meeting of minds and interests.[2]

Introduction

It is often remarked that understanding the past is difficult enough without then attempting the near-impossible task of trying to predict the future. Nonetheless, a reasonably intelligent analyst back in the mid-1980s could be forgiven for making at least two predictions with some degree of confidence: one, that the USSR would remain in its essentials the same – that is, economically inefficient, politically repressive, globally challenging, but strategically incapable or unwilling to give up its increasingly costly possessions in Eastern and Central Europe; and two, that even if China could look forward to better times in a post-Mao age – difficult to imagine otherwise – it would take generations before it could ever become a serious actor on the world stage. Few back then could have imagined, and none as far as we know did, that the Soviet system of power would implode in little under ten years; or that backward, communist-led China would have become the second-largest economy in the world in just over 20 years. China was of course beginning to change by the late 1980s. Incomes were rising. Foreign investors were beginning to take note. Growth was on the up. The country was clearly on the move – so much so that *The Economist* talked in November 1992 of 'one of the biggest improvements in human welfare anywhere at any time', and six months later, *Business Week* of 'breathtaking changes'. Still, all this was taking place in a country where hundreds of millions of ordinary Chinese were poor, where China's overall weight in the international economy remained pathetically low, where an inefficient state sector remained dominant, and where all manner of obstacles still stood in the way of further economic reform.³

For all these reasons, and no doubt a few more besides, most experts would more likely have put their money on Russia succeeding than China. With its vast energy wealth, educated work force, proximity to Europe, and emerging democratic polity, Russia's future looked decidedly more rosy than that of China with its limited resources, ageing population, sclerotic party leadership, and huge rural hinterland. Certainly the events of Tiananmen Square did not encourage much optimism about China's future. Singaporean leader Lee Kuan Yew may have been right to have been upbeat about China.⁴ But his was only one voice among many during the 1990s; and even a few years after he had made his optimistic forecast, there were still people warning us not to buy into the hype then being propagated about a new China rising within the most dynamic region in the world. The so-called Asian miracle was nonsense on stilts according to leading economist Paul Krugman.⁵ Moreover, all this frenzied talk about China's rise was so much hot air, claimed Gerald Segal in a much quoted-article. Segal was insistent. China was, and would remain, a middle-ranking power that had the rhetorical potential to frighten a few of its insecure neighbours. But it had little chance of ever becoming a serious international actor. The world could rest easy. China was not about to shake things up in spite of Napoleon's much earlier warning that one day it might.⁶

The quite unexpected decline of one communist superpower and the exponential rise of another raises all sorts of interesting and difficult questions. Much, of course, has been written about why Sovietologists failed to anticipate the decline of the Soviet system.⁷ But much the same might be said about the failure of many Sinologists to predict the opposite about China. One can only speculate. Were analysts so mesmerized by their own liberal prejudices that they could not contemplate the possibility of a communist-led polity managing a successful economy?⁸ Or did the end of the Cold War itself lead many in the West to think that history really had come to an end and that liberalism had triumphed? Either way, the speedy and dramatic transformation of China from economic backwater to the world's number-two economy was something that only a few foresaw.⁹ Moreover, many of those who did talk in the 1990s of China 'awakening' or the dragon 'roaring' could not have envisaged how far China would rise or the impact this would then have on the international system.¹⁰ Certainly, nobody in the 1990s speculated (as some did a decade later) of China one day 'ruling the world'.¹¹

The sheer speed of China's ascent produced two very distinct literatures. On the one side stood what might loosely be called the 'economists' who together seemed to be uniformly enthusiastic about China's economic rise – and for several good reasons.¹² First, China's economic ascent, they pointed out, had helped the rest of the international economy remain on course during some very turbulent times. By mass-producing cheap goods, China had also improved choice for millions of people around the world while helping keep global inflation in check. China, moreover, had spawned an extraordinarily large, cash-rich middle class who had become hooked on high-end Western products from Armani to the top-five wines of Bordeaux. Finally, for those in the field of development economics, China had shown the way and, in the process, taken hundreds of millions of ordinary Chinese out of poverty.[13]

Scholars of international relations were more divided. Liberals certainly hoped that China would one day become a responsible great power with a stake in the international order.[14] Realists, on the other hand, were much less sanguine. China's economic transformation might have made China wealthy; however, this wealth had also made China more powerful. This in turn raised a series of critical questions about whether or not China would be able to rise peacefully,[15] about what would happen to the liberal order when it had risen, and finally about its relationship with other actors in the international system, especially the United States.[16] China may have been what one writer called a 'fragile superpower'.[17] Nevertheless, by the time Obama entered the White House, there was more than a little to be concerned about.[18] China was fast modernizing its military; it had come out of the economic crisis of 2008 more rapidly than the United States; and it was becoming an increasingly influential player in the Global South. It was also beginning to challenge American hegemony in the Asia-Pacific region. Whether its power was as formidable as some claimed was doubtful.[19] But it clearly represented a challenge.[20]

If China's relationship with the United States has received more than its fair share of attention the same could not be said of its equally complex relationship with another important state with which it has had an even closer history: Russia. The two countries did after all share one of the longest land borders in the world. The old USSR was for many years a close ally of the Chinese communists. And though Russia may have abandoned communist rule while China has not, since the beginning of the 21st century the two had developed increasingly close links – so much so that by the time Xi became president in 2013 China had come to regard Russia as an indispensable friend (even if it didn't call Russia an 'ally'), while Russia under Putin had come to view China and Russia as having a very special relationship'.[21] But in spite of mounting evidence that the two had formed what they themselves defined as a strategic partnership there were many analysts who still doubted whether the relationship was an especially close one.[22] Relations between the two countries might have improved, but there were limits to how close they would ever become.[23] In the words of one writer, the relationship would forever remain 'non-committal and asymmetrical', more an 'axis of convenience' than a real meeting of minds.[24] Indeed, according to this view, the two countries had little in common culturally,[25] were rivals in many parts of the world (most obviously Eurasia), and whose economic ties to the West would always be more important than their economic links with each other.[26] Moreover, because one of the two economies was far more powerful than the other, the less powerful of the two (Russia) was bound to fear becoming dependent. The two were thus destined to be very uneasy bedfellows.[27]

In what follows, I want to challenge what many years ago was, and in many ways still is, the prevailing view about Russia and China.[28] I do so not because I believe there are no differences between the two countries or because I am unaware of the potential for competition and rivalry. Rather, I do so for an altogether different reason, which is to explain what the various sceptics seem unable to: why it is that China and Russia have managed to form an increasingly close relationship in spite of what most experts predicted might happen. Nor can the relationship simply be understood in its own bilateral terms: it also has to be understood in terms of its opposition to something else and that something, quite obviously, is the West and the leader of the West in the shape of the United States. Some, of course, would insist that this still does not add up to classic balancing behaviour;[29] that neither China nor Russia has a positive vision of a new world order;[30] and that there remain subtle and sometimes not-so-subtle differences in the ways in which Russia and China conduct themselves abroad.[31] Nor can it be ruled out that their different national identities might force them apart in the future.[32] Nonetheless, it is impossible to ignore the self-evident fact that what increasingly binds the two together – more so than ever since the great financial crash of 2008 followed a few years later by a breakdown in relations between Russia and the West – has become more important than what separates them. Moreover, there is every reason to think the relationship will get closer as time goes by. Naturally, this does not mean they do not have other interests, including in China's case a very great interest in maintaining strong relations with the rest of the world economy. Nor does either want to challenge world capitalism as an economic system. But this does not detract from the main argument being advanced here: namely, that China has found a good friend in Russia and that Russia has clearly discovered one in China.[33]

To make good on my claim, I have divided the essay into several parts. In the first section, I examine the collapse of the USSR and why this cataclysmic event has such importance for the ways in which contemporary Russia and modern China together view the world and each other. Next, I then look at their positions on international affairs, focusing in particular on their critique of American power and US policies in the world system. In the third section, I go on to look at four key areas where China and

Russia now cooperate regularly: inside the permanent five (P5) of the UN; as part of the Shanghai Co-operation Organization; within the BRICS organization; and over their preferred trade architecture for the Asia-Pacific.

Finally, I reflect on the future in the light of the crisis in Ukraine. Here I differ from those who seem to think that the crisis exposed deep fault lines in the Sino-Russian relationship. I take a rather different view, which, stated bluntly, is that the crisis has revealed something quite different: namely, that China has been prepared to abandon certain basic principles in order to maintain its relationship with Russia, while Russia has been more than willing to appease China in order to make sure it can keep the Chinese on their side. Nothing, of course, is predetermined. But if one were to make a prediction (a fool's errand to be sure), it would be that a Russia increasingly under siege from what it now perceives as being a permanently hostile West, and a China still confronted by an America that stands as the principal obstacle to its ambitions in the Asia-Pacific, have come to the not illogical conclusion that there is nothing to lose, and probably much to be gained, from moving even closer together. That this presents a challenge to the West is obvious, though whether or not it constitutes a serious threat is much less clear. This, I believe, will in part depend just as much on how the West responds to what is happening as it will on policies devised in either Moscow or Beijing. In an age of improving Sino-Russian relations, there is still much the West can do to shape the future. But it will only be able to do this if it abandons the now-outdated view that the relationship is 'vulnerable, contingent and marked' only 'by uncertainties.' In short, it will only be able to think straight about China and Russia together when it abandons what I would term here old ways of thinking about their emerging relationship.[34]

United by history

> The People's Republic of China and Russia are more aware of the world's problems than the United States because they have gone through terrible wars unleashed by the blind egoism of fascism.[35]

One of the basic reference points in the ongoing debate about the durability of the China–Russia relationship is history, or more exactly what happened in their history to create what many still believe is a serious barrier to the establishment of trust between the two. The list of grievances on the Chinese side in particular is indeed a long one, going right back to the unequal treaties of the 19th century, through Stalin's efforts to stop the Chinese Communist Party coming to power in 1949, and on to the great split between the two communist states between the early 1960s and the late 1980s. Yet history, as we know, is always contested terrain, and one could just as easily make the case that the past has the potential to unite rather than divide. After all, if it had not been for the USSR, the Chinese Communist Party would never have come into being in the first place; and though Stalin was never less than ambiguous about Mao, in the end the Soviet Union did provide the People's Republic of China with massive support in its early formative years. Moreover, the USSR and China did fight on the same side in the Second World War, a fact the world was graphically reminded of in the spring of 2015 when the Chinese president was the guest of honour in Moscow standing next to Putin as the tanks and troops rolled by during the victory parade, and four months later when Putin attended another massive event in Beijing celebrating China's victory over Japan. The two leaders, moreover, used both occasions not just to recall times gone by, but to demonstrate how far their relationship had improved. Indeed, Xi's visit to Russia and his appearance at the Moscow commemorations, according to one Chinese official, 'pushed the China-Russia all-round strategic partnership relationship to a new level,' while Russia's equally active participation in China's celebrations, according to Putin himself, marked yet another major step forward in a fast-maturing relationship.[36]

But it was not just the war that united the two. So too did a more recent event: the collapse of the Soviet project itself between 1989 and 1991. The reasons why a once mighty superpower with an extensive industrial base, a huge military capability, and a powerful apparatus of controls finally imploded has been analyzed at length in the West. However, the collapse of Soviet communism has perhaps been of even greater interest to those states directly and indirectly involved themselves: namely, Russia and China. The official line in Russia initially was that the end of the Cold War and the implosion of the USSR were more or less inevitable given the burdens of empire and the more efficient character of their capitalist competitor. But all was not lost, it was felt. Indeed, precisely because these seismic changes appeared to open up the way to deep economic reform at home and a much-improved relationship with the West, there was good reason to think they would lay the foundation for greater prosperity at home and huge economic opportunities abroad. In fact, for a while, with Clinton in the White House calling for a deep strategic partnership with Russian reform (see Chapter 3) there looked to be every chance that Russia would be able to come to terms with its much-reduced role in world politics, not to mention its diminished influence in its former imperial space.[37]

Whether there was ever any chance of a new cooperative relationship being built between post-communist Russia and the United States remains an open question. What is not open to question is how quickly this early vision of a 'new deal' began to lose its allure. The shift from what has been described as the pro-Western phase in Russian thinking to something quite different evolved through several stages. In simple chronological terms, however, the decline in the relationship began as early as 1990 when the West refused large-scale economic aid to Russia; it then continued after 1993 with the enlargement of NATO; the relationship was further compromised as Russian nationalists and communists began to mobilize their not inconsiderable base of support at home; and it was finally provided with a more material form as the Russian economy imploded because of what many in Russia saw as a deliberate Western plan to reduce the country to the status of a Third World country. Certainly, long before Putin assumed office, there was a sizeable group of Russians who insisted that having given away everything to the West between 1989 and 1991, Russia had received nothing in return other than broken promises and a raft of policy suggestions that had impoverished the majority and allowed a narrow band of oligarchs to seize control of the nation's assets.[38]

In terms of his policies, Putin did not at first seem to represent a break with those pursued by his predecessor, Yeltsin. But very soon it became clear that he had a strategy of sorts, at the heart of which was a drive to consolidate as much power in his own hands while aligning his own political fortunes with those of Russian state power.[39] Though not opposed at first to working with the West, or even the United States, his basic outlook was infused with an underlying suspicion of the Western world and what he appeared to view as a Western desire to ensure that Russia remained weak and dependent. The consequences of this for both Russia and its near abroad – not to mention Russia's relations with the United States and the European Union – were deeply significant. Putin also added a 'dash of history' to justify his new stance and did so by turning to a group of patriotic 'Eurasianists,' who were more than happy to provide him with a story that best suited his purpose. At the heart of this was the very strong belief that Russia was not merely different from the 'liberal' West: the West, it was argued, was almost congenitally hostile to Russia. This had been true for the greater part of the 19th century. It remained true for the whole of the Soviet period. And it continued to be true into the 21st century. In fact, according to Putin's apologists, the end of the Cold War and the collapse of the USSR itself were all part of a larger Western plan to ensure the West's and the United States' continued primacy. This is why 1989 and what followed in 1991 were not the progressive 'liberating' events portrayed in much Western literature but rather well-organized regime-changing plots backed by certain traitors at home like Gorbachev.[40]

Unsurprisingly, this particular narrative was one that found a ready audience in China. In fact, the Chinese had been saying very much the same ever since the collapse of Soviet power back in 1989: in part because they opposed political reform per se and in part because Gorbachev's reforms had posed a very real danger to Chinese communist rule itself. Indeed, as we knew then (and have found out more since) during that fateful year, Beijing did as much as it was then possible for it to do to prevent the collapse from happening; and, when that proved impossible, they then took their own draconian measures in the June of 1989 to ensure that the contagion did not bring down communist rule at home. Always hostile to Gorbachev, and from the outset opposed to what they viewed as his dangerously destabilizing efforts to liberalize the Soviet system – Deng Xiaoping later commented that even though Gorbachev may have looked 'smart,' he was in fact 'stupid' – the Chinese had little trouble in agreeing with Putin's less than positive analysis of both 1989 and the final denouement of Soviet power later in 1991. And why not? After all, what had happened to the USSR could just as easily have happened to China itself.[41]

In rather typical Stalinist fashion, the Communist Party then went on to draw all sorts of 'lessons' about how to make sure that what had happened to the Soviet Union did not happen to China.[42] This was not a task they took lightly. Commissions were set up and study groups created, tasked with the crucial job of explaining what had destroyed the other communist superpower. As has been observed, the collapse of the Soviet Union following hard on the heels of communist collapse in Eastern Europe and East Germany 'was a deeply disturbing experience for the Chinese communists'.[43] It was also a deeply complicated problem, which might in part explain why it took a several study groups over many years (not to mention an eight-part television series called *Preparing for Danger in Times of Safety [Ju'an siwei] – Historic Lessons Learned from the Demise of Soviet Communism*) before they could come to any firm conclusions. Even then, the conclusions at which they arrived at were not entirely consistent. Nor did they necessarily agree with Putin that the collapse of the Soviet Union had been a catastrophe. After all, once the USSR had disintegrated, China itself no longer faced a united rival on its northern and eastern borders. That said, China in the end did concede that what had happened contained lessons for both states: the first, that while economic reform might be necessary one should make sure that this did not threaten the integrity of the state; and the second, that one should forever remain wary of the West's intentions, especially when the West dressed up its geostrategic ambitions in liberal rhetoric. Herein lay the most obvious lesson of all: namely, that whatever else may have divided them in the past, and might divide them in the future, both states had a very strong interest in supporting the other against those who challenged their sovereign right to rule in a particular way. By so doing, they would not only be protecting themselves at home from dangerous ideas born in the West. They would, ironically, also be upholding the fundamental Westphalian principle of non-interference on which the whole international system had rested for centuries and would hopefully continue to do so for decades to come.[44]

Unipolarity and its dangers

> China opposes hegemonism and power politics in all their forms, does not interfere in other countries' internal affairs and will never seek hegemony or engage in expansion.[45]

The lessons drawn from the collapse of Soviet power thus provided China and Russia with a common point of historical reference. But it was the structure of the new international system that concerned them more. Both, of course, recognized that the world had changed for ever and that both would now have to sink or swim in a word dominated by the market. There could be no going back to the past. On the other hand, the world as seen from Beijing and Moscow was not one in which either could feel especially comfortable. For one thing, the established rules governing the world had all been written by the West. The metaphorical table around which the main players then sat was also made and designed in the West. And sitting at the top of the table, of course, was the established hegemon: the United States.

To add material insult to injury, in this world the United States not only possessed a vast amount of power – soft and hard – but an extensive alliance system as well, which not only reminded China and Russia of how few genuine friends they had themselves; it also contributed in significant ways to America's ability to place pressure on the two countries. The United States may have proclaimed its innocence, insisting that the last thing it was thinking about when it enlarged NATO was to encircle Russia, or that when it decided to tilt to Asia under Obama it was looking to contain China rather than engage it. However, that is not how things were viewed in either Moscow or Beijing. Indeed, for the Chinese, the so-called tilt (accompanied as it was by what they saw as a change in US military doctrine)[46] was seen as a highly aggressive act, and the only legitimate response, it was felt, was to fight fire with fire, which it did with an 'outpouring' of increased 'anti-American sentiment' in China itself followed up by what looked to many as a final abandonment in practice, if not in theory, of the tried and true Deng principle of keeping a low profile.[47] To underscore the point, it also began to refer to the US less frequently as a global partner – though such language did not disappear entirely from the Chinese foreign policy discourse[48] – and more as a potential rival that would forever seek to maintain its position of primacy in Asia through the manipulation of its still highly dependent allies.[49]

This in turn connected to a wider debate in which China and Russia had been engaged for some time about the structure of the world system after the Cold War; one thing that emerged was neither felt that their interests, singly or collectively, could be fulfilled in a system in which power was so heavily concentrated in the hands of a single hegemon, especially when that hegemon happened to be a liberal power like the United States of America.[50] This analysis not only flowed from their very strongly held realist belief that hegemony by definition conferred great status on the hegemon. The concentration of power in the hands of a single power, they believed, was also likely to encourage greater assertiveness by the power. Clinton may have resisted the temptation for a while, though not entirely, as the NATO-led bombing of Kosovo showed; but post-9/11, the situation changed dramatically. Buoyed up by an American public fearful of yet another attack, and taking full advantage of the freedom afforded it by the much-debated unipolar 'moment', the United States launched a war on terror with the ostensible goal of combating global jihad (of which the Chinese and Russians approved), but with the unwritten purpose (which they did not) of reasserting US power after what many on the Republican political right saw as a post-Cold War decade of drift.[51] The lesson drawn in China and Russia from all this was obvious: until and when the distribution of power in the international system had become more evenly distributed – in short had become 'multipolar' – then the world would not only remain a deeply disturbed place, but one in which their voices would remain marginal at best, and insignificant at worst.[52]

China and Russia's various efforts to challenge what they saw as America's global pre-eminence also brought both into direct opposition with what they viewed as something equally challenging: the Western idea of 'humanitarian intervention', or to give its more official title, the international community's right to protect individuals when sovereign states failed to uphold certain basic norms. In theory, neither power was opposed to the basic principles of the *Responsibility to Protect* (R2P). That said, the two clearly felt deeply uncomfortable with the whole drift in Western thinking, which in their view allowed the West to bring outside pressure to bear on what they regarded as recalcitrant states. This attempt to 'interfere into the internal affairs of other states' under the cover of humanitarianism proved to be deeply worrying for the Russians and the Chinese. Not only did it undermine the UN system based on the original Charter of 1945 and the principle of sovereignty; it also provided a green light for the West to force change from without on states with whom the West either happened to disagree or with whom both China and Russia may have had significant economic and strategic relations.[53] But this was not all. Their even greater fear was that if the democratic West was given the green light to change or overthrow dictatorial regimes in, say, Iraq or Libya, this opened up the theoretical possibility at least of Western countries legitimately demanding change in Russia and China as well. In this sense, their hostility to intervention was not just because they looked at the world differently; it was because they worried that under the guise of advancing the rights of the human, or protecting peoples from their less-than-perfect governments, the West could use the doctrine of humanitarianism as a Trojan horse with the purpose of weakening their own control at home.[54]

This would be less important, of course, if either China or Russia, or both, happened to agree with the kinds of values that America and most of its allies were seeking to promote. But this was clearly not the case. Indeed, viewed from the vantage point of Putin's Kremlin or China's leadership compound in Beijing, Zhongnanhai, the values espoused by the West looked deeply problematic. It was one thing doing business with the West. It was something else altogether when engagement with the West led – as the Chinese and Russians clearly feared it might – to ideological contamination. The market may have been neutral politically, but the West as a project was not, and faced with such a challenge the two countries together took different, but not entirely dissimilar, countermeasures.[55] These included, in the Chinese case, an extensive system of censorship reinforced in the age of the web by an increasingly intrusive set of controls over the internet.[56] Russia may not have constructed the same system of controls. Nevertheless, under Putin, the flow of information was to be severely curtailed by a media that was now either completely state controlled or run by the friends of the president. Like the Chinese, the Russians also spent an inordinate amount of time and effort trying to curtail flows of information from the outside world in an attempt to uphold what some Russians now called 'internet sovereignty'.[57] Those close to Putin even spoke of the West having launched what they called an 'information war' against Russia, one that they had no intention of losing. Indeed, in one typically forceful statement (one of several), the Russian foreign minister not only linked US aggression back to the Cold War and an unreformed Cold War mentality, but to American exceptionalism and what he termed the belief by Americans that they possessed an 'eternal uniqueness', one that allowed them to resist any form of external interference into their affairs but made it perfectly acceptable for them to become deeply involved in the affairs of others.[58]

Finally, in this ongoing ideological battle against the liberal West, both China and Russia identified any form of internal dissent with some assumed Western plot to undermine their respective systems. In the case of Russia, the presumed link between opposition at home and the machinations of some unnamed Western agencies was now regularly made in the media. Indeed, in 2014, a TV programme was broadcast purporting to show that there were still many traitors in Russia, all of them, including a number of NGOs, supported by (and obviously working for) the West. Others were portrayed in harsher terms still, most notably the Ukrainians, who were now systematically portrayed in the wider Russian press as being little more than stalking horses for the Americans and their dangerous allies in Brussels. China may have adopted a somewhat (though only somewhat) less bellicose approach. Nonetheless, in its own ongoing struggles against all those who would challenge the idea of the 'harmonious society', it was rarely, if ever, reluctant not to associate dissent at home with acts of subversion from abroad. Nor has it been backward in coming forward in sanctioning those in the West whom it deemed to have overstepped the ideological mark – as Norway found out to its cost back in 2010 when the Nobel Peace Prize committee had the temerity to award the prize to the jailed human rights activist, Liu Xiaobo. Whether or not Beijing viewed the award as a Western plot was unclear. What was clear, however, was the impact it had on the official mind in China, reinforcing its basic belief that Western countries (even small ones like Norway) were engaged in subtle and sometimes not-so-subtle forms of subversion whose ultimate purpose was regime change in China.[59]

China and Russia: international cooperation

> Russia and China attach great importance to cooperation within multilateral formats, including the UN, G20, BRICS, the SCO.[60]

If, as I have suggested here, China and Russia adhere to a broadly similar view of the world while together asserting their right to protect themselves from what they both regard as that bearer of ideological contamination known as the liberal West, how has their increasingly close strategic partnership manifested itself at the international level? Here again, the standard answer has been that in spite of a certain tactical convergence on specific issues, one should not overstate the extent of their collaboration.[61] Indeed, in the midst of the crisis occasioned by the Russian intervention in Ukraine, one respected Western newspaper made a very direct comparison between the 'constructive' approach being pursued by the Chinese and the 'increasingly dangerous' approach adopted by the Russians. It was high time, the paper went on, for the 'provocative' Russians to learn something from the more pragmatic Chinese. Whether Putin ever read the advice coming from the *Financial Times* is, of course, unknown. But one suspects that if he had, he might have wondered why the editorial made no mention of the tacit support he was already receiving from the Chinese in his efforts to undermine Ukrainian sovereignty. He may have also noted that the editorial also forgot to mention the fact that in the years leading up to the Ukrainian crisis, the apparently 'irresponsible' Russians and the 'well-behaved' Chinese had been working increasingly closely together on a range of significant international issues in a number of key international forums.[62]

The first, and perhaps most important, arena where China and Russia had been working closely together over the years was in the United Nations, where both occupied seats as Permanent Members of the UN Security Council. Their approaches were not identical, to be sure. Indeed, China appeared to be less willing than Russia to deploy its veto, usually preferring to use the less controversial strategy of abstention when faced with resolutions it opposed. Moreover, on some issues involving international security (Iran's nuclear programme, for example) China was willing to support measures such as sanctions. Nonetheless, like Russia, it consistently resisted the use of force by the West against recalcitrant regimes, and more generally opposed any form of economic pressure being applied to states deemed to be guilty of human rights abuses. In 2006, for example, it effectively prevented any action being taken against Sudan over its genocidal behaviour in Darfur; in 2007, it then stymied the UN over Myanmar; and a year later acted once again to protect Mugabe's Zimbabwe from criticism. China together with Russia then repeatedly vetoed UN motions aimed at censure of Russia's close ally in the Middle East – Syria. A year later they also vetoed an Arab League Plan calling for political change in Syria. Resolutions calling for sanctions against Bashar al-Assad were also vetoed, as was a UN draft resolution in May 2014 backed by 65 countries calling for the crisis in Syria to be referred to the International Criminal Court.[63] And so it went on, causing something close to a storm in the UN and the wider Arab world. One writer even accused the two of 'kneecapping' the Security Council.[64] But all to no avail. In fact, at a 2014 meeting in Beijing, the two appeared to congratulate the other for having prevented a Western intervention, which in their view would not only have made matters much worse but would have undermined any moves toward a far distant 'peaceful resolution' of the conflict.

If increased political cooperation in the United Nations pointed to more than just a coincidental meeting of minds over specific issues, then China and Russia's formal membership of the sometimes underestimated Shanghai Co-operation Organization (SCO) pointed to something of equal significance: a proven longer-term ability to cooperate in matters relating to hard security. Of course, the SCO was not, and was never intended to be, the Eurasian equivalent of NATO. However, over time it became more than the sum of its disparate parts. A Chinese initiative, in the first instance, with the purpose of promoting some degree of regional coordination where before there had been none, the SCO thereafter took on several roles, which included a counterterrorism function, a sharing of intelligence, and an increasingly high degree of military cooperation – especially between China and Russia.[65]

At first China was keen to stress that even if no Western power was likely to play a role in the SCO, this did not mean that its purpose was anti-Western or anti-American as such. However, even if the SCO sought 'no open confrontation' with the United States, it was difficult to think of it not having some broader strategic purpose, especially after 9/11, when the United States began to increase its presence in Central Asia. This certainly worried the ever-sensitive Chinese, though given their own concerns about terrorism, they were prepared to concede some temporary US presence. But within a couple of years the two together demanded of the West and the US that they remove their forces from SCO members' territories. They in turn linked this specific demand to a wider debate about the kind of international system they sought and the role the SCO might play in creating a new 'world order,' one in which no single power (here meaning the United States) would have a 'monopoly in world affairs' or be able arrogate to itself the right to interfere 'in the internal affairs of sovereign states.' Furthermore, at its various meetings, China and Russia started to behave as if the SCO formed the kernel of a powerful new security organization constructed on principles very different from those found in the liberal West. Underwritten politically by what has become known as the 'Shanghai spirit,' with its strong emphasis on non-interference, stability, and diversity, the SCO thus soon came to form part of wider Chinese and Russian strategy with the purpose of establishing deeper cooperation between the two powers.[66]

If both China and Russia worked together in maintaining and strengthening the SCO as a regional security organization, the same could just as easily be said of an even more famous organization, which started life back in 2001 as an acronym invented by Goldman Sachs economist Jim O'Neill.[67] Initially the idea of the BRICS (Brazil, Russia, India, China, and South Africa) was pooh-poohed by most conventional economists; and even after the organization had begun to take on a life of its own, there were still those who repeated the line that the countries that constituted the BRICS were too different to be viewed as a united bloc. Even so, the simple idea of the BRICS not only helped redefine the way many people came to see the world. As an organization it also showed enormous creativity, especially after the financial crash of 2008, thus helping undermine the belief that only the West had answers to the economic challenges facing the world.[68] Certainly, ever since its first summit in 2009, the BRICS has assumed ever-greater importance; and within the BRICS organization itself, China and Russia worked closely together, fashioning common positions, attacking in one breath Western-style structural reforms, and then, in another, the unequal character of the world's financial system and the privileged role enjoyed by the US dollar. They were equally vocal on global governance issues, arguing that the current distribution of voting power on the International Monetary Fund and the World Bank was much too heavily weighted in favour of the Europeans and the Americans. At the Brazil summit in 2014, the two also helped the BRICS establish two banks that would, they hoped, challenge the primacy of the IMF and the World Bank. Whether or not these various efforts could ever weaken, let alone undermine, the West's grip on the levers of financial power was not at all clear. Still, it was not without significance (or irony) that a body that had been invented in the West by a Western economist working for a Western investment bank, many years later looked like it was now providing both China and Russia with a platform from which they were able to launch a critique of the West.[69] Moreover, though some BRICs were more economically more significant than others, the fact remained that what had started life as an acronym had only a few years later become what one Russian analyst termed a 'full fledged organization' with regular summit meetings, an international presence and an ability to set agendas that were more often than not directed against the West.[70]

Finally, in any assessment of the China–Russia relationship, one should not underestimate the importance of wider trade questions relating to the Asia-Pacific region. Indeed, in what has rapidly become a battle between the United States and China over which body should define the trade agenda regarding the Pacific, it is not insignificant that Russia rushed into support China which favoured the Asia-Pacific economic cooperation (APEC) while taking great exception to American efforts to establish its own parallel organization in the shape of the Trans-Pacific Partnership (TPP).[71] Not only did it do so because both countries were at first excluded from TPP; it acted thus because, like China, it sought to thwart America's much-vaunted 'tilt to Asia,' of which TPP was seen as being a vital part. Making its own very strong claim to be as much an Asian power as a European one – some have even talked of a 'Russian tilt to the East' – Russia was certainly very highly active on the diplomatic front. Indeed, at the APEC summit hosted by the Chinese in Beijing in November 2014, it could not have been more engaged or Putin more vocal. It was quite 'obvious', Putin noted in one interview, that the TPP was nothing more than 'just another American attempt to build an architecture of regional economic co-operation' from which the US in particular 'would benefit'. But the effort would fail, he continued, and would do so in large part because the Americans had gone out of their way to exclude 'two regional players' in the shape of Russia and China. Thus having stressed the dubious motives of the Americans, Putin then emphasized how close Russia now was to China, noting that 'relations between the two countries' had never been better. Indeed, according to Putin, they had 'reached the highest level' in our 'entire history'.[72] The Chinese president did not appear to digress from this assessment. Nor did the official Chinese press, which continued to rail against what it saw as an American-led strategy of returning to Asia by opening 'the door' to the Asian 'market' as part of an even wider, and more insidious, effort to encircle China itself.[73]

Conclusion: China, Russia, Ukraine and beyond

China does not want the South China Sea dominated by Americans. Russia does not want the West – the United States and Europe – to penetrate what Moscow perceives as 'its sphere of influence'. In short, Russia and China do not want a world dominated by the United States.[74]

The crisis in Ukraine posed what initially looked like a diplomatic problem for China. After all, what Russia was doing went directly against something to which China had for so long been opposed: secession. Yet in spite of trying to appear even-handed – even suggesting at one point that matters should be settled through negotiation, not force – when push came to proverbial shove, China still came down on the Russian side.[75] Indeed, as the crisis unfolded, China appeared to suggest that if anybody was to blame, it was not so much its close friend Putin but a meddling West that had failed to understand history or the 'complexities of the Ukrainian issue'. Furthermore, far from attacking Russia, China went out of its way two months later at the BRICS summit in Brazil to ensure that it escaped any form of censure at all.

China's diplomatic attempts to sound even-handed in public while scolding the West for acting irresponsibly undoubtedly helped the Russians in their moment of diplomatic need. China, meanwhile, took full advantage of the situation to enhance its own position by exploiting Russia's self-evident need for diplomatic and economic cover. Certainly, the much-vaunted gas deal signed in May 2014 was one that worked to China's advantage. Indeed, as was observed at the time, China drove an especially 'hard bargain'.[76] But with the Russian economy now under increased pressure, China was perfectly happy to exploit the situation to its own advantage. Nor did the diplomatic initiatives end there. Indeed, as if to make the point even 'clearer than the truth' to those who may have been wondering about the health of the relationship, the two countries signed yet another energy deal in November. Then, as if to drive the point home, they confirmed they were planning even more naval exercises together, this time, however, in the Mediterranean, not off the Chinese mainland.[77] At around the same time, China also signed a major new arms deal with Russia. Certainly, if China was feeling uncomfortable in supporting Russia, as some Western analysts speculated at the time, it was certainly not showing.[78]

Naturally enough, none of this seemed to make much difference to those who had always doubted the staying power of the relationship. Thus, a short while after China and Russia had signed a massive new gas deal, one analyst was still reassuring his readers that the relationship was still 'more superficial than strategic'.[79] A few months later, another pundit was claiming that the Russian and Chinese leaders were not really 'buddies'.[80] And by the beginning of 2015, yet another writer was suggesting that even if China and Russia might have looked like they were getting on extraordinarily well, the relationship with China could not deliver what Russia really needed.[81] Some pundits even began to speculate that the relationship was about to take a tumble.[82] But nothing of the sort happened. Indeed, far from sputtering or coming to a halt, the relationship continued to move forward, and did so, as leaders in both Moscow and Beijing pointed out, for a very simple reason that it was in their interest for it to do so. As Putin made clear at the time (and Xi did not demur) the continued 'expansion of the Russian-Chinese partnership' met and presumably would continue to 'meet the interests and strategic goals of our two countries'.[83]

The question then remains, how might the relationship evolve in the future? Our numerous sceptics obviously think that underlying differences would in the end push the two countries apart. Thus far, though, there was little evidence to indicate this was likely to happen. Indeed, why should it? The relationship had already realized major strategic and political gains for the two sides. The two were even beginning to look towards deepening their economic ties. The partnership also allowed the two countries to confront together what both agreed was their biggest joint problem: namely an American-led international order. Things could, of course, change. Thus the two could decide that the liberal order was one within which they could realize their ambitions. Russia could abandon its great power ambitions. China could give up on its goals in the East and South China seas, even accept that the United States had a right to be an Asian power. But as we know, the chances of any of this ever happening in practice were virtually nil. The scene was thus set for a continued standoff, one consequence of which would be to reinforce the belief in Moscow and Beijing that in a hostile international environment one should stick close to one's friends, because in an insecure world such friends, warts and all, were central to achieving one's long-term objectives, which in their case meant greater political security at home, having fewer obstacles to realizing their ambitions in their own neighbourhood, and ultimately creating a more equal international system in which the United States and its allies had less control over what happened. And as long as they continued to share these basic goals then there was every chance the two would continue to travel together along the same path they had been moving along since the beginning of the 21st century.[84]

PART IV

Trump: Turbulence in the Age of Populism

As a BBC journalist remarked not long after Donald Trump was elected:

> Very few people thought he would actually run, then he did. They thought he wouldn't climb in the polls, then he did. They said he wouldn't win any primaries, then he did. They said he wouldn't win the Republican nomination, then he did. Finally, they said there was no way he could compete for, let alone win, a general election. Now he's President-elect Trump.[1]

No doubt some then expected that he would very quickly be 'domesticated' and behave like any ordinary 'decent' Republican. Some even entertained the hope that the establishment, which included more than a few Republicans – the 'adults in the room' – would gradually pull him back towards the centre and that America would once again return to normal. He was, after all, a businessman and a billionaire, and thus far men like him tended to act just like businessman and billionaires had always done in the past: as upholders of the status quo. However, anybody who had studied Trump's campaign and the speeches he made when on the presidential trail should have known that he was not your average candidate. Very rich he may well have been; however, inspired in part by what had happened in the UK where the Brexiteers had scored a stunning victory over their rivals by calling on ordinary people to 'take back control', and in part by a group of advisers like Steve Bannon who sensed that a radical populist platform would appeal to enough Americans, Trump became the attack dog candidate of the 2016 election. And attack he did: the rich and the powerful, whom he said had benefited from globalization while working-class Americans had been losing their jobs; China, for taking advantage of a trade system that worked in its favour; European 'free riders' who refused to spend their own money on their own defence; immigrants, who were flooding into the country over the US–Mexican border; Muslims, who 'hated us'; and of course, all liberals who, he claimed, controlled the media and ran the intelligence services, not to mention those bastions of political correctness – the universities. In this section, Chapter 9 looks at Trump in the context of the broader movement known as populism. In Chapter 10, I provide an overview of his four years in office and the legacy he left behind.

9

Populism, Trump and the Crisis of Globalization[1]

The spectre of populism

> A spectre is haunting Europe – the spectre of communism. All the powers of old Europe have entered into a holy alliance to exorcise this spectre: Pope and Tsar, Metternich and Guizot, French Radicals and German police-spies.[2]

Well, it would seem that there is another very different spectre haunting Europe in the 21st century, but it is no longer communism. That clearly has been consigned into that proverbial dustbin of history. But there is another dangerous 'ism' threatening the liberal world order, and that 'ism', of course, is something that has come to be known as populism. Of course, there have been varieties of populism in the past: Russia had its own species of the same during the 1870s and 1880s; a similar though politically less radical version of populism grew up in the United States during the 1890s and reappeared in different iterations several times thereafter (McCarthyism was in its own way a populist revolt against liberalism); and then, of course, there were the many varieties of populism, which as a student I was told was the main problem in Latin America during the post-war years. Peronism in Argentina was, it seemed, a particularly nasty kind of populism – largely, I gathered, because Peron liked speaking to the masses and did not much like the British. So, in some regards the study of what is known as populism is not new. Indeed, I can well recall reading my first book on the subject in 1969 when I was studying politics; and that was a rather fine LSE study edited by the very great duo of Ernest Gellner and Ghiţa Ionescu, titled *Populism: Its Meanings and National Characteristics*.[3]

So we might conclude that there is nothing new here. But that would be wrong; for clearly there is something rather significantly new happening in the modern world. For one thing, the populist 'problem' (if that's what it is) appears to have migrated towards Europe where it did not have much of a hold before; and for another, it has assumed a much more widespread form. Indeed, whereas previous populisms were specifically national in character, this new populism has assumed a more international form. Furthermore, if the pundits are to be believed, this new populism is much more of a challenge than anything we have witnessed in the past. Certainly, if we were to listen to most European leaders it would appear to have become the political challenge of our age. A former German finance minister, Wolfgang Schäuble, definitely thought so. Not a man to mince his words, Schäuble talked of a rising tide of 'demagogic populism', which if not dealt with frontally and decisively could easily threaten the whole European edifice. A Chatham House report came to much the same conclusion. 'The trend of rising support for populist extremist parties', its author wrote, 'has been one of the most striking developments in modern European politics' – one which not only poses a challenge to Europe alone but to democracy itself.[4] The then-KPMG chair, John Veihmeyer, was in no doubt either about the challenge Europe was now facing. The 'rise of populism in Europe' he opined in late 2016, was and remains the biggest threat of all to the continent's stability; a much bigger threat, he went on to stress, than Brexit.[5] Brexit worried him, he conceded. But the more general recent rise of 'anti-system, populist' and 'quite extreme political parties' in Western Europe worried him much more and did so not just because of the threat it posed to Europe alone but to globalization more generally.

But was this just a European phenomenon? Clearly not. Across the Atlantic in the US, a similar if not exactly identical dragon emitting all sorts of unpleasant and noxious sounds was to arise in the shape of Donald Trump, one of the very few billionaires in modern history who also laid claim to being a 'man of the people'. But billionaire or not this quite extraordinary political phenomenon – a combination of Jay Gatsby and Howard Hughes with a dash of William Randolph Hearst thrown in for good measure – delivered shock and awe in equal amounts. Indeed, by tapping into popular discontent in what Gavin Esler termed nearly 20 years ago the 'United States of anger', he was to shake the US establishment (not to mention their European partners) to its very core by saying things one is not supposed to say in polite company, taking pot shots along the way against globalization (un-American), the liberal press (fake news), parts of the judiciary and the intelligence agencies (part of the deep state), climate change (a hoax), human rights (you've got to deal with the world as it is), the idea of democracy promotion, immigration, and of course the EU itself (Brexit is a wonderful thing, he opined on more than one occasion).[6]

Moreover, it was not just Trump who railed against the elites and the powerful during the 2016 US presidential campaign. Bernie Sanders may have termed himself a socialist (and still does), but some of his targets – most obviously the corporations, which he claimed had sold the American worker short, and the Wall Street financiers – were broadly similar to those identified by Trump. But if Sanders and Trump together can be classified as populists, then who, one wonders, is not now a populist? And where do the ideological fault lines lie? Should Jeremy Corbyn not also be defined as a populist? After all, he claimed to speak on behalf of the 'many' rather than the 'few'. But then, so too do the true Brexiteers who, in their rush to win over white working-class voters, talked quite volubly of governing in favour of the 'left-behinds' and the 'just about managing' in order to make Britain a country that works for everyone and not just the rich and powerful. But this has also been the dominant narrative of such left-wing political parties such as Syriza in Greece and Podemos in Spain. This cannot be said of the National Front in France, of course. But there is no more rampant populist in Europe today than Marine Le Pen, who has waxed lyrical against the European Union and its twin – 'rampant globalization' – both of which have, in her words, been 'endangering' French 'civilization'. Indeed, while the successful former banker Emmanuel Macron made his appeal to those who were better educated in prosperous cities like Lyon and Toulouse, Le Pen spent most of her time campaigning in the run-down towns of the north-east, speaking to workers whose parents (if not they themselves) had once voted for the Communist Party.

Liberals confront populism

Populism would thus seem to defy easy political pigeon-holing. But most liberal writers on the subject seem to be united on one thing: they don't much like populism and have tended to approach the subject with a mixture of enormous surprise mixed in with a strong dash of ideological distaste. In fact, even the most cursory glance at the literature (with a few notable exceptions) reveals what I would call a distinct 'cosmopolitan' bias against populists and populism. Nor has this gone unnoticed. Indeed, in a piece in *MoneyWeek* by John Stepek, he made the entirely fair point that as far as he could make out 'the bulk of opinion columns' dealing with populism tended to fall into two main categories: sneering or patronizing.[7]

The controversial UK-based sociologist, Frank Furedi, was more scathing still. Populism, he argued, had virtually become a term of abuse directed against anybody critical of the status quo. Worse, it implied that the revolt facing the West today was not a legitimate response to deep-seated problems but was rather the problem itself.[8] There is certainly something to this. It's clearly shown, for example, in the way populists are invariably described. How could we ever forget the use of the word the 'deplorables' made famous or infamous by Hillary Clinton in her description of Trump's supporters during the 2016 presidential campaign? But this was only the tip of a very large liberal iceberg. Other epithets deployed have included – and this is only a sample – irrational, racist, xenophobic, losers, dangerously illiberal, economically illiterate, morally inferior, and of course the best epithet of all: 'pig thick'. Even when populists participate in, and win, elections or referendums, they are still castigated as being a threat to democracy. This was clearly the conclusion arrived at in one recent and influential book on the subject. Populists may claim to talk in the name of the people, argued Jan-Werner Müller in his well-reviewed study, but one should not be deceived.[9] When populists actually assume power, he warned, they will create an authoritarian state that excludes all those not considered part of the proper 'people'. Beware the populists therefore. They may talk the democratic talk, but hidden behind all that rhetoric is a dangerously anti-democratic impulse.

This antagonism to populism may be understandable, given that so much of what some populists have said is deeply concerning. Moreover, as their critics have legitimately pointed out, their policies can be, and in Trump's case have proven to be, deeply disturbing. Still, we face a quandary. On the one side, there are the analysts of populism who tend in the main to look at the phenomenon all the time holding their noses as if there were a bad smell in the room. On the other side, there are millions of very 'ordinary people' out there who actually vote for such movements. If nothing else, it says something about the state of the West when you have the overwhelming bulk of public intellectuals lining up on one side to critique populism – some more fairly than others, to be sure – and millions of their fellow citizens voting in their droves for parties and individuals of whom most experts and academics appear to disapprove. Trump may not be everybody's choice, but he did after all win the US presidential election in 2016. Equally, Brexit only won by a few hundred thousand votes; however, the 'Leave' campaign gathered in more votes than 'Remain' and did so because it tapped into something important. And while Viktor Orbán has proved to be a highly contentious prime minister in Hungary, in 2014 his Fidesz party won 44 per cent of the popular vote, and 52 per cent in 2019. The point being made here is a simple but important one. We do not have to like or agree with populists, and we should not forget our role as critic, but we should at least try to distance ourselves from our own political or ideological preferences, move beyond moral outrage at something so many of us might not like, and instead seek to understand what is happening here. Because something clearly is. And what is that something? We should not exaggerate. Nor should we conclude that the world we have known is about to collapse. It is not. But the tectonic plates are shifting. The mood across the West has turned sour. Many millions of people are obviously very unhappy with the old order and have expressed their alienation by voting against the establishment in very large numbers. This has expressed itself through different political parties. It has taken different forms in different countries. Each nation has its own peculiarities. But the new populism is more than just a reflection of national exceptionalism. There is something much more widespread going on here. Moreover, this something is not happening in the developing countries or the poor Global South where billions have little or nothing. Rather, it is taking place in the rich and democratic West. Moreover, it clearly constitutes a distinct threat to the old order. Francis Fukuyama certainly seems to think so. Having become an academic superstar back in 1989 by talking in grandiloquent terms about the 'end of history' and the victory of liberalism over all its main ideological rivals, he is now worried that the liberal moment may be over.[10] Indeed, in his view, the real threat to the West today may not be coming from rising powers like China or revisionist states like Russia – challenges from without, in other words – but instead, it is coming from within. And according to Fukuyama, it is not just Europe or the United States that will have to live with the consequences. It will be the liberal order *tout court*.

What is populism?

But what, then, is populism? The answer to this simple question is by no means clear. But one can, I suppose, say that populism reflects a deep suspicion of the prevailing establishment; that this establishment in the view of most populists does not just rule in the common good but conspires against the people; and that the people, however defined, are the true repositories of the soul of the nation. Populists like Trump, for example, also tend in the main to be nativist and suspicious of the outside world; more often than not they are sceptical of the 'facts' as provided to them by the establishment press; and in most cases they don't much like experts. Nor in general do they like big cities and the metropolitan types who happen to live in them. They are (to use a term made popular by David Goodhart) the 'somewheres' – that is to say, people who want to be part of somewhere as opposed to those who are the 'anywheres'.[11] Indeed, the fault line in Britain he argues (and the same would be true of the United States too) is between those who come from 'somewhere' – that is to say, people rooted in a specific place or community: usually a small town or in the countryside, socially conservative, often less educated – and those who come from 'anywhere': footloose, often urban, socially liberal, university educated and who tend to feel at home nearly everywhere. But it is the 'somewheres' we have to understand, for it is they after all who constitute the real basis of the populist revolt.

But one should beware of assuming that because populist voters tend to be less well educated that all populists are fools. This would be a mistake. Indeed, even if most supporters of populist parties have less formal education, this does not mean they are irrational. Nor does it make populist thinkers stupid or unthinking. They are not. Those who planned Brexit in the UK had a much better grasp of politics than their opponents. Meanwhile, across the Atlantic, the Trump team and the populists (unlike their critics) had a very clear plan. Indeed, it was their very big thinkers and strategists like Steve Bannon who plotted the campaign that finally won Donald Trump the White House by focusing on precisely those issues – immigration, unfair trade and free-riding allies – that traditional conservatives in the Republican Party (not to mention the Clinton people) had hitherto ignored.

But what has caused this surge of support for populism across the West? There are at least three competing narratives.

One was provided by Moisés Naím, former editor of the magazine *Foreign Policy*. Populism has to be taken seriously he agrees. But it has no intellectual coherence. It is merely a rhetorical 'tactic' that demagogues around the world have always used, and will continue to use, to gain power and then hold on to it. As Naím puts it:

> The fact is that populism is not an ideology. Instead, it's a strategy to obtain and retain power. It has been around for centuries, recently appearing to resurface in full force, propelled by the digital revolution, precarious economies, and the threatening insecurity of what lies ahead.[12]

This, however, does not make populism any the less dangerous. Indeed, populism is invariably divisive, thrives on conspiracy, finds enemies even where they do not exist, criminalizes all opposition to it, plays up external threats, and more often than not insists that its critics at home are merely working for foreign governments. Yet one would be wasting one's time – he implies – seeking some deeper cause for this particular phenomenon.

A second view is that populism in its modern iteration is a search for meaning in what the sociologist Tony Giddens earlier termed a 'runaway world' of globalization – a world which according to Giddens at least is 'shaking up our existing ways of life, no matter where we happen to be'. Moreover, this world, says Giddens, is emerging in 'an anarchic, haphazard, fashion [...] fraught with anxieties', as well as scarred by deep divisions and a feeling that we are all 'in the grip of forces over which we have no control'.[13] Indeed, not only do we have no control, but because of the speed and depth of the changes across traditional frontiers, many citizens feel as if the world is not just passing them by but undermining their settled notion of identity born in more stable, more settled times. This loss has been felt by everybody. But it has been experienced most by an older cohort of white people who simply want to turn the clock back to a time when the people in their towns looked like them, sounded like them and even had the same traditional loyalties as most of them: an age, in other words, when there were fewer immigrants and even fewer Muslims living among them. Globalization and socioeconomic factors in this account obviously play a role, as Giddens makes clear. But, according to this narrative, at the heart of the modern populist problem is not so much economics as identity and meaning driven by a set of inchoate but nonetheless key questions about who I am, what I am, and do I still live in my own country surrounded by people who share the same values and allegiances?

There is, however, a third way of understanding populism, and this argues that modern populism is less the result of an identity crisis, as such, and much more the result of what the Indian economist Arvind Subramanian (former adviser to Indian Prime Minister Narendra Modi) has termed 'hyper-globalization'.[14] This latest form of globalization, he notes, began slowly in the 1970s, accelerated rapidly in the 1980s, took off in earnest in the 1990s, and continued to accelerate thereafter – until, that is, the crash of 2008. For years the results of this 30-year headlong drive towards the future only seemed to be positive and beneficial. Indeed, according to the many defenders of globalization, the new economic order generated enormous wealth, drew in once previously closed economies, drove up the world's GDP, encouraged real development in countries that had for years been poor, and most important of all in terms of human welfare, helped reduce poverty too. Not surprisingly India, China and the developing countries loved this new world order. They were its beneficiaries. But for the West more generally it has through time created all sorts of downside problems. As a number of writers have pointed out, wealth became ever more concentrated in the hands of the few.[15] Middle-class incomes stagnated. Meanwhile, many of the working class in Western countries found themselves losing their jobs, either because jobs were going elsewhere or by a rush of cheap imported goods largely coming from the new emerging economies, most obviously China. And to add to their economic woes immigration, it was claimed, was undercutting the price of their labour. Thus what may have been great for the corporations and the consumer – not to mention the Chinese – turned into an economic tsunami for the traditional bastions of labour.

A crucial component part of what might be described as a materialist interpretation of populism has also been provided by James Montier and Philip Pilkington. They do not deny the fact that globalization has important downsides. But their point is that the very real crisis facing the Western economies is not just down to globalization in the abstract, but what they more precisely term 'a broken system of economic governance' the result they insist of the West adopting a certain menu of free market economic policies in the 1970s. 'Neoliberalism' as it is often referred to, contained within it at least three 'significant economic policies' that have fuelled the populist backlash:

the abandonment of full employment as a desirable policy goal and its replacement with inflation targeting; [...] a focus at the firm level on shareholder value maximization rather than reinvestment and growth; and the pursuit of flexible labour markets and the disruption of trade unions and workers' organizations.[16]

Taken together, this new neoliberal order, they believe, has not only skewed the balance towards capital and away from labour; the regime it has created has also given rise to lower inflation, lower growth rates, lower investment rates, lower productivity growth, increasing wealth and income inequality, diminished job insecurity, and a seriously deflationary bias in the world economy. Moreover, instead of the 2008 crisis undermining this order, it has only made things much, much worse. And given all this, we should not be so surprised that there has been a backlash in the form of populism. The only surprise perhaps is that it did not happen earlier. Someone like Trump espousing the views he did was simply waiting to happen.

Further reflections on populism

One thing that writers often leave out of their accounts of populism – or perhaps do not stress enough – is the enormous impact long term that the failure of communism and the collapse of the USSR has had (and still has) on the world in which we live. Before 1989 and 1991 there seemed to be some kind of balance in the world: some built-in limit to the operation of the free market. However, by the 1990s, all this had been swept aside. The years 1989–91 also led to a high degree of hubris and over-confidence in the West. Anything was now possible, and even if it caused pain to some, this was a price worth paying for the general good; and anyway there was now no serious opposition. Or any alternative. So one could press on regardless.

Nor did policy makers quite figure out what it might mean for the West if massive low-wage economies like China were to join the world market club. Many economists will no doubt tell you (and still do) that free trade is always a good in the long term. Ricardo said so, Adam Smith said so, Keynes said so, even Milton Friedman said so. So it must be for the best. Moreover, if jobs have been lost in the EU and the US, this it seems has little to do with free trade and more with new labour-saving technologies. In fact, all those manufacturing jobs in Europe and the US would have had to go anyway because of technology and automation. Thus it is unfair to blame China, as of course Trump did throughout his campaign and after. But there is ample evidence to suggest a rather different narrative: that in fact millions of jobs were lost in the West because of new emerging economies joining in the game. It is not merely a populist myth.

I would also wish to suggest that populism was and is very much an expression in the West of a sense of powerlessness: the powerlessness of ordinary citizens when faced with massive changes going on all around them; but the powerlessness too of Western leaders and politicians who really do not seem to have an answer to the many challenges facing the West right now. Many ordinary people might feel they have no control and express this by supporting populist movements and parties who promise to restore control to them. But in reality, it is the established political parties, the established politicians, and the established structures of power as well, which are equally powerless – powerless, as many believe, to stop the flow of migrants from the Middle East and Africa, powerless to control the borders of their own nation-states. Powerless when faced with a terrorist threat, powerless to prevent off-shoring and tax avoidance, and powerless too to reduce unemployment to any significant degree across most of the Eurozone.

Now this might have been finessed but for two other factors: one, quite clearly was the 2008 financial crisis. As we have already suggested, this not only delivered a major blow to Western economies; it also undermined faith in the competence of the establishment, from the bankers to the economists at the LSE. Who, after 2008, would ever believe the experts again? Or think they might be on your side? The other factor here was a series of major setbacks in the field of foreign policy ranging from Iraq to Libya. These not only did enormous damage to the Middle East, but exposed the West and Western leaders to the charge of being incompetent and lacking in strategic nous. It was no coincidence of course that one of the themes Trump returned to time and again was the Iraq war – a clear demonstration in his view that the 'establishment' simply could not be trusted with America's security.

Finally, the more general phenomenon of populism was the political reflection – an expression of a deep fear, no less – that the old Western-dominated order led by the US and Europe was rapidly being undermined by an irreversible shift in global power away from the West. After all, for the last few years we have heard the same mantra being uttered by the bulk of our so-called public intellectuals: namely, that the 'rest', viewed here as either Asia, China or that interesting combination known as the BRICs, will sometime soon be running the world. Meanwhile, we have been informed by the same Jeremiahs that the poor old West is on the way down. As I have argued elsewhere, this view of an enormous power shift leading to either a post-American, post-Western or even a post-liberal world order has been much exaggerated. Nevertheless, it has become for many the new truth of our age; almost the common sense of our times. And it has had consequences, intended or otherwise. One of these has been to make many people living in the West feel deeply uncertain about their future. This in turn has made many of them look to those politicians and movements who say they will stand up for the West; or, in the American context, make America great again. Moreover, the view that a power shift was or is underway has also helped those in the UK make the case for Brexit. Indeed, in the UK the argument that the EU in particular was in terminal decline, and that one had to look to other parts of the world economy – China and India most obviously – clearly played an important role in mobilizing the case for Brexit.

Conclusion: populism and the future of globalization

Finally, to what degree does populism pose a serious threat to globalization? The simplest answer to this is not as much some alarmists would lead you to believe – at least that is what the 'facts' tell you if you measure globalization by such indicators as cross-border financial flows, international tourism, and foreign direct investment. By any measure, the world is not de-globalizing. Nor is it likely to do so as long as its five biggest economic actors – the European Union, the United States, China, India and Japan – continue to support policies that favour more integration not less, more extensive supply chains not fewer, and see continued advantage economically by being part of a world market. To this degree the forces in favour of globalization would still appear to be far stronger than those pitted against it. Yet, as the populist revolt in the West reveals only too clearly, those who feel they have lost rather than won as their once cherished national economies have become more and more open to the outside world, have become increasingly vocal, and vocal in a negative way. Martin Wolf has also made the important point that even if globalization might not be in rapid reverse, it is beginning to lose its dynamism; and to add to the West's woes, there is now much greater ambivalence across the West as a whole about the benefits of free trade and trade deals.[17] It is not just Trump who has attacked trade deals such as NAFTA and TPP. In Europe too there would seem to be less and less support for large multilateral trade deals, while the UK, of course, voted in 2016 to get out of the largest single market in the world. Globalization may still be secure. However, the case for it is no longer being made with anything like the same confidence we found ten or 15 years ago. And if the unpicking of what Simon Fraser has termed 'the pro-globalization orthodoxy of the post-Cold War period' continues, then we could very well find ourselves facing even more challenges to the liberal economic order in the future.[18] The populist backlash, one suspects, still has a long way to run.

10

Trump's World: The Legacy

There have been many shocks in American electoral history but probably none more shocking than the election of Donald Trump in November 2016. Hardly any pollsters ever thought he could win; when he did it was by a mere 80,000 votes spread across the three crucial 'swing states' of Wisconsin, Michigan and Pennsylvania; and as if to rub salt into Democratic wounds, he didn't even win the majority of the votes cast across the country as a whole.[1] Yet, after one of the more bruising campaigns in recent times, he secured the White House against one of the most experienced US politicians of modern times. Inspired in part by what had earlier happened in the UK when the British voted to leave the European Union – the first great shock of 2016 – Trump the outsider managed to tap into a vein of discontent among millions of working-class Americans who either felt that their position in society was under threat from changes at home and abroad,[2] or found it difficult to connect with an increasingly liberal Democratic Party whose candidate only rarely seemed to speak to their concerns or connect with their fears. Nor did Trump ignore other important sources of support. Indeed, as a result of a very well organized campaign which left no stone unturned, he scored very heavily among three other significant constituencies: the evangelical right (80 per cent of whom voted for him),[3] the US military (who voted 2-to-1 in his favour),[4] and the better off and the wealthy who were attracted to his banner by promises of tax breaks and deregulation. With enough additional support coming from Latinos and even women (and Clinton losing some ground among African-Americans, Latino and younger voters) it turned out to be a winning combination.[5]

How and why Trump won an election he was predicted to lose will no doubt be debated for years to come.[6] But one thing became clear even as the dust began to settle: that a political earthquake had occurred which was bound to have huge consequences both for the United States and for the rest of the world. For Trump was not just a 'normal politician' tasked with running the nation, but rather an insurgent who far from uniting the US 'under one flag' set out to exploit its many divisions, and who instead of making the usual comforting noises about the United States being the indispensable nation working with allies to solve problems together made it abundantly clear that there was only one country in which he was interested and that was the United States. Nor did he try to hide any of this in his election campaign directed at his mainly white 'USA'-chanting audiences.[7] As has been observed, 'race and racism have always coursed through American politics', but they very soon became a central feature of the contest in 2016. Trump, of course, claimed that he was looking for 'the vote of every African-American and Hispanic citizen'.[8] On the other hand, his references to Mexicans as 'rapists' and Muslims as 'hating us' made it abundantly clear to whom he was appealing and why. Nor did he ever pass up on the opportunity of pointing out that for eight years the nation had been led by an African-American who might not even be an American, and who also happened to be the darling of the liberals in the media, Hollywood and the universities, all of whom endorsed ideas which were gradually eating away at good old American values such as love of nation and the right to bear arms. But the rot stopped here he insisted, and by voting for 'me'[9] Trump promised decent hard-working Americans (usually living outside the main metropolitan centres of power) that their voice would now be listened to.[10]

Thus a populist wave that began with Brexit in June 2016 reached the US in stunning fashion just five months later. Portraying his opponents as being in hock to the wealthy and representative of a distant elite who had been selling the country short for years while getting it involved in all sorts of pointless wars abroad, Trump and his closest adviser Steve Bannon very quickly figured out which issues would resonate mostly deeply with Trump's potential base. His portrayal of a nation under siege being taken for a proverbial ride by both its enemies and friends certainly played well to the gallery. But nothing played so well as his ability to tap into a deep-seated nativist hostility to immigration and free trade policies which taken together were, he claimed, undermining the wages of Americans while destroying the country's manufacturing base. As he made clear in one of his many speeches invariably delivered before adoring blue-collar crowds, America had for years been betrayed by all 'our politicians' who 'have aggressively pursued a policy of globalization'. This may have made the financial elite who donated to politicians 'very, very wealthy'. But for most workers it had caused nothing but misery. A new course was necessary, therefore. Indeed, until the US changed direction and abandoned the failed project of globalism and replaced it with the credo of Americanism – which it would only be able to do under Trump – the United States would continue on its downward path.[11]

In what follows we shall look at what followed Trump's successful campaign of 2016. In the first section we shall look at what he did during his first year when he started putting into practice some of the policies designed to make 'American great again'. We shall then examine his official national security strategy as set out in December 2017. The following section will look at some his key policies, but focus in particular on what his administration defined as the greatest challenge facing the US in the 21st century: China. Finally, we will assess how successful Trump was in realizing his original goals. Here opinion remains deeply divided in the US between those (80 per cent of all Republicans) who insist that he set America on the right course, and others (85 per cent of all Democrats) who insist with equal passion that far from making 'America great again' he achieved quite the opposite. Either way, there is no doubting the disturbing impact that he had during his four-year term – one which concluded in his last year in office with a deadly pandemic, which he at first denied was significant (and which almost certainly lost him the White House), an election which the overwhelming majority of his followers then claimed he had won, followed a few weeks later with a physical assault on Congress itself by thousands of his loyal supporters. In 2016 Trump entered office in a flurry of fevered speculation as to why he might have won: he left it four years later with a country more divided than ever and its reputation abroad in tatters.[12]

America First

> As long as I hold this office, I will defend America's interests above all else.[13]

American presidents are invariably judged by what they say and do during their first 100 days. Trump was no different and lost very little time in making it clear that having won the election he would not be deviating from the pledge he had made during his campaign of putting America and Americans first. His inaugural address set the tone for what followed. His message was hardly a reassuring one for those who may have hoped he might be moving back to occupy the middle ground. The speech was pure Trump with attacks on corrupt and venal politicians reaping all the rewards while middle- and working-class families struggled as 'jobs left' and 'factories closed', leaving them with little hope and even less to look forward to. Moreover, while all this was taking place at home, foreign countries were flourishing at 'America's expense'. Indeed, America found itself in the bizarre position, according to Trump, of spending trillions and trillions of dollars overseas, while America's infrastructure was falling into disrepair and decay. It was pure madness, he went on, making 'other countries rich while the wealth, strength and confidence of our country dissipated over the horizon [...] with not even a thought' being spared 'about the millions and millions of American workers that were left behind'. This 'American carnage' as he defined it, 'stops right here and stops right now'.[14]

Trump's early attempt to link American woes at home with its entrapment into a multilateral order which worked to the advantage of every other nation except the United States not only had the advantage of portraying the US as victim, it also provided some sort of justification for many of the controversial measures he then went on to take. This began straight away with an announcement to start work on that 'big beautiful wall' between the US and Mexico, went on with the decision to pull out of one of Obama's signature policies, the Trans-Pacific Partnership (another one of those hated multilateral trade deals), continued with the decision to withdraw from the Paris Climate Agreement (a ruse thought up by others to make the US economically uncompetitive), and concluded in October when Trump made it clear he was taking the first step to pull the US out of the Iran nuclear deal, which Obama had signed up to in January 2016. Over the same 12 months Trump also imposed a travel ban on seven Muslim countries – though, significantly, not Saudi Arabia – called ISIS a bunch of 'loser terrorists', referred to the North Korean leader as 'rocket man' in charge of a rogue state, which the US threatened to obliterate, and in a provocative speech delivered to the United Nations not only complained that the US was subsidizing an organization which kept on attacking one of America's best friends in the form of Israel, but railed (once again) against all those 'mammoth multinational trade deals' that had led to millions of job losses in America. Espousing what he termed a 'principled realism' Trump wrapped all this up in a strong defence of the nation-state and sovereignty, a move which not only reinforced his basic message that he would always place America 'first' but also implied that the US would no longer be as bothered as it had been in the past about the political practices of other regimes. It was no coincidence, perhaps, that following Trump's UN speech in which he declared that all sovereign nations should find their own way and that America would not be seeking to 'impose' its 'way of life on anyone' that Russian Foreign Minister Sergei Lavrov announced that he very much welcomed Trump's words.

While Trump was delivering on his promise of asserting America's right to promote its own interests rather than anybody else's, his administration quickly turned its attention to a part of the world that had preoccupied all post-Cold War presidents since Clinton: namely, the Middle East. Here Trump seemed to adopt the line that if Obama had been in favour of pursuing a certain policy, then he was against it and would therefore do the opposite. Thus if Obama had at times talked about supporting change in the region – especially in the wake of the Arab Spring, Trump instinctively opted for the status quo. If Obama tried (as he did) to be as even-handed as it was ever possible to be for an American president in relation to Israel, then he, Trump, would prove his loyalty to the Jewish state by moving to have Jerusalem declared to be Israel's capital and cutting off support for the Palestinians. And if Obama had had ethical or political qualms about the some of the region's Sunni dictatorships, Trump seemed to have none at all. Indeed, his first foreign trip was to Saudi Arabia where he not only had what was seen as a most positive meeting with Prince Salman, but also a most profitable one as well, after he signed off on a large arms deal worth $350 billion. Finally, of course, there was the crucial issue of Iran with which Obama had struck a deal in the hope of limiting its nuclear programme, and hopefully its ambitions in the wider region too. Trump and his advisers had never hidden their views about either the deal or Iran, which in their collective view was run by a group of dangerous radicals fundamentally opposed to Israel and hostile to America's Sunni allies.

But perhaps Trump's most significant move in the wider region had less to do with building bridges to the Middle East's more significant actors, but of finding ways of abandoning those commitments the US had made ever since the attack of 9/11. A strong critic of Bush's original decision to go into Afghanistan and Iraq – except for the more limited purpose of eliminating international terrorism – Trump was at least consistent when it came to what he viewed as unwinnable wars in countries in which the US, in his view, did not have a vital interest. In Iraq, therefore, he conducted a short-term war against ISIS before declaring victory and removing most American ground forces. Meanwhile, his administration opened up a line of communication with the Taliban leadership in Doha, culminating with the February 2020 announcement that all US forces would be out of Afghanistan the following year on the condition that if and when the Taliban took over (the implicit assumption here being that they would) they would not harbour international terrorists – even though many AQ militants were fighting alongside the Taliban – and that they would engage in direct negotiations with the Afghan government itself (which so far had been locked out of the discussions). Sold as a negotiated settlement of what President Biden himself later called this 'forever war', the deal in effect amounted to a Taliban diplomatic triumph whose only consequence was to demoralize those battling against the Taliban back in Afghanistan and prepare the way for their final takeover a year later. As even some in the Trump administration later confessed, the agreement 'did little more than provide cover for a pull-out that Mr Trump was impatient to begin before his re-election bid'.[15]

If Trump's reorientation of US policy towards the Middle East shocked his critics at home, then his views on Europe had much the same impact across the Atlantic – so much so that when EU leaders heard the news that he had won the election in November 2016 they convened an emergency meeting to deal with what many there saw as nothing less than a disaster for the transatlantic relationship. They had several reasons to be concerned. Here after all was the leader of the free world who not only supported the UK decision to leave the European Union, but who talked of the EU less as a partner and more as a competitor, which had only been created in the first place to take advantage of the US on trade. Indeed, according to Trump, nobody treated America 'worse than the European Union', and within the EU no country treated the US quite as badly when it came to trade and spending on defence as Germany did. Nor did Trump spare NATO and when asked long before he entered the White House what he thought of the most successful alliance in history, he wondered if it was not 'obsolete'.

Even Trump's various trips to Europe between June and July 2017 did nothing to calm most European nerves. Having shoved the Montenegrin prime minister out of the way to get to the front of a NATO photo-op, he proceeded to lecture US allies in a most undiplomatic way on their lack of spending on defence. In Helsinki, he then appeared to side with Putin against his own intelligence agencies while failing to condemn Russian meddling in the democratic process across the West. He then railed against Germany (once again), this time over its support for the Nord Stream pipeline. On a brief but controversial visit to London he once again reiterated his very strong support for Brexit; and as if it to confirm his opposition to the wider European project, visited Poland in July to demonstrate his support for the populist government there, which had come into power in 2015 expressing similar views to his own on the importance of sovereignty and why it was important to limit immigration. Indeed, in a speech delivered to cheering supporters of the government, he praised Poland – the 'proud nation' of Copernicus, Chopin and Pope John Paul III – for saving Europe from Bolshevism in 1920, for surviving 40 years of communism, for its love of God, for its very special relationship with the United States, and most important of all, perhaps, for continuing to uphold the values of Western civilization. Here Trump waxed lyrical about independent nations like Poland and America, which were founded on family, 'bonds of culture, faith and tradition'. These bonds not only made us 'who we are', but were now under attack from various 'forces', which were attempting to 'undermine our courage, sap our spirit, and weaken our will to defend ourselves and our societies'. Trump did not mention who or what these unspecified 'forces' might be, but it was perfectly obvious who or what he was talking about: namely, liberals in America as well as in Europe who no longer knew what Western values were and why they needed defending.

In the end, though, Trump knew that he would be judged not by what he did or said abroad, but rather by what he did at home, and in particular how successful he was in bringing jobs home while unleashing that mighty engine known as the American economy. A property developer who had made a reputation (at least, in his own eyes) of being able to strike a deal, it was hardly surprising that he looked at the United States less as a seasoned politician but rather through the eyes of a businessman, though not one very much liked by the wider business community, it seems. In fact, if anybody was trusted when it came to managing the American economy, it had been Obama – who had helped pull America out of the recession while saving two of the big three auto companies – as well as Hillary Clinton whose support among the corporations far exceeded that of Trump whose constant beating of the populist drum and attacks on companies 'shipping jobs abroad' drove many of the biggest companies into the welcoming arms of the Democrats.[16] Indeed, the list of the major businesses supporting Clinton in 2016 almost read like a 'who's who' of American capitalism with strong backing coming from the tech sector and corporations with major overseas interests, as well as many of the big firms on Wall Street.[17]

Trump, though, had at least one advantage, which he exploited to the full: the US economy itself, which by the time he took over may not have been in rude health – growth stood at only 2.5 per cent in 2016 – but had recovered significantly from the worst of the 2008 crisis, largely because of the measures Obama had taken in the eight years before.[18] Trump, of course, conceded nothing to his predecessor, instead painting a picture with the economy in headlong decline before he took over, and then bouncing back once he had entered the White House! Still, the various measures he did take, from cutting corporate taxes to reducing regulations (especially those covering the energy sector) did lead to something of a surge, reflected in the very speedy rise in the Dow Jones index from around 16,000 in January 2017, to over 22,000 by August, to just under 25,000 by the end of the year. Whether this was a result of his measures, the underlying strengths of the American economy, or most likely, historically low interest rates didn't really matter much. In a nation looking for some good news after so many difficult years, Trump could claim – as any politician would – that this was all down to him. Trump may just have got lucky.[19] That said, there was no getting away from the fact that growth by the end of his first year in office was up to over 3 per cent, the stock market was on a roll, and unemployment falling – even if the economy was a good deal smaller than it would have been had there been no financial crisis, that wages remained relatively flat, and that the number of high-paying jobs were much scarcer than they had been a decade earlier.[20]

A new national security doctrine?

In the end, Trump's actions will matter far more than his words. And no matter how much fanfare this strategy document gets, foreign governments will likely continue to take their cues from the president himself.[21]

Every administration sees as one of its important tasks the drawing up of an official document outlining its National Security Strategy (NSS). Neither a blueprint for action nor a precise roadmap, the purpose of such documents lies in indicating, in the broadest terms possible, the long-term goals and specific threats facing the nation. Regarded by some critics as mere window dressing, and others as making the everyday business of conducting foreign policy look a lot more coherent than it really is, the Trump team managed to bring out its own 68-page document with a typically upbeat introduction written by Trump himself. In this he not only reiterated his key goal of putting 'America First' – but the American people also elected me to make 'America great again' and that is precisely what I have done, he insisted. He also claimed some early successes, notably in confronting the two rogue states of Iran and North Korea while at the same attacking the sources of 'radical Islamist terrorism', most obviously in Syria where the US (apparently with no help from the Kurds, Iran or Hezbollah) had managed to 'crush' Islamic State on the battlefield.

The document itself was a curious hybrid that seemed to be caught between two stools, one of which gave expression to Trump's populist view of the world and another which reflected the foreign policy outlook of its more mainstream authors. Thus, whereas Trump was always deeply reluctant to call out Russia on anything (though felt he had to when speaking in Poland), the authors of the NSS did not mince their words when it came to talking about Russia, arguing that with China it was one of the great challenges facing the United States. The document also talked of the importance of allies and alliances in ways that Trump rarely did. It then went on to praise international institutions built by the United States, even though Trump had denigrated nearly all of them both before and after having come into office. The NSS also insisted that 'diplomacy' was 'indispensable', even though Trump himself had little or no idea what being diplomatic meant and had already instructed his Secretary of State, Rex Tillerson to cut the State Department budget by a third![22]

There were also areas where the document said very little at all. Most obviously, there was no mention at all of climate change. Indeed, when it did refer to 'energy' issues it was not in terms of carbon emissions leading to climate change, but rather the threat posed to the US economy because of 'anti-growth energy agenda' promoted by the climate change lobby. Not only were such activities economically harmful, it argued, they were also coming at a time when for the 'first time in generations' the US stood on the cusp of becoming the 'energy dominant nation' of the world. Nor was there any mention of democracy or democracy promotion as a US goal. Susan Rice, former national security advisor, even pointed out that the strategy document 'fails to mention the words 'human rights'', while the editorial board of the *Washington Post* regretted that the strategy contained 'no commitment to promot[ing] democracy and human rights'.[23] Finally, far from celebrating America's part in building a world economy from which the US among others had drawn strength – something that had been stressed in both Bush Jnr's and Obama's previous NSS reviews – Trump's NSS was wholly negative with its authors complaining that other countries have 'exploited the international institutions' which 'we helped to build'.

Given all these limits it was hardly surprising that the NSS ran into a storm of criticism, a good deal of it coming from more traditional Republicans. Hence, a former Bush official believed that the disconnect between what large parts of the document said (those bits to which one could not take exception) and what Trump himself had been doing in 2017, made it difficult to take the new NSS seriously. The deputy managing editor of the influential journal *Foreign Policy* agreed. Indeed, according to Kate Brennan, the discrepancies and silences in the document rendered it 'practically meaningless. Another seasoned observer of the American foreign policy scene (Roger Cohen) even called the whole project a 'farce', while a Republican foreign policy expert, Kori Schake – adviser to John McCain in 2008, no less – believed the NSS was utterly 'implausible as a description of the president's actual views' or a 'likely template for its priorities or spending'.[24]

Yet, in its own way the 2017 strategy document did provide some insights into how American policy makers within the Trump administration looked at the world. Their collective view was a decidedly conservative one informed by one central argument: that the United States had lost its way and that as a result was no longer viewed or treated with respect. In part, this may have been the consequence of the 2008 crisis. But the source of the problem ran deeper and might even be traced back to the end of the Cold War. Victory over the USSR was no doubt most welcome. Yet being a 'lone superpower' was not without its problems, especially if it bred – as the NSS claimed it did – a certain 'complacency' based on the illusion that the unipolar moment would go on forever. What compounded this problem was something even more dangerous, perhaps: the acceptance in certain policy circles of a distinctly liberal view of the world which took it as read that as new actors emerged onto the world stage they could easily be integrated into an American-led world order. Indeed, successive administrations, it was argued, Republican as well as Democrat, all seemed to have bought into the idea that rival powers (even China) could be tamed by being drawn into 'international institutions and global commerce'. This, however, was a false promise which ignored something very basic about the world: that competition and great power rivalry was not some accidental feature of the system but a basic fact of international life.

This of course led the NSS to possibly its most important conclusion of all: that among all the new actors in the world it was China with its sense of historical mission, its ever-expanding economy and its rapidly modernizing military that presented the greatest challenge of all. Led after 2013 by a dedicated communist who no longer felt it was necessary to hide China's ambitions under a bushel, America faced a rival second to none. The time had come therefore to reset policy towards China, even if this upset US allies or even those US corporations with interests in China. For years now, many in the liberal establishment had justified their benign approach to China on the grounds that one day it would become a trusted member of the international community. But it was clear that this stakeholder strategy had failed. A new approach based on a hardheaded realism was in order.

Trump and China

> He's now president for life. President for life. No, he's great. And look, he was able to do that. I think it's great. Maybe we'll have to give that a shot some day.[25]

For the last two to three years of his term in office Trump devoted more time to China than any other single issue. Trump himself, however, seemed to have no particular animus towards China because it was run by a Communist Party, or because of its appalling record on human rights. Indeed, in his first meeting with Xi Jinping at his Florida home in April 2017, many issues were discussed from North Korea to trade, but the issue of human rights was never raised. As one analyst later put it, 'In Trump, China found an American leader who seemed focused on transactional politics and trade deals, rather than human rights and Chinese foreign policy.'[26] Trump's lack of diplomatic finesse may have worried various China experts in the United States, as had his various attacks on China during his presidential campaign. Even so, the relationship through 2017 seemed to settle down with Trump announcing later in the year that not only were China and the US going to become 'strategic partners' but that the relationship between the two leaders was 'outstanding'. As Trump put it in his own folksy way in October, President Xi himself was just 'a terrific guy' with whom he liked 'being with a lot'.[27]

None of this, however, could change the fact that since 2011 at least Trump had been convinced that China had been taking economic advantage of the United States. Nor could he easily row back from what he had said against China during his presidential campaign, given how many times he had attacked it for stealing American know-how, manipulating its currency to keep China's goods cheap, and taking away American jobs. There was, moreover, the even more significant problem, as Trump saw it, of those burgeoning trade deficits and America's loss of manufacture caused in large part, he insisted, because of China. Never much interested in foreign countries as such, Trump did not bother much with geopolitics, something he left to his various advisers like Herbert Raymond McMaster and John Bolton. They, in turn, were not much interested in economics, rather seeing China in classically realist terms of a rising power, which like all rising powers through history was duty bound to challenge the established hegemon. Either way, they all arrived at the same policy conclusion: that something would have to be done about China both for economic and national security reasons. The problem then was to work out what could be done and with what instruments at America's command.

The most obvious weapon in the US arsenal was of course trade and waging what became regularly referred to from 2018 onwards as 'trade war'. Urged on by his two hardline trade advisers – Robert Lighthizer and Peter Navarro – Trump initiated a series of fairly far-reaching measures primarily aimed at reducing Chinese access to the US market. It started slowly in late 2017 when Lighthizer instructed officials to consider 'whether to investigate any of China's laws, policies, practices, or actions that may be unreasonable or discriminatory and that may be harming American intellectual property rights, innovation, or technology'. It then became more serious by January 2018 when President Trump approved tariffs on $8.5 billion in imports of solar panels and $1.8 billion of washing machines. In April the administration then went on to identify over a thousand Chinese products covering $46.2 billion of US imports. More followed in June when Trump directed the Office of the US Trade Representative to identify an additional $200 billion worth of Chinese goods for additional tariffs at a rate of 10 per cent. In July, during an interview, Trump said he was ready to impose tariffs on all US imports from China, which in 2017 totalled well over $500 billion. A month later, in August, Trump then signed what became known as the John S. McCain National Defense Authorization Act containing two key provisions on monitoring some foreign investments in the United States and outbound transfers of technology.[28]

How effective these measures proved to be remains a source of some disagreement. Trump's policy certainly had more than its fair share of critics who among other things pointed out that his aggressive stance did little to open up China's economy, change its economic behaviour, reduce US trade deficits or bring anything other than a handful of jobs back home. Unsurprisingly, Trump's defenders (fewer in number) took a rather different line, pointing out that by being tough China was in the end forced back to the negotiating table where some kind of first-stage 'deal' was finally signed in the autumn of 2019. The deal was by no means perfect.[29] On the other hand, it did lead to changes to China's economic and trade regime and a commitment by China to make substantial additional purchases of US goods and services in the coming years, supported by a strong dispute resolution system that ensured prompt and effective implementation and enforcement.[30] It also had the added advantage of providing Trump with something he craved and needed most: positive headlines followed by an upward bump in the stock market. Indeed, his main goal now, it seemed, was to sell what he called this 'terrific trade deal' to the American people, an increasingly difficult task as news began to come out of China about a dangerous virus.[31] Trump, however, was not deterred, even praising China for the great job it was doing in managing the health scare. They are 'getting it more and more under control' he declared on 26 February. A few days later he spoke in an equally upbeat fashion of China 'making tremendous progress' while reminding his audience (just in case they had forgotten) that the relationship with China was now 'very good', so much so that we're beginning to work on 'another trade deal – a big one'.[32]

It was perhaps only a matter of time before Trump stopped boasting about his trade agreement with China and started attacking his old friend Xi and the Chinese regime for not only having caused the pandemic, but possibly doing so deliberately. Trump even gave COVID-19 a typically provocative name: 'China virus'. Inevitably China responded, insisting that Trump was only calling it that as a way of avoiding responsibility for America's own inadequate response to the crisis. When Trump then floated the idea in spring 2020 of seeking reparations from China, both for having caused the virus and then covering up what had happened, Beijing once again reacted furiously. They became even more incensed when Trump (supported by the Democrats in a rare show of unity) then decided to back Hong Kong, and in July ended all preferential treatment for the island in retaliation for the mainland's passing of a new security law. China could not let that interference into what it saw as its own internal affairs pass without responding and went on to attack America, this time pointing to its failure to deal with its own problems at home, in particular those flowing from race and police behaviour towards African-Americans.

The deterioration in US–China relations to the point where some experts were even beginning to speculate that this could very easily end in open conflict may or may not have done something to bolster Trump's position at home. Nonetheless, as the pandemic spread and the numbers of American deaths began to soar, many more Americans started to ask serious questions about the Trump administration, and how well (or more precisely how badly) it was handling the crisis. Moreover, once the health crisis began to hit the US economy, Trump's ratings – except among his loyal followers – began to take a hit which no amount of bluster could hide. Herein was Trump's greatest challenge perhaps. Hitherto he had been able to claim that the American economy had been doing well under his stewardship; indeed, even some of those who may not have approved of Trump were at least prepared to concede that he had done a reasonable job when it came to the economy. This however became an increasingly difficult 'sell' as the

US economy plummeted, unemployment and poverty began to soar, and the underlying inequalities in American society were exposed by a disease which Trump himself had first suggested was just like flu and then failed to deal with in anything like a competent fashion. It may well have been coincidence, but in the same month that Trump was finally voted out of office in November, COVID-19 killed more Americans than in any other month in 2020. Trump had said he would make America his first priority and America great again. As the body count continued to rise with no end in sight, making those bold claims rang increasingly hollow for the millions of Americans who seemed to think otherwise and finally voted him out of office.

Conclusion: after Trump?

> For all the visible damage the president has done to the nation's global standing, things are much worse below the surface.[33]

Perhaps no single president since the Second World War has had such a disruptive impact on American politics or on America's position in the wider world as Trump. Very much part of that wider global phenomenon known as modern populism, there was, however, something distinctly 'American' about Trump's style of politics with its overt anti-intellectualism, hostility to liberal elites and ingrained suspicion of the outside world. Indeed, the parallels between mainstream American populism going all the way back to the late 19th century and Trump are striking.[34] Back then, populist ideologues appealed to those living in rural America and in small towns with little access to a college education. So, too, did Trump. Historically, populism was also prone to conspiracy thinking. Moreover, like its 21st-century successor, earlier populists were also deeply suspicious of banks and bankers. Trump's base of support may well have been wider, and the way he mobilized it using very modern means quite different. Nonetheless, many of those who rallied around his flag, like those populists of old, tended to see the world as a threat and hard-working citizens being taken for a ride by those wealthy people back East who were not just distant but downright indifferent to the needs of ordinary Americans. There was, however, one vital difference. The first populists did not take over the White House, whereas Trump did. Moreover, the populist surge of the late 19th century occurred when America was not yet a central actor in the international system.

Trump has often been compared to a 'wrecking ball' who deliberately went out of his way to destroy a well-established system of global governance with the express purpose of keeping everybody else off balance while he (and hopefully the United States too) picked up the pieces left behind. A transactional politician who saw the world in purely zero-sum terms and America as having been suckered by others, it was hardly surprising that he took the hostile positions he did on international organizations, international treaties and trade agreements unless they could be shown (which they never could, he believed) to have benefited the United States. This no doubt played to his own nativist base back home. Nevertheless, its impact on America's standing in the world was nothing less than devastating, leaving the US in a more isolated position by 2020 than at any time since the end of the Second World War.

Even so, Trump still managed to maintain a very high level of support within the United States itself. Tapping into several sources of resentment while articulating a programme that clearly appealed to many constituencies at home – the white working class and the wealthy, born-again Christians, as well as those whose primary interest was in maintaining the right to bear arms – Trump proved to be the most consequential American politician of his age. The past master at exploiting fear and stoking up racial tensions (while all the time denying he was racist), Trump had no problem in painting a picture of America under siege from its enemies within, whether this was from the Black Lives Matter movement or their 'anarchist comrades' who despised authority and whose only objective was the destruction of everything that was dear to Americans, including a good part of their history. Trump also deployed something that had not been heard of for years: a 'red scare'. Indeed, he was the first political leader since the 1960s who played on the old trope that America was facing a very real threat in the shape of socialism, and that unless he was re-elected the private enterprise system would not survive. As Larry Kudlow, the president's top adviser on economics, argued at a conference nine months prior to the November election, the really dangerous virus facing America was not COVID-19 – that will 'not sink the American economy', he insisted – but rather the 'socialism coming from our friends [the Democratic Party] on the other side of the aisle'.[35] Trump could not have agreed more, and indeed fought the election in November on the promise of stopping the ideological rot. As he put it, 'This election will decide whether we save the American Dream or whether we allow a socialist agenda to demolish our cherished destiny.'[36]

The chances of Joe Biden's election leading to that which Trump claimed he most feared were of course zero. But even if America was unlikely to become the radical dystopia predicted by Trump, there was every chance it would remain profoundly divided between the over 74 million Americans who voted for him and the 80 million or so who voted for Biden. Moreover, with most Republicans continuing to believe that Trump was victorious, and with Trump standing in the wings like some American de Gaulle waiting to be called back to save the country from those who stole the election back in 2020, the United States hardly looked like that 'shining city on the hill' or the 'hope of mankind' that many Americans felt it had been since the nation first came into being. Historians may one day try and make sense of the Trump phenomenon. Meanwhile, American democracy and the world order which Trump tried to unmake confront a legacy with which both will be living with for years to come.

PART V

Biden: Is America Back?

Few successful candidates have ever entered the White House with quite so much experience as Joe Biden or with so many challenges to deal with. Sworn into office only a couple of weeks after the assault on Congress in a city where over 25,000 troops had been drafted in to maintain order, the circumstances of his inauguration were extraordinary by any measure. Faced by an outgoing president who refused to accept defeat in a deeply polarized nation where the COVID-19 pandemic still continued to kill Americans in great numbers – on the day when Biden officially became president the virus had already claimed over 400,000 lives – Biden faced an uphill struggle even to restore some degree of normality into American political life, let alone successfully tackle the many problems the US was facing both at home and abroad. As one newspaper of a decidedly liberal bent commented at the time, the passing of power from what it called a 'dangerous man' to one set on healing his country was a relief. Even so, American democracy still remained at peril. Biden, however, was clear in his own mind that if America was to regain its equilibrium it had to end what he termed 'this uncivil war' that was pitting red state against blue state, 'rural versus urban, conservative versus liberal'. He was equally clear that the foreign policy he would be pursuing would be very different from that of his predecessor, and that once elected he would repair America's 'alliances and engage with the world once again'. Biden did at least attempt to make good on this promise, much to the relief of US allies around the world. Yet, one suspects that his foreign policy will be increasingly viewed through the prism of Afghanistan and his controversial decision to pull US forces out by a specific date. Meanwhile, he faces a whole range of other problems, one of which of course is the increasingly deep divide within America itself. The United States may indeed remain the most powerful country in the world, but one suspects that until it can heal itself, then there is every chance it will remain what one American called many years ago a 'crippled giant' with more power at its disposal than any other nation in the world, but so polarized at home that it will be unable to use it wisely or well.

11

After the Deluge or Whither the Empire?

As we argued at the beginning of this volume, 30 years before Joe Biden became President of the United States, the international system stood on the cusp of something quite extraordinary and quite unexpected too: namely, a world in which America appeared to be facing neither serious opposition to its values nor to its power. As we indicated, there were several reasons why even the least sanguine American may have felt confident back then. The Soviet Union had just retreated from Eastern Europe. A year or two on, it collapsed. Then around the world, as socialism retreated in Europe, a number of leaders – even those who had once proclaimed the virtues of planning – began singing the praises of the market. Meantime, the term 'globalization', which was a concept that had hardly been used before 1990, began to gain traction among policy elites and would soon go on to define the new international economy of the post-Cold War era.[1] One American writer even coined a term to describe this transition from one age marked by division and war to another where the liberal sun would forever shine: the 'end of history'. We were not just witnessing the end of one bloody century, according to Fukuyama: a new door was opening through which we could glimpse a bright future in which liberal democracy would become the ideal to which every country would aspire. Even that least visionary of US presidents, George Bush Snr, sensed that something was in the air, and indeed was moved to announce in early 1991 the possibility of building a 'new world order' in which all the 'nations of the world, East and West, North and South' could 'prosper and live in harmony'. The fact that Bush proclaimed his new order on the eve of a devastatingly successful military operation against Iraq led by Washington only confirmed what many now thought was self-evident: that there had never been anything quite so impressive as the United States in international affairs.[2]

It is worth recalling all this if only to get some sense of how far the world has changed since those heady days when anything and everything seemed possible for the United States. Indeed, so heady were they that a number of writers – as we saw earlier – even started talking of America as being the new Rome on the Potomac. In fact, so assured did the United States seem, in 2001 it supported China's membership of the World Trade Organization – a self-confident move if ever there was one; then in early 2003 it mobilized a vast 'coalition of the willing' whose ambitious goal was nothing less than the defeat of the most powerful army in the Middle East and the overthrow of the Ba'athist regime in Iraq. As we know, both moves would come back to haunt America. At the time, however, they were viewed as yet more evidence that the world would now be organized around American principles and power, and that others, including those 'old laggards' in Europe, had better wake up to the fact.[3]

It is often said that the most dangerous moment in the history of all great powers is either when they take their position in the world for granted or assume their position is invulnerable. So it has been in the past, and so it was with the United States as ten very good years gave way to a long 20 years' crisis, during which the debate shifted dramatically from one of talk about another American century to an acceptance (at least among some writers) that the world order it had built was fast coming to an end.[4] There had of course been many debates before about whether or not the United States would remain dominant forever. But now the discussion began to move outside the corridors of academe to reach a much wider reading public with one popular book after another appearing with some wonderfully lurid titles such as *After America: Get Ready for Armageddon*,[5] *America: The Farewell Tour*,[6] and even *Disintegration: Indicators of the Coming American Collapse*.[7] Naturally enough, different writers focused on different issues, with as many seeking the cause of the malaise at home – growing inequality, the decline of the middle class and stagnant living standards – as its declining position in the world.[8] Nor did all writers agree that the US was in terminal decline.[9] Nevertheless, the once influential idea – that the American empire was unassailable and the liberal order it had created secure – started to look decidedly unconvincing to students of the US scene. As yet another volume on the decline of the US suggested, the issue was not whether or why America had stopped being 'great', but 'when'.[10]

Which leads logically enough to Trump who was swept into office vowing to make America 'great again' after years in which America in his view had been on the slide. As we argued in Chapter 10, Trump may have been the great disrupter who did as much harm to the idea of America as he did to America's real standing in the world. That said, we still need to remind ourselves that there were deep-seated reasons why he got elected in the first place, why he then amassed nearly 75 million votes in 2020, and even after the assault on Congress in January 2021 still remained the most important player in the Republican Party. On the other hand, there is little doubt the relief that was felt around the world (except perhaps in Putin's Russia) when he lost the election to Biden. Nor was there much doubting the tasks facing Biden as he looked to deal with an ongoing pandemic at home while also trying to build bridges across the ideological divide within the US itself. Much was made of Biden's age and the fact that he was the oldest person ever to have become president. But even some sceptics conceded that during his first few months in office he displayed almost boundless energy passing one measure after another including a COVID-19 package in March amounting to nearly $2 trillion followed in July 2021 by a $3 trillion 'recovery plan'. He was equally active abroad, reassuring old allies that the US still valued them, that America remained committed to the liberal international order, and that on such key questions such as climate change it would no longer be sitting at the back of the class denouncing the idea but would now be leading from the front. With an experienced team now directing US foreign policy it really did seem that America had after a four-year detour returned to the mainstream.

Nothing, however, prepared either his team, the United States or the world at large for the fallout which followed Biden's announcement in April 2021 to pull out all US forces from Afghanistan by the end of August. Though Trump had prepared the way by negotiating a deal with the Taliban in Doha the previous year, few expected Afghanistan to fall to the militants in just under two weeks when all the intelligence suggested that the Taliban either could not win militarily, or that it would take months of heavy fighting before they would be able to do so. Nor did what followed bring much, if any comfort, to the Biden team. Images of helicopters taking off from the roof of the American Embassy in Kabul brought back painful memories of what had happened in Vietnam in 1975 when the United States was forced to withdraw in a state of near panic. Nor were critics slow in drawing out what they saw as the implications of the Taliban victory. As one observer among many others put it, not only was what happened a massive setback militarily that would embolden Islamist militants in other parts of the world, it was yet another indication in his view that the 'American era' was over. Obama may have taken it as read that the world was becoming 'post-American'. Biden only seemed to confirm it.[11]

But where did all this leave the United States more generally, and where did analysts think it was heading? There were at least two very distinct views about this – by far and away the most influential being that however hard Biden had worked during his first year in office at uniting Americans and restoring America's credibility abroad, its future looked to be anything but bright. Following as it did a less than brilliant record when it came to dealing the COVID-19 crisis, and faced with an American electorate less and less inclined to support an activist foreign policy abroad – over 70 per cent of Americans initially claimed they supported a withdrawal from Afghanistan[12] – it was little wonder that so many pundits believed that the empire was at last coming to an ignominious end.[13] Nor, it seemed, did ordinary Americans appear to care that much. Faced by a host of problems at home and the need to rebuild America from the bottom up, why, they asked, should America pay other nations' bills when there was a crying need to sort out its own problems at home?[14] Furthermore, the very idea that any one power could take on the responsibility and cost of running the world was always a nonsense. If anything, what we were now witnessing, at least according to some writers, was less American decline and more a rebalancing within the international system, from a period when the US was the only serious player to one where there were now several.[15] Moreover, according to a number of leading realist writers, the crisis facing the US was not so much the result of having a deficit of power, but of foolishly deploying that power after the Cold War in the pursuit of impossible-to-achieve liberal objectives, as in fact happened in Afghanistan. As John Mearsheimer among others argued, the coming of the unipolar order led to a 'moment' of liberal hubris that not only poisoned US relations with countries which were clearly not liberal (and never likely to become so), but also encouraged foolish interventions abroad and the pursuit of hyper-globalizing free trade economic policies, which in the end resulted 'in lost jobs, declining wages, and rising income inequality throughout the liberal world' itself. Little wonder the United States now found itself in a cul-de-sac.[16]

Others of a perhaps less pessimistic frame of mind might concede that the US was facing some really big challenges, and that the US had a great deal of patching up to do following the dark days of Trump and the unilateral decision taken by Biden to get out of Afghanistan. However, with Trump now gone and the 'adults' back in charge of the ship of state, there was no reason, they insisted, why America could not continue to head up a group of powerful liberal democracies institutionally represented by the G7 and militarily united within NATO. As Robin Niblett of Chatham House reminded us, though much damage had been done to US credibility by what had happened both under Trump and Biden, this did not necessarily weaken America's 'key alliances' or the transatlantic relationship.[17] Moreover, in spite of these setbacks, the wider Western order which many now regarded as being in steep decline still possessed some formidable assets. In fact, taken together, the Europeans and the Americans not only continued to dominate the International Monetary Fund and the World Bank,[18] they also remained the largest source of foreign direct investment in the world, and between them accounted for about a third of global GDP, a third of world trade and 42 per cent of trade in services. There was, of course, the very real issue of China. However, its global economic reach was not quite as great as some seemed to believe.[19] Meanwhile, most of its neighbours did not trust it.

It also had few serious 'allies', except Russia. Nor was its future as secure as China itself seemed to believe. Indeed, it ran the very real danger of underestimating the power of the one country whose power it should have been taking much more seriously: the US. The noted China analyst Wang Jisi was no doubt correct when he argued that the US had been driven over many years by a fear of a 'rising' China. But one could equally well argue that in spite of its oft-repeated assertion that the US was on the way down, China still faced a very formidable rival in the shape of the United States.[20]

The future, therefore, was perhaps a little less dire than some appeared to think.[21] Trump in his way, and Biden in his, may have damaged America's image. But none of this really changed the basic facts on the ground, and what these facts told us was that in 2021 the US still accounted for: '24% of global GDP and 48% of business activity'; nearly half of the companies created over the last 25 years (since 1995), worth $100 billion; and 27 of the 43 companies set up over the past 50 years (since 1971), worth over $100 billion.[22] The US could also lay claim to seven out of the top ten corporations, eight of the top ten universities, more Nobel prizes than any other nation (over 130 since 2000), not to mention the almighty dollar. Even some of its individual states were economically bigger than most countries: California, for example, had a GDP larger than that of the UK; in economic terms Texas was bigger than Canada; the Netherlands was smaller than Florida; and Pennsylvania 'outgunned' Turkey. Geography and demography also favoured the United States. In fact, not only was the US 'big, young, and highly educated',[23] it was almost oversupplied with critical raw materials, quite unlike China whose dependency on others for oil and food, for example, made it potentially vulnerable to external shocks.[24] To add military might to these economic assets, the US also spent more on national security than the next ten countries put together (over $700 billion in 2021) while sitting at the centre of a system of alliances which spanned the great globe itself. Much, of course, has been made of the US getting out of Iraq and Afghanistan. However, it is worth reminding ourselves that even in spite of these setbacks, it still had 800 military bases around the world located in just under 70 countries.[25] The proverbial American titan may have become weary with its reputation damaged and its soft power tarnished. However, for all that, it still remained the only titan in town.[26]

Naturally, none of this is meant to imply that the US was likely to do a very good job at playing titan. Indeed, if the past 20 years was anything to go by, there was a very good chance that it would not. Nor was this just because the world had become more complex or its rivals more dangerous. It also had a great deal to do with what was happening inside the United States itself. Two costly wars in the Middle East certainly did not help; but as writers have been pointing out for many years, with or without Iraq and Afghanistan, a number of other factors including 'the absence of a compelling foreign policy narrative' and 'the rise of hyper-partisanship in Washington' have split the country right down the middle, thus making foreign policy that more difficult.[27] A powerful nation may not become any the less powerful by virtue of being divided. On the other hand, without some degree of consensus at home it is difficult to imagine the US forging anything like a coherent grand strategy which Americans might be willing to support. Viewed from this perspective, the US's biggest foreign policy problem in the 21st century will not be caused by a lack of power, or even a bungled withdrawal from Afghanistan – though that will no doubt prove to be damaging enough – but by what has been going on in America itself. As one of the gurus of the liberal post-Cold War order, Francis Fukuyama, has observed, the challenges facing the US today are likely to derive less from a changing international order (though this should not be underestimated) and more from political polarization at home.[28] Many years ago, Tip O'Neill, the then-Speaker of the House of Representatives, once quipped that 'all politics' – including presumably foreign policy – was 'local' and would be shaped by domestic factors as much as external ones. What was true back then when O'Neill uttered his wise warning to Americans, remains equally true today.

Notes and References

Introduction

1. 'Thomas Jefferson to James Madison, 27 April 1809', Founders Online, National Archives, https://founders.archives.gov/documents/Jefferson/03-01-02-0140.
2. Robert Kagan, *Dangerous Nation: America's Foreign Policy from Its Earliest Days to the Dawn of the Twentieth Century*, New York: Knopf, 2006.
3. Morgenthau's reflections on the land of his adoption are to be found in his *The Purpose of American Politics*, New York: Alfred A. Knopf, 1960.
4. Quote from Gerald Friedman, 'The sanctity of property in American economic history', Working Paper Series no. 14, Political Economy Research Institute, University of Massachusetts Amherst, 2001, https://scholarworks.umass.edu/cgi/viewcontent.cgi?article=1008&context=peri_workingpapers.
5. Fareed Zakaria, *From Wealth to Power: The Unusual Origins of America's World Role*, Princeton, NJ: Princeton University Press, 1998.
6. Alan Greenspan and Adrian Wooldridge, *Capitalism in America: A History*, New York: Penguin Random House, 2018, p. 89.
7. Still one of the best general (and most popular) works on the period remains Walter LaFeber, *The New Empire: An Interpretation of American Expansion 1860–1898*, Ithaca, NY: Cornell University Press, 1963.
8. Michael H. Hunt, *The American Ascendancy: How the United States Gained & Wielded Global Dominance*, Chapel Hill, NC: University of North Carolina Press, 2007, p. 87.
9. Kathleen Burk, *Old World: New World: The Story of Britain and America*, London: Little Brown, 2009, p. 362.
10. W.T. Stead, *The Americanization of the World, or, the Trend of the Twentieth Century*, London/New York: H. Markley, 1901.
11. The Princeton University historian Paul Frymer has argued: 'Race and racism drove American expansion, both as a conquering imperialism for white Europeans and a willingness to ignore the indigenous populations that lived on the land as having equal rights and human value.' www.princeton.edu/news/2017/11/29/frymer-discusses-building-American-empire.
12. Paul Frymer, 'Race, class and the building of an American empire, 1789–1860', unpublished paper, www.asanet.org/sites/default/files/savvy/sectionchs/documents/frymer.pdf.
13. www.thebritishacademy.ac.uk/publishing/review/33/Americas-forgotten-empire.
14. Daniel Immerwahr, *How to Hide an Empire: A History of the Greater United States*, New York: Farrar, Straus and Giroux, 2019.
15. For a critique of the idea of America as a 'reluctant empire' see Andrew J. Bacevich, *American Empire: The Realities and Consequences of US Diplomacy*, Cambridge, MA: Harvard University Press, 2002.

16. For an elaboration of this point see G. John Ikenberry's now classic *After Victory: Institutions, Strategic Restraint, and the Rebuilding of Order after Major Wars*, Princeton, NJ: Princeton University Press, 2001.
17. Walter B. Slocombe, 'A crisis of opportunity: the Clinton administration and Russia', in Melvyn Leffler and Jeffrey W. Legro (eds), *In Uncertain Times: American Foreign Policy after the Berlin Wall and 9/11*, Chapel Hill, NC: Cornell University Press, 2011, pp. 78–9.

Chapter 1

1. An earlier version of this chapter was published in Michael Cox, *US Foreign Policy After the Cold War: Superpower without a Mission? (Chatham House Papers)*, Pinter Publishers/Royal Institute of International Affairs, 1995, pp. 21–37, 130–2, and is published with permission.
2. 'Unveiling the National Export Strategy', *Business America: The Magazine of International Trade*, 4 October 1993.
3. Mickey Kantor, 'US trade policy and the post-cold war world', statement before the Senate Finance Committee, Washington DC, 9 March 1993 (*US Department of State Dispatch*, 4:11, 15 March 1993, p. 144).
4. Lester Thurow, *Head to Head: The Coming Economic Battle among Japan, Europe, and America*, New York: William Morrow and Company, 1992, pp. 14–17.
5. Michael Borrus, Steve Weber and John Zysman with Joseph Willihnganz, 'Mercantilism and global security', *The National Interest*, Fall 1992, pp. 21–9.
6. The phrase can be traced back to James Carville, who was a strategist for Bill Clinton's successful 1992 presidential bid, https://politicaldictionary.com/words/its-the-economy-stupid.
7. Jeffrey E. Garten, 'Challenges of the global marketplace: if you don't win, you lose', presentation to the Royal Institute of International Affairs, London, 11 July 1995.
8. Martin Fletcher, 'Rough diamond Clinton cuts tough deals on trade', *The Times*, 15 February 1994.
9. Quote from Jeffrey E. Garten speech, 'The Clinton administration's trade priorities for 1994 and reflections on Europe', *Atlantic Outlook*, 28 January 1994, pp. 1–2.
10. 'Clinton on foreign policy issues', The Reference Center, United States Information Service, Embassy of the United States of America, London, 1992.
11. For Jeffrey Garten's views see his article 'Clinton's emerging trade policy: act one, scene one', *Foreign Affairs*, 72:3, 1993, pp. 182–9.
12. Peter F. Cowhey and Jonathan D. Aronson, 'A new trade order', *Foreign Affairs*, 72:1, 1993, pp. 183–95.
13. Martin Walker, 'The end of the imperial presidency', paper presented at 'Kennan, the Cold War, and the Future of American Foreign Policy' conference, School of International Relations, University of California, 27–29 January 1995.
14. Jean-Pierre Lehmann and Stephen Thomsen, 'Washington thinking on trade', *International Affairs*, 69:3, 1993, pp. 527–45.
15. For Tyson's views on trade see also Rudiger W. Dornbusch, Anne O. Krueger and Laura D'Andrea Tyson, *An American Trade Strategy: Options for the 1990s*, Washington, DC: The Brookings Institution, 1990.
16. Garten was Undersecretary of Commerce for International Trade, 1993 to 1995.
17. Jeffrey E. Garten, *A Cold Peace: America, Japan, Germany, and the Struggle for Supremacy*, New York: Times Books, 1993.
18. Garten, see note 9.

19. Theodore H. Moran, *American Economic Policy and National Security*, New York: Council on Foreign Relations Press, 1993.
20. For a brief guide to Theodore Moran's economic thinking see his article, 'An economics agenda for neorealists', *International Security*, 18:2, 1993, pp. 211–15.
21. Ira C. Magaziner and Robert B. Reich, *Minding America's Business: The Decline and Rise of the American Economy*, New York: Vintage Books, 1983; and Robert B. Reich, *The Next American Frontier: A Provocative Program for Economic Renewal*, New York: Penguin Books, 1984.
22. Robert B. Reich, *The Work of Nations*, New York: Vintage, 1992.
23. James Adams, 'Business swings behind Clinton', *The Sunday Times*, 25 October 1992.
24. Leonard Silk, 'Head off a trade war', *The New York Times*, 4 February 1993.
25. Michael Prowse, 'A Prussian in the White House', *Financial Times*, 21 February 1994.
26. Adrian Hamilton, 'A whiff of US imperialism', *The Observer*, 12 December 1993.
27. Paul Krugman, 'Competitiveness: a dangerous obsession', *Foreign Affairs*, 73:2, 1994, pp. 28–44.
28. Nora Lustig, Barry P. Bosworth and Robert Z. Lawrence (eds), *North American Free Trade: Assessing the Impact*, Washington, DC: The Brookings Institution, 1992.
29. Mickey Kantor, 'Regional arrangements facilitate global trade', *Atlantic Outlook*, 22 October 1993, pp. 1–2.
30. David E. Sanger, 'Clinton in Seattle for Pacific talks to seek markets', *The New York Times*, 19 November 1994; Roger Cohen, 'Like the US, Western Europe steps up its trade with Asia', *The New York Times*, 24 November 1993.
31. 'GATT deal', *Daily Telegraph*, 15 December 1993.
32. Figures about world trade after GATT from Martin Wolf, 'Doing good, despite themselves', *Financial Times*, 16 December 1993.
33. Nancy Dunne, 'A round sceptic seeking a square deal', *Financial Times*, 2 December 1993.
34. *Towards a National Export Strategy*, Report to the United States Congress, Washington DC, 30 September 1993. The importance of the report in creating America's first national export strategy was emphasized in Clinton's national security reviews. See, for example, 'A national security strategy of engagement and enlargement', The White House, February 1996, p. 19.
35. Jurek Martin and Nancy Dunne, 'Turning the moribund into mainstream', *Financial Times*, 21 February 1994.
36. Don E. Kash and Robert W. Rycroft, 'Nurturing winners with federal R&D', *Technology Review*, November–December 1993, pp. 58–64.
37. Deborah Shapley, 'Clintonizing science policy', *The Bulletin of the Atomic Scientists*, December 1993, pp. 39–43.
38. On the Saudi deal see Thomas L. Friedman, 'Saudi Air to buy $6 billion in jets built in the US', *The New York Times*, 17 February 1994.
39. Garten, see note 7.
40. Manuel Saragosa, 'US pressure on trade deals in Asia pays off', *Financial Times*, 17 November 1994.
41. Nancy Dunne and Michael Cassell, 'Big Brother lends a hand', *Financial Times*, 15 February 1995.
42. David M. Lampton, 'America's China policy in the age of the finance minister: Clinton ends linkage', *China Quarterly*, 139, 1994, pp. 597–621.

Chapter 2

1. An earlier version of this chapter was published in Michael Cox. G John Ikenberry and Takashi Inoguchi (eds), *American Democracy Promotion: Impulses, Strategies, and Impacts*, Oxford University Press, 2000, pp. 218–39, and is published with permission.
2. Torbjørn L. Knutsen, *The Rise and Fall of World Orders*, Manchester: Manchester University Press, 1999. The issue is explored for the post-Cold War era in John C. Hulsman, *A Paradigm for a New World Order*, Basingstoke: Macmillan Press, 1997.
3. George F. Kennan, *American Diplomacy: 1900–1950*, London: Secker and Warburg, 1953.
4. John Mearsheimer, 'Introduction', George F. Kennan, *American Diplomacy: Sixtieth-Anniversary Expanded Edition*, Chicago, IL: University of Chicago Press, 2012, www.mearsheimer.com/wp-content/uploads/2019/06/Introduction.pdf.
5. The best discussion on the Bush foreign policy is by the British scholar, Steven Hurst. See his *The Foreign Policy of the Bush Administration: In Search of a New World Order*, London: Pinter Publishers, 1999.
6. Richard Haass, *The Reluctant Sheriff: The United States after the Cold War*, Washington, DC: The Brookings Institution, 1997, esp. pp. 60–3.
7. In his first major foreign policy speech at Georgetown on 12 December 1991, Clinton argued that Bush had not only 'coddled China' but more generally seemed to 'favor stability and his personal relations with foreign leaders over a coherent policy of promoting freedom and economic growth'. In his next address to the Foreign Policy Association on 1 April 1992 he continued his attack, adding that, aside from appeasing China, Bush had also 'poured cold water on Baltic and Ukrainian aspirations for independence' and had failed to recognize 'Croatia and Slovenia'. In the summer issue of the *Harvard International Review*, Clinton was in even more expansive form. 'President Bush', he opined, 'too often has hesitated when democratic forces needed our support in challenging the status quo. I believe that President Bush erred when he secretly rushed envoys to resume cordial relations with China barely a month after the massacre in Tiananmen Square; when he spurned Yeltsin before the Moscow coup; when he poured cold water on Baltic, Ukrainian, Croatian and Slovenian aspirations for independence; and when he initially refused to help the Kurds.' On 13 August in a speech given to the World Affairs Council in Los Angeles, he again assailed Bush, not just for being indifferent to democracy and the 'democratic revolution' but in daring to criticize Israel, 'America's only democratic ally in the Middle East'. Finally, in an address delivered at the University of Wisconsin in Milwaukee on 1 October 1992, Clinton more or less accused Bush of being 'un-American' and of not appearing to be 'at home in the mainstream pro-democracy tradition of American foreign policy'. Cited in 'Clinton on foreign policy issues', London: United States Information Service, n.d.
8. For a classic example of the way Wilson has been portrayed in the modern foreign policy debate, see Robert W. Tucker, 'The triumph of Wilsonianism', *World Policy Journal*, 10:4, 1993–94, pp. 83–99.
9. Michael Hunt, *Ideology and US Foreign Policy*, New Haven, CT: Yale University Press, 1987.
10. Bill Clinton, 'A national security strategy of engagement and enlargement', The White House, February 1996, pp. i, ii, 2, 32–3.
11. Bryan Jones (ed.), *The New American Politics: Reflections on Political Change and the Clinton Administration*, Boulder, CO: Westview Press, 1995.
12. I discuss this point at greater length in Michael Cox, *US Foreign Policy after the Cold War: Superpower without a Mission?*, London: The Royal Institute of International Affairs, 1995.
13. Douglas Brinkley, 'Democratic enlargement: the Clinton doctrine', *Foreign Policy*, 106, 1997, pp. 111–27.

14. For a critique of Clinton's fear of foreign policy engagement, see Jim Hoagland, 'Signs of global decline in America's ability to command respect', *The International Herald Tribune*, 21 April 1995.
15. Clinton's speech can be found in 'Clinton warns of perils ahead despite Cold War's end', London: United States Information Service, 28 September 1993.
16. Anthony Lake, 'Lake says US interests compel engagement abroad', London: United States Information Service, 22 September 1993.
17. Fareed Zakaria, 'Internationalism as a way of life', *World Policy Journal*, 12:2, 1995, pp. 59–61.
18. Jacob Heilbrunn, 'Lake Inferior', *The New Republic*, 20 and 27 September 1993, pp. 29–35.
19. For a very small sample of the attacks made on Clinton's Wilsonian or neo-Wilsonian views see, *inter alia*, Fareed Zakaria, 'Is realism finished?', *The National Interest*, 30, 1992–3, pp. 21–32; Robert W. Tucker, 'Realism and the new consensus', *The National Interest*, 30, 1992–93, pp. 33–6; Christopher Layne, 'Kant or cant: the myth of the democratic peace', *International Security*, 19:2, 1994, especially pp. 47–9; John Mearsheimer, 'The false promise of international institutions', *International Security*, 19:3, 1994–95, esp. p. 5; Godfrey Hodgson, 'American ideals, global realities', *World Policy Journal*, 10:4, 1993–94, p. 16; and Richard Haass, 'Paradigm lost', *Foreign Affairs*, 74:1, 1995, pp. 43–58.
20. For a useful summary of the arguments for and against democracy promotion, see Christopher Layne and Sean M. Lynn-Jones (eds), *Should America Promote Democracy?*, Boston, MA: MIT Press, 1998.
21. De Tocqueville, *Democracy in America* [1835], London: Oxford University Press, 1946, p. 370.
22. Daniel J. Boorstin, *The Genius of American Politics*, Chicago, IL: Chicago University Press, 1958.
23. Bill Clinton, 'A new covenant for American security', speech delivered at the Georgetown University School of Foreign Service, Washington, DC, 12 December 1991.
24. Strobe Talbott, 'The new geopolitics: defending democracy in the post-Cold War era', speech delivered at Oxford University, 20 October 1994.
25. Doh Chull Shin, 'On the third wave of democratization', *World Politics*, 47:1, 1994, pp. 135–70.
26. Doh Chull Shin, 'On the third wave of democratization', p. 136.
27. Samuel Huntington, *The Third Wave Democratization in the Late Twentieth Century*, Norman, OK: University of Oklahoma Press, 1992, p. 58.
28. Francis Fukuyama, *The End of History and the Last Man*, New York: The Free Press, 1992, pp. 39–51.
29. Michael Doyle, 'Liberalism and world politics', *American Political Science Review*, 80:4, 1986, pp. 1151–69; and Bruce Russett, *Grasping the Democratic Peace: Principles for a Post-Cold War World*, Princeton, NJ: Princeton University Press, 1993.
30. Warren Christopher, 'US strategy to defend human rights and democracy', *US Department of State Dispatch*, 6:15, 10 April 1995, p. 295.
31. Clinton, see note 23.
32. Talbott, see note 24.
33. For a more sceptical view of the relationship between academic theory and foreign policy practice, see Thomas Carothers, 'Think again: democracy', *Foreign Policy*, 107, 1997, pp. 11–18.
34. Michael Cox, 'The necessary partnership: the Clinton presidency and post-communist Russia', *International Affairs*, 70:4, 1994, pp. 635–58.
35. Strobe Talbott, 'Democracy and the national interest', *Foreign Affairs*, 75:6, November/December 1996.

36 Clinton, see note 23.
37 Clinton, see note 10, p. 32.
38 Governor Bill Clinton, 'Democracy in America', speech delivered at the University of Milwaukee, Wisconsin, 1 October 1992.
39 Lake, see note 16, p. 5.
40 Talbott, 'Democracy and the national interest', p. 52.
41 President Bill Clinton, 'American leadership and global change', *US Department of State Dispatch*, 4/9, 1 March 1993, pp. 113–18.
42 Anthony Lake, 'American power and American diplomacy', *US Department of State Dispatch*, 5/46, 14 November 1994, pp. 766–9.
43 Anthony Lake, 'The need for engagement', *US Department of State Dispatch*, 5/49, 5 December 1994, pp. 804–7.
44 Lake, 'The Need for Engagement', p. 805.
45 Talbott, 'Democracy and the national interest', pp. 48–9.
46 Jacques Attali, 'The crash of Western civilization: the limits of market and democracy', *Foreign Policy*, 107, 1997, p. 58.
47 Irwin Stelzer, 'A question of linkage: capitalism, prosperity, democracy', *The National Interest*, 35, 1994, pp. 29–35.
48 Fareed Zakaria, 'Democracy and tyranny', *Prospect*, December 1997, pp. 20–5.
49 Douglas Brinkley, 'Democratic enlargement: the Clinton doctrine', esp. pp. 117, 120–1.
50 Talbott, 'Democracy and the national interest', pp. 54–5.
51 Lake, see note 16, p. 3.
52 Warren Christopher, 'America's fundamental dedication to human rights', *US Department of State Dispatch*, 6:6, 6 February 1995, p. 76.
53 Talbott, 'Democracy and the national interest', p. 51.
54 Bill Clinton, speech to the Los Angeles World Affairs Council, 13 August 1992.
55 Warren Christopher, statement to the Senate Foreign Relations Committee, 14 February 1995 (USIS European Wireless File, 15 February 1995, p. 4).
56 Arthur S. Link, *The Higher Realism of Woodrow Wilson and Other Essays*, Nashville, TN: Vanderbilt University Press, 1971; David F. Trask, *The United States in the Supreme War Council: American War Aims and Inter-Allied Strategy, 1917–1978*, Middletown, CT: Wesleyan University Press, 1961; and David F. Trask, *The AEF and Coalition Warmaking, 1917–1918*, Lawrence, KS: University Press of Kansas, 1993.
57 N. Gordon Levin, *Woodrow Wilson and World Politics: America's Response to War and Revolution*, New York: Oxford University Press, 1980; and Lloyd Gardner, *Safe for Democracy: The Anglo-American Response to Revolution, 1913–1923*, New York: Oxford University Press, 1984.
58 Arthur S. Link, *Wilson*, vols 3, 4 and 5, Princeton, NJ: Princeton University Press, 1960–65.
59 Frederick Calhoun, *Power and Principle: Armed Intervention in Wilsonian Foreign Policy*, Kent, OH: Kent State University Press, 1986.
60 A question raised in the important intervention in the democratic peace debate by Ido Oren, 'The subjectivity of the "democratic peace": changing US perceptions of imperial Germany', *International Security*, 20:2, 1995, pp. 147–84.
61 Sidney Bell, *Righteous Conquest: Woodrow Wilson and the Evolution of the New Diplomacy*, Port Washington, NY: Kennikat Press, 1972, pp. 10–28.
62 Bell, see note 61, p. 17.
63 Lloyd Ambrosius, *Woodrow Wilson and the American Diplomatic Tradition*, New York: Cambridge University Press, 1987) esp. pp. 30, 77, 119–22.

64 Allen Lynch, 'Woodrow Wilson and the principle of "national self-determination": a reconsideration', unpublished manuscript, October 1999, p. 35.
65 David Fromkin, 'What is Wilsonianism?', *World Policy Journal*, 11/1, Spring, 1994, p. 108.
66 Oren, see note 60, p. 178.
67 Fromkin, see note 65, p. 107.
68 E.H. Carr, *The Twenty Years' Crisis, 1919–1939*, London: Macmillan, 1951.
69 Carr, see note 68, p. 14.
70 Thomas Carothers, *Aiding Democracy Abroad: The Learning Curve*, Washington, DC: The Carnegie Endowment, 1999.

Chapter 3

1 The chapter title is taken from Stephen Cohen, *Failed Crusade: America and the Tragedy of Post-Communist Russia*, New York: W.W. Norton & Company, 2000. A version of this chapter first appeared in David Lane (ed.), *The Legacy of State Socialism and the Future of Transformation*, Rowman & Littlefield Publishers, 2002, pp. 225–40 and appears here with permission.
2 Michael Cox, *US Foreign Policy after the Cold War: Superpower without a Mission?*, London: The Royal Institute of International Affairs, 1995.
3 'A strategic alliance with Russian reform', *US Department of State Dispatch*, 4:15, 12 April 1993.
4 'Securing US interests while supporting Russian reform', *US Department of State Dispatch*, 4:13, 29 March 1993.
5 Stephen White, 'Rethinking the transition: 1991 and beyond', in Michael Cox (ed.), *Rethinking the Soviet Collapse: Sovietology, the Death of Communism and the New Russia*, London: Pinter Publishers, 1998, pp. 135–49.
6 'Reforming Russia's economy', *The Economist*, 11 December 1993, pp. 27–9.
7 The term 'near abroad' is used by the Russian Federation to refer to the 14 Soviet successor states other than Russia.
8 Strobe Talbott, 'America must remain engaged with Russian reform', *US Department of State Dispatch*, 5:5, 31 January 1994.
9 Charles Krauthammer, 'Honeymoon over, the two powers must go their own way', *International Herald Tribune*, 26–27 February 1994.
10 Helen Dewar, 'Senate backs Talbott for State Department,' *The Washington Post*, 21 February 1994.
11 Zbigniew Brzezinski, 'The premature partnership,' *Foreign Affairs*, 73:2, 1994, pp. 67–82.
12 Michael R. Gordon, 'Perry says caution is vital to Russian partnership', *The New York Times*, 15 March 1994.
13 Anders Aslund, 'Russia's success story,' *Foreign Affairs*, 73:5, 1994, pp. 58–71.
14 'Russia's reforms in trouble', *The Economist*, 22 November 1997.
15 John Lloyd, 'Yeltsin leaps into the abyss', *The Times*, 24 March 1998.
16 James Meek, 'Russia stares into the abyss,' *The Guardian*, 2 April 1998.
17 'Domino effect: how a little market like Russia set off a global chain reaction,' *The Wall Street Journal Europe*, 22 September 1998.
18 Martin Mafia, 'In Russia, the liberal Western model has failed,' *International Herald Tribune*, 5–6 September 1998.
19 George Friedman, 'Russian economic failure invites a new Stalinism,' *International Herald Tribune*, 11 September 1998.
20 William Safire, 'Primakov is no short-termer,' *International Herald Tribune*, 18 September 1998.

21. Celestine Bohlen, 'Gorbachev's economists back at the helm,' *International Herald Tribune*, 16 September 1998.
22. Steven Erlanger, 'Economy shift in Russia worries US, Albright says,' *The New York Times*, 3 October 1998.
23. Strobe Talbott, 'Dealing with Russia in a time of troubles', *The Economist*, 21 November 1998.
24. The previous section draws on published statements released on the US Embassy website, London.
25. Alexei Arbatov, 'Russian national interest', in Robert D. Blackwill and Sergei Karaganov (eds), *Damage Limitation or Crisis?*, London: Brassey's, 1998, pp. 55–76.

Chapter 4

1. An earlier version of this chapter was published in Ken Booth and Tim Dunne (eds), *Worlds in Collision: Terror and the Future of Global Order*, Basingstoke/New York: Palgrave Macmillan, 2002, pp. 152–61, and appears with permission.
2. The quickest book off the publisher's block dealing with 9/11 must have been Fred Halliday's thoughtful *Two Hours that Shook the World*, London: Saqi Books, 2001.
3. Adam Garfinkle, 'September 11: before and after', *Foreign Policy Research Institute*, 9:8, 2001.
4. Peter Beaumont and Ed Vulliamy, 'Focus – American power: armed to the teeth', *The Observer*, 10 February 2002.
5. Paul Kennedy, 'The eagle has landed', *Financial Times*, 2–3 February, 2002.
6. Margaret Thatcher, 'Go ahead and make the world a safer place', *International Herald Tribune*, 12 February 2002.
7. 'Muslims are strongly at odds with the US, survey shows', *Financial Times*, 27 February 2002.
8. *Financial Times*, 12 September 2001.
9. 'Three central Asian nations seem open to US military', *Wall Street Journal Europe*, 21–22 September 2001.
10. Anatol Lieven, 'Fighting terrorism: lessons from the Cold War', Policy Brief no. 7, October 2001, Carnegie Endowment for International Peace; and Walter A. McDougall, 'Cold War II', *Orbis*, December 2001.
11. Fred Iklé, *Every War Must End*, New York: Columbia University Press, 1971.
12. As Dan Plesch of the Royal United Services Institute put it: 'The current rise in US military spending ought to be compared to the decision in the First World War to order up more cavalry when the first wave had been mown down by machine-guns', quoted in *Observer*, 10 February 2002.
13. Barney Frank, 'Why Obama can – and must – cut defense spending', *The Atlantic*, 12 December 2002.
14. Ashton B. Carter, 'The architecture of government in the face of terrorism', in *International Security*, 26:3, 2001/02, p. 5.
15. Irene Khan, 'Curtailing freedom', *The World Today*, 58:2, 2002, pp. 7–8.
16. Brian Knowlton, 'On US campuses, intolerance grows', *International Herald Tribune*, 12 February 2002.
17. Hans von Sponeck and Denis Halliday, 'The hostage nation', *The Guardian*, 29 November 2001; Evan Thomas, 'Chemistry in the war cabinet', *Newsweek*, 28 January 2002.
18. Julian Borger and Ewen MacAskill, 'US targets Saddam', *The Guardian*, 14 February 2002.
19. Paul Rogers, 'Right for America, right for the world', *The World Today*, 58:2, 2002, pp. 13–15.

20. Charles William Maynes, 'US unilateralism and its dangers', *Review of International Studies*, 25:3, 1999, p. 516.
21. As Paul Kennedy (see note 5) observed rather cryptically at the time of the initial intervention into Afghanistan, the US did 98 per cent of the fighting, the British, 2 per cent, while the Japanese 'steamed around Mauritius'.
22. Peter Beaumont and Ed Vulliamy, 'Armed to the teeth', *The Observer*, 10 February 2002.
23. See in particular Chris Patten's attacks on what he called the US 'instinct' to go it alone, in the *Financial Times*, 15 February 2002.

Chapter 5

1. An earlier version of this chapter was published in *Review of International Studies*, 30:4, 2004, pp. 585–608, and appears with permission.
2. Michael Ignatieff, 'Empire lite', *Prospect*, 20 February 2003, p. 36.
3. On the role played by war in the formation of great states, see Philip Bobbitt, *The Shield of Achilles: War, Peace and the Course of History*, London: Penguin Books, 2002.
4. John T. McNay, *Acheson and the Empire: The British Accent in American Foreign Policy*, London/Columbia, MO: University of Missouri Press, 2001.
5. On the scale of American preponderance in 1945, see Donald White, 'The nature of world power in American history: an evaluation at the end of World War II', *Diplomatic History*, 11:3, 1987, pp. 181–202.
6. For one of the better studies of the American empire, see Ronald Steel, *Pax Americana*, London: Hamish Hamilton, 1967.
7. Niall Ferguson, *Colossus: The Rise and Fall of the American Empire*, London: Allen Lane, 2004, p. 68.
8. Toynbee, it has been observed, 'attended Winchester and studied classics at Oxford, both of which were intended to prepare young men for service in an enlightened Empire'. Quoted from Cornelia Navari, 'Arnold Toynbee (1889–1975): prophecy and civilization', *Review of International Studies*, 26:2, 2000, p. 289.
9. G. John Ikenberry, 'Rethinking the origins of American hegemony', *Political Science Quarterly*, 104:3, 1989, p. 377.
10. According to one of the principle American theorists of hegemonic stability, it was E.H. Carr in *The Twenty Years' Crisis* who first 'demonstrated that a liberal world economy world must rest on a dominant liberal power'. See Robert Gilpin, *Global Political Economy: Understanding the International Economic Order*, Princeton, NJ: Princeton University Press, 2001, fn. 52, pp. 100–1.
11. Even the best American study on the subject uses the term 'empire' to apply to every other power other than the United States. See Michael W. Doyle, *Empires*, London/Ithaca, NY: Cornell University Press, 1986.
12. A point made by Dimitri K. Simes in his useful 'America's imperial dilemma', *Foreign Affairs*, 82:6, 2003, p. 93. On foreign reflections on the American empire, see, for instance, Raymond Aron, *The Imperial Republic: The United States and the World, 1945–1973*, London: Weidenfeld & Nicolson, 1975; Geir Lundestad, 'Empire by invitation? The United States and Western Europe, 1945–1952', *Journal of Peace Research*, 23:3, 1986, pp. 263–77; and Susan Strange, 'The future of the American empire', *Journal of International Affairs*, 42:1, 1988, pp. 1–18.
13. William Appleman Williams, *Empire as a Way of Life*, New York: Oxford University Press, 1980.
14. William Appleman Williams, 'The frontier thesis and American foreign policy', *Pacific Historic Review*, 24, 1955, p. 379.
15. Charles S. Maier, 'An American empire', *Harvard Magazine*, 105:2, 2002, pp. 28–31.

16. Ronald Wright, 'For a wild surmise', *Times Literary Supplement*, 20 December 2002, p. 3.
17. George Bush speeches to cadets at West Point, June 2002, and to veterans at the White House, November 2002.
18. Michael Mann, *Incoherent Empire*, London: Verso Press, 2003.
19. Alfredo Valladao, *The Twenty-First Century Will Be American*, London: Verso, 1996.
20. David Campbell, 'Contradictions of lonely superpower', in David Slater and Peter J. Taylor (eds), *The American Century: Consensus and Coercion in the Projection of American Power*, Oxford: Blackwell, 1999, pp. 222–42.
21. Quote from Dimitri K. Simes, 'America's Imperial Dilemma', *Foreign Affairs*, p. 93.
22. I discuss this in my *US Foreign Policy After the Cold War: Superpower Without a Mission? (Chatham House Papers)*, London: Pinter Publishers/Royal Institute of International Affairs, 1995.
23. For a critique of Clinton's lack of military purpose see the detailed David Halberstam, *War in a Time of Peace: Bush, Clinton and the Generals*, New York: Simon & Schuster, 2001.
24. On the American renaissance in the 1990s, see Bruce Cumings, 'Still the American century', in Michael Cox, Ken Booth and Tim Dunne (eds), *The Interregnum: Controversies in World Politics, 1989–1999*, Cambridge: Cambridge University Press, 1999, pp. 271–99.
25. This section draws heavily from the excellent first-hand description provided by Nicholas Lemann, 'The next world order: the Bush administration may have a brand-new doctrine of power', *The New Yorker*, 24 March 2002, www.newyorker.com/magazine/2002/04/01/the-next-world-order.
26. The document which summed up these hegemonic thoughts was put together by a group of defence intellectuals in 1992 led by Paul Wolfowitz, Richard Perle, Albert Wohlstetter, I. Lewis Libby and Zalmay Khalilzad.
27. Charles Krauthammer, 'The new unilateralism', *The Washington Post*, 8 June 2001, p. 29.
28. James Woolsey, Interview by Galina J. Michkovitch, *Prospect*, 20 September, 2003, pp. 20–3.
29. For a sample of this kind of thinking, see the neoconservative magazine *The Weekly Standard*.
30. To see how European allies responded to the Bush doctrine, see Philip H. Gordon and Jeremy Shapiro, *Allies at War: America, Europe and the Crisis Over Iraq*, Washington, DC: The Brookings Institution, 2004.
31. William Kristol and Robert Kagan, 'Towards a neo-Reaganite foreign policy', *Foreign Affairs*, July–August, 1996, pp. 23–35.
32. I discuss European criticism of the early Bush policies in my 'Europe and the new American challenge after September 11: crisis – what crisis?', *Journal of Transatlantic Studies*, 1:1, 2003, pp. 37–55.
33. In one of the more significant studies edited and authored by key figures on the new right, nearly every other threat was mentioned from China to Iraq, but little was said about the Sunni-inspired terrorism articulated and practised by Bin Laden. See Robert Kagan and William Kristol (eds), *Present Dangers: Crisis and Opportunity in American Foreign and Defense Policy*, New York: Encounter Books, 2000.
34. For the best analysis of the ideological roots of the Bush foreign policy see Brian C. Schmidt and Michael C. Williams, 'The Bush doctrine and the Iraq War: neoconservatives versus realists', *Security Studies*, 17:2, 2008, pp. 191–220.
35. Niall Ferguson, 'We're an empire now': the United States between imperial denial and premature decolonization', *Macalester International*, 16:8, 2005, https://digitalcommons.macalester.edu/macintl/vol16/iss1/8.

NOTES AND REFERENCES

36. Quoted in Christopher Hitchens, 'Imperialism, superpower dominance, malignant and benign', *Slate*, 10 December 2002, https://slate.com/news-and-politics/2002/12/american-imperialism-then-and-now.html.
37. Quote from Andrew Bacevich, cited in Niall Ferguson, 'The empire that dares not speak its name', *The Sunday Times*, 13 April 2003.
38. G. John Ikenberry, 'The illusions of empire', *Foreign Affairs*, 83:2, 2004, pp. 154–62.
39. Dominic Lieven, 'Empire, history and the contemporary global order', 2005 Elie Kedourie Memorial Lecture, The British Academy, 24 February, www.thebritishacademy.ac.uk/documents/2012/pba131p127.pdf.
40. It remains a moot point as to whether or not territorial expansion was even constitutional. Gary Lawson and Guy Seidman, *The Constitution of Liberty: Territorial Expansion and American Legal History*, New Haven, CT: Yale University Press, 2004.
41. In a letter to James Madison in 1809, Thomas Jefferson wrote that 'no constitution was ever so well calculated as ours for extensive empire'. Quoted in Lawson and Seidman, see note 40.
42. I discuss this in my 'America and the world', in Robert Singh (ed.), *Governing America: The Politics of a Divided Democracy*, Oxford: Oxford University Press, 2003, pp. 13–31.
43. Doyle, see note 11.
44. John Gallagher and Ronald Robinson, 'The imperialism of free trade', *Economic History Review*, 2nd series, 6:1, 1953, pp. 1–25.
45. This point is outlined in terms of IR theory by Robert Gilpin, *Global Political Economy: Understanding the International Economic Order*, Princeton, NJ: Princeton University Press, 2001, pp. 97–102.
46. A point made by G. John Ikenberry in his 'Rethinking the origins of American hegemony', *Political Science Quarterly*, 104:3, 1989, pp. 375–400.
47. For a later discussion of the 'uneasy place' that self-determination 'occupies' in the history of US foreign relations, see Brad Simpson, 'The United States and the curious history of self-determination', *Diplomatic History*, 36:4, September 2012, pp. 675–94.
48. See the chapter on 'Imperial anticolonialism', in William Appleman Williams, *The Tragedy of American Diplomacy*, Cleveland, OH: World Publishing, 1959.
49. On British suspicion of American moral rhetoric, see Niall Ferguson, *Empire: How Britain Made the World*, pp. 348–52.
50. On the more general uses of self-determination as a means of advancing US influence, see Michael Cox, G. John Ikenberry and Takashi Inoguchi (eds), *American Democracy Promotion: Impulses, Strategies, Impacts*, Oxford: Oxford University Press, 2000.
51. John Wacher (ed.), *The Roman World*, 2 vols, London: Routledge, 1990, p. 139.
52. 'Empire is the rule exercised by one nation over others both to regulate their external behavior and to ensure minimally acceptable forms of internal behavior within the subordinate states.' Quoted in Stephen Peter Rosen, 'An empire, if you can keep it', *The National Interest*, 71, 2003, p. 51.
53. 'The US does not and indeed no nation-state can today form the centre of an imperialist project.' Cited in John Hardt and Antonio Negri, *Empire*, Cambridge, MA: Harvard University Press, 2000, pp. xiii–xiv.
54. Joseph Nye Jr, *The Paradox of American Power: Why the World's Only Superpower Can't Go It Alone*, New York: Oxford University Press, 2002.
55. Joseph Stiglitz, *Globalization and Its Discontents*, London: Penguin Books, 2002, p. 24.
56. Robert Hunter Wade, 'The invisible hand of the American empire', *Ethics & International Affairs*, 17:2, 2003, pp. 77–88.
57. The main reason cited by the United States for not joining the International Criminal Court. See Dominic McGoldrick, Peter Rowe and Eric Donnelly (eds), *The Permanent*

International Criminal Court: Legal and Policy Issues, Oxford/Portland, OR: Hart Publishing, 2004, pp. 400–52.

58 For a further elaboration of the issues raised in this section see my 'The empire's back in town: or America's imperial temptation – again', *Millennium*, 32:1, 2003, esp. pp. 14–22.

59 Michael Mann, 'The first failed empire of the 21st century', in David Held and Mathias Koenig-Archibugi (eds), *American Power in the 21st Century*, Cambridge: Polity, 2004.

60 'America's world', *The Economist*, 23 October 1999, p. 15; and John M. Owen, 'Why American hegemony is here to stay', Pax Americana or International Rule of Law, Symposium, 16 January 2003.

61 Dominic McGoldrick, *From '9–11' to the Iraq War 2003: International Law in an Age of Complexity*, Oxford/Portland, OR: Hart Publishing, 2004.

62 On Clinton as a more effective empire builder than George W. Bush, see Chalmers Johnson, *The Sorrows of Empire: Militarism, Secrecy and the End of the Republic*, pp. 255–6, London: Verso, 2004.

63 Fareed Zakaria, 'Arrogant empire', *Newsweek*, March 2003.

64 Robert Kagan, 'America's crisis of legitimacy', *Foreign Affairs*, 83:2, 2004, pp. 65–87.

65 Joseph S. Nye Jr, *The Paradox of American Power: Why the World's Only Superpower Can't Go It Alone*, New York/London: Oxford University Press, 2002.

66 See the critical comments by a former undersecretary of state to Clinton and a senior adviser to Senator Kerry on foreign policy. James E Rubin, 'Political dynamite', *Financial Times Magazine*, 3 April 2004.

67 Charles Grant, 'Comment', Centre for European Reform, May 2003.

68 Joseph M. Grieco, 'Let's get a second opinion: allies, the UN and US public support for war', unpublished manuscript, June 2002.

69 Niall Ferguson, see note 7, p. 293.

70 Wade, see note 56.

71 Robert Brenner, 'The crisis in the US economy', *London Review of Books*, 25:3, 2003, pp. 18–23.

72 Precisely the point made by Bush's first Secretary of the Treasury, Paul O'Neill, who was later sacked for pointing out that massive tax cuts for the rich combined with huge defence outlays was likely to lead to serious deficit problems. See Ron Suskind, *The Price of Loyalty: George W. Bush, The White House, and the Education of Paul O'Neill*, New York: Simon & Schuster, 2004.

73 George Soros, *The Bubble of American Supremacy: Correcting the Misuse of American Power*, Australia: Allen & Unwin, 2004.

74 After having concluded that the situation in Iraq by May 2004 was as difficult as the one that had driven the United States out of Vietnam, one former Clinton official argued: 'We now have to admit that the American position is untenable.' Richard Holbrooke, quoted in *International Herald Tribune*, 11 May 2004.

75 The title on the cover of one well-known US magazine said all that most Americans wanted or needed to know about Iraq: 'State of siege' (*Time*, 163:16, 19 April 2004). In the same issue one poll showed that, whereas in April 2003 over 50 per cent of Americans felt safer because of having got rid of Saddam, a year later the figure had fallen to 40 per cent.

Chapter 6

1 Tim Worstall, 'Ben Bernanke: the 2008 financial crisis was worse than the Great Depression', *Forbes*, 27 August 2014.

NOTES AND REFERENCES

2 Roger Altman, 'The great crash, 2008: a geopolitical setback for the West', *Foreign Affairs*, 88:1, 2009.
3 'When our opponents say this nation is in decline, they are dead wrong. This is America. We still have the best workers in the world and the best entrepreneurs in the world. We've got the best scientists and the best researchers. We've got the best colleges and the best universities. [...] So, no matter what the naysayers may say for political reasons, no matter how dark they try to make everything look, there's not a country on Earth that wouldn't gladly trade places with the United States of America.' Barack Obama, speech, 8 September 2012, www.presidency.ucsb.edu/documents/remarks-campaign-rally-seminole-florida.
4 Two authors whom Obama read were both strong proponents of globalization. See Fareed Zakaria, *Post-American World*, New York: W.W. Norton & Company, 2008; and Thomas Friedman, *The World is Flat*, revised edn, New York: Farrar, Straus and Giroux, 2007.
5 James Mann, *The Obamians: The Struggle Inside the White House to Redefine American Power*, New York: Penguin Books, 2012, p. 179.
6 'Obama has placed the least emphasis on a "top dog" image of the United States. Instead, he has stressed the need for the United States to integrate itself into a changing world rather than stomp around arrogantly and blindly.' Cheng Li, 'Assessing US–China relations under the Obama administration', Washington, DC: The Brookings Institution, 30 August 2016.
7 Brent Budowsky, 'Obama's speech opposing the Iraq War' [October 2002], cited in *Huff Post*, 25 May 2011.
8 Timothy F. Geithner, *Stress Test: Reflections on Financial Crises*, New York: Random House Business Books, 2014, p. 1.
9 Jesse Holcomb, 'How the Lehman Bros crisis impacted the 2008 presidential race', Pew Research Center, 19 September 2013.
10 This paragraph draws heavily from Ben S. Bernanke, Timothy F. Geithner and Henry M. Paulson Jr, *Firefighting: The Financial Crisis and Its Lessons*, London: Profile Books, 2019, esp. pp. 4–5.
11 Gautam Mukunda, 'The social and political costs of the financial crisis, 10 years later', *Harvard Business Review*, 25 September 2018.
12 Elise Gould, 'Decades of rising inequality in the US', Economic Policy Institute, 27 March 2019.
13 Geithner, see note 8, p. 357.
14 Stephen S. Poloz, 'The legacy of the financial crisis: what we know and what we don't', BIS, 3 November 2014, www.bis.org/review/r141104b.pdf.
15 Martin Wolf, *The Shifts and Shocks: What We've Learned from The Financial Crisis*, London: Penguin Books, 2014.
16 The strong case for globalization is laid out in a number of books, the two most popular probably being Jagdish Bhagwati, *In Defence of Globalization*, New York: Oxford University Press, 2004; and Martin Wolf, *Why Globalization Works*, New Haven, CT: Yale University Press, 2004.
17 Gordon Brown, *Beyond the Crash: Overcoming the First Crisis of Globalisation*, London: Simon & Schuster, 2010.
18 Graeme Wheeler, 'Thoughts on globalization and the global financial crisis', *The World Bank*, 13 November 2008.
19 Zakaria, see note 4, p. xxiii.
20 This issue has been dealt with at length in G. J. Ikenberry, *Liberal Leviathan: The Origins, Crisis and Transformation of the American World Order*, Princeton, NJ: Princeton University Press, 2011.

21. James W. Fulbright, *Crippled Giant: American Foreign Policy and Its Domestic Consequences*, New York: Vintage Books, 1972.
22. Jeffrey A. Bader, *Obama and China's Rise: An Insider Account of America's Asia Strategy*, Washington, DC: The Brookings Institution, 2012.
23. John Mearsheimer, 'China's unpeaceful rise', *Current History*, 105:690, 2006, pp. 160–2.
24. Jin Canrong, 'How America's relationship with China changed under Obama', World Economic Forum, 14 December 2016.
25. 'US public, experts differ on China policies', Pew Research Center, 18 September 2012.
26. Danielle Kurtzleben, 'Report: America lost 2.7 million jobs to China in 10 years', US News, 24 August 2012.
27. Will Kimball and Robert E. Scott, 'China trade, outsourcing and jobs', Economic Policy Institute, 11 December 2014.
28. Daron Acemoglu, David Autor, David Dorn, Gordon H. Hanson and Brendan Price, 'Import competition and the great US employment sag of the 2000s', *Journal of Labor Economics*, 34:1, 2016, pp. 141–98.
29. Cory Bennett, 'GOP hopefuls blame Obama's China policy for data breach', The Hill, 6 June 2015.
30. Jeremy Diamond, 'Trump slams globalization, promises to upend economic status quo', CNN *Politics*, 28 June 2016.
31. One business magazine summed up the view of the majority of US corporations in the following way: 'Beat up on China all you want – the truth is that companies overwhelmingly want to be there.' Kenneth Rapoza, 'Why American companies choose China over everybody else', *Forbes*, 3 September 2019.
32. Salvatore Babones, 'Hillary Clinton, Donald Trump, and China', Aljazeera *Live*, 17 September 2016.
33. Stephanie Condon, 'Obama: "We welcome China's rise"', CBS News, 20 January 2011.
34. Mann, see note 5, p. 99.
35. Quote from https://fgerges.net/publications/books/obama-and-the-middle-east-the-end-of-Americas-moment.
36. Colin Dueck, *The Obama Doctrine: American Grand Strategy Today*, Oxford: Oxford University Press, 2015.
37. Mann, see note 5, p. 257.
38. Fawaz Gerges, *Obama and the Middle East: The End of America's Moment?*, New York: St Martin's Press, 2012.
39. Martyn Frampton and Ehud Rosen, 'Reading the runes? The United States and the Muslim Brotherhood as seen through the Wikileaks cables', *The Historical Journal*, 56:3, 2013, pp. 827–56.
40. James Reinl, 'Obama aide: how we got it wrong in Yemen', TRT World, 14 February 2019.
41. Fyodor Lukyanov, chair of the Russia Council on Foreign and Defence Policy, quoted in Courtney Weaver, 'Putin looks past Obama to Trump, *Financial Times*, 30 December 2016.
42. Angus Roxburgh, 'Putin began by embracing the West. Now, he wants revenge', *The Guardian*, 12 August 2019.
43. Steven Pifer, 'US–Russia relations in the Obama era: from reset to refreeze?', *OSCE Yearbook 2014*, IFSH, 2015, pp. 111–23.
44. Edward Lucas, *The New Cold War: How Russia Menaces both Russia and the West*, London: Bloomsbury Publishing, 2008.
45. Angela Stent, 'US–Russia relations in the second Obama administration', Washington, DC: The Brookings Institution, 31 December 2012.
46. 'Russia', Gallup historical trends, https://news.gallup.com/pol/1642.russia.aspx.

47 Ali Watkins, 'Obama team was warned in 2014 about Russian interference', *Politico*, 14 August 2017.
48 Maria Lipman, 'How Russia has come to loathe the West', European Council on Foreign Relations, 13 March 2015.
49 Charles Grant, 'Is the EU to blame for the crisis in Ukraine?', Centre for European Reform, 1 June 2016.
50 See, for example, John Mearsheimer, 'Why the Ukraine crisis is the West's fault: the liberal delusions that provoked Putin, *Foreign Affairs*, 93:5, 2014, pp. 77–89.
51 Kate Connolly, 'Obama lambasts Putin: you're wrecking Russia to recreate Russian empire', *The Guardian*, 8 June 2015.
52 Abigail Abrams, 'Here's what we know so far about Russia's 2016 meddling', *Time*, 18 April 2019.
53 'Obama leaves office on high note, but public has mixed views of his accomplishments', Pew Research Center, 14 December 2016.
54 There were four nuclear summits in all: in Washington (2010), Seoul (2012), the Hague (2014) and Washington (2016). See Amandeep S. Gill, *Nuclear Security Summits: A History*, Cham: Palgrave Macmillan, 2020.
55 'The Trans-Pacific Partnership', The White House Archives: President Barack Obama, https://obamawhitehouse.archives.gov.
56 Letter by J.L. Frydman, *Financial Times*, 27 October 2020.
57 Steve Walt, 'Barack Obama was a foreign policy failure', *Foreign Policy*, 18 January 2017.
58 Richard Wike and Jacob Poushter, 'Obama's international image remains strong in Europe and Asia', Pew Research Center, 29 June 2016.
59 Patricia Sabga, 'The economic insecurity behind Donald Trump's triumph', Aljazeera Live, 16 November 2016.

Chapter 7

1 A version of this chapter was first published as 'Too big to fail': the transatlantic relationship from Bush to Obama' in *Global Policy*, Volume 3, Supplement 1, December 2012, pp. 71–8, and appears here with permission. My earlier published contributions on this topic include 'Martians and Venutians in the new world order', *International Affairs*, 2003, 79(3), pp. 521–32, and 'Beyond the West: terrors in transatlantia', *European Journal of International Relations*, 11(2), 2005, pp. 203–33.
2 Leon Trotsky, *Europe and America: Two Speeches on Imperialism*, New York: Pathfinder Press, 1984.
3 John M. Roberts, *Penguin History of the World*, London: Allen Lane, 2002, pp. 789, 945.
4 Geir Lundestad, *The United States and Western Europe since 1945: From 'Empire by Invitation' to Transatlantic Drift*, Oxford: Oxford University Press, 2003.
5 See, for example, Irwin M. Wall, *The United States and the Making of Postwar France, 1945–1954*, New York: Cambridge University Press, 1991.
6 Michael Cox, 'Beyond the West: terrors in transatlantia', *European Journal of International Relations*, 2005, 11(2), pp. 203–33.
7 Freddy Gray, 'The Pacific president', *The Spectator*, 19 January 2013, www.spectator.co.uk/article/the-pacific-president.
8 See also Barry Buzan, 'Will the 'global war on terrorism' be the new Cold War?', *International Affairs*, 82(6), 2006, pp. 1101–18.
9 Dr Rice, 'Remarks by National Security Advisor Condoleezza Rice on terrorism and foreign policy', The White House Archives: President George W. Bush, 29 April 2002.

10. 'The Pearl Harbor of the 21st century took place today', Bush noted in his diary on the night of 11 September 2001. Cited in Bob Woodward, *Bush at War: Inside the Bush White House*, New York: Simon & Schuster, 2002, p. 37.
11. John L. Gaddis, 'A grand strategy of transformation', *Foreign Policy*, 133:50, 2002, pp. 50–7.
12. Michael Cox, *US Foreign Policy after the Cold War: Superpower without a Mission? (Chatham House Papers)*, London: Pinter Publishers/Royal Institute of International Affairs, 1995.
13. 'Fifty-six per cent of Americans and Europeans do not feel that the values of Islam are compatible with the values of democracy.' *Transatlantic Trends 2006*, p. 4.
14. 'Large numbers of Americans and Europeans agree on the importance of global threats, with the largest increase over the past year in those who see Islamic fundamentalism as an 'extremely important' threat [...]', *Transatlantic Trends 2006*, p. 4.
15. Robert Kagan, 'Power and weakness', *Policy Review*, 113, 2002, pp. 3–28.
16. Michael Howard, 'What's in a name? How to fight terrorism', *Foreign Affairs*, 81:1, 2002, pp. 8–13.
17. Bradley Graham and Josh White, 'Abizaid credited with popularizing the term "long war"', *The Washington Post*, 3 February 2006. President Bush also sought to place the enemy in the camp of fascism, hence his brief use of the term 'Islamo-fascism' to describe jihadists of all shapes and sizes.
18. Buzan, see note 8, p. 112.
19. Paul Wilkinson, *International Terrorism: The Changing Threat and the EU's Response*, Chaillot Paper 84, Paris: European Union Institute for Security Studies, 2005.
20. Lawrence Wright, *The Looming Tower: Al-Qaeda and the Road to 9/11*, New York: Knopf, 2006.
21. Fred Halliday, *The Making of the Second Cold War*, London: Verso, 1984.
22. Adam Quinn and Michael Cox, 'Fear and loathing in Brussels: the political consequences of anti-Americanism', in R. Higgott and I. Malbašić (eds), *The Political Consequences of Anti-Americanism*, London/New York: Routledge, 2008, pp. 93–107.
23. Peter Baldwin, *The Narcissism of Small Differences: How America and Europe are Alike*. Oxford: Oxford University Press, 2009.
24. Simond de Galbert, 'Are European countries really "free riders?"', *The Atlantic*, www.theatlantic.com/international/archive/2016/03/obama-doctrine-europe-free-riders/475245.
25. Tom Rosentiel, 'Strengthen ties with China, but get tough on trade', Pew Research Center, 12 January, 2011, http://pewresearch.org/pubs/1855/china-poll-Americans-want-closer-ties-but-tougher-trade-policy.
26. Hillary Clinton, 'America's Pacific century', *Foreign Policy*, November 2011, www.foreignpolicy.com/articles/2011/10/11/Americas_pacific_century?page=full.
27. D.S. Hamilton and J.P. Quinlan (eds), *The Transatlantic Economy 2012*, School of Advanced International Studies, John Hopkins University, https://archive.transatlanticrelations.org/publication/transatlantic-economy-2012.

Chapter 8

1. A version of this chapter was first published in Asle Toje (ed.), *Will China's Rise Be Peaceful?*, Oxford University Press, 2018, pp. 321–48 and appears here with permission.
2. Yun Sun, 'China–Russia relations: alignment without alliance', 7 October 2015, The Stimson Center, www.stimson.org/2015/china-russia-relations-alignment-without-alliance.

3. This section draws heavily from Liu Binyan and Perry Link, 'A great leap backward?' *The New York Review of Books*, 8 October 1998, www.nybooks.com/articles/1998/10/08/a-great-leap-backward.
4. Zuraidah Ibrahim 'Lee Kuan Yew was ahead of the curve when he predicted China's emergence,' *South China Morning Post*, 24 March 2015, www.scmp.com/news/asia/article/1745715/lee-kuan-yew-was-ahead-curve-when-he-predicted-chinas-emergence.
5. Paul Krugman, 'The myth of Asia's miracle,' *Foreign Affairs*, December 1994, pp. 62–78.
6. Gerald Segal, 'Does China matter?' *Foreign Affairs*, September–October 1999, pp. 24–36.
7. Michael Cox (ed.), *Rethinking the Soviet Collapse: Sovietology, the Death of Communism and the New Russia*, London: Pinter Publishers, 1998.
8. Will Hutton, *The Writing on the Wall: China and the West in the 21st Century*, London: Little, Brown, 2006.
9. No doubt some will claim they foresaw China's economic rise a quarter of a century before it happened; and no doubt a few were better positioned to see the economic writing on the wall before the beginning of the great economic takeoff. Among some of the more perceptive Sinologists, see the work of Allen Whiting, Steven Fitzgerald and Stuart Harris, who did, to be fair, foreshadow a more positive economic future for China, despite the massive domestic challenges and international scepticism that continued to prevail during the 1980s and 1990s.
10. Nicholas D. Kristof and Sheryl WuDunn, *China Wakes: The Struggle for the Soul of a Rising Power*, London: Nicholas Brealey Publishing, 1994. See also Daniel Burstein and Arne de Keijzer, *Big Dragon: The Future of China: What It Means for Business, the Economy, and the Global Order*, New York: Touchstone, 1999.
11. Martin Jacques, *When China Rules the World: The Rise of the Middle Kingdom and the End of the Western World*, London: Penguin/Allen Lane, 2009.
12. James Kynge, *China Shakes the World: The Rise of a Hungry Nation*, London: Phoenix, 2006.
13. Peter Goodman, 'In Davos, deepening worries about China and the global economy,' *International Business Times*, 22 January 2016, www.ibtimes.com/davos-deepening-worries-about-china-global-economy-2276048.
14. G. John Ikenberry, 'The rise of China and the future of the West: can the liberal system survive?', *Foreign Affairs*, 87:1, 2008, pp. 23–37.
15. Barry Buzan and Michael Cox, 'China and the US: comparable cases of "peaceful rise"?', *The Chinese Journal of International Politics*, 6, 2013, pp. 109–32.
16. Ted C. Fishman, *China Inc.: How The Rise of the Next Superpower Challenges America and the World*, New York: Scribner, 2006.
17. Susan Shirk, *China: Fragile Superpower*, New York: Oxford University Press, 2008.
18. Jeffrey A. Bader, *Obama and China's Rise: An Insider's Account of America's Asia Strategy*, Washington, DC: The Brookings Institution, 2012.
19. Michael Cox, 'Power shifts: economic change and the decline of the West?', *International Relations*, 26:4, 2012, pp. 369–88.
20. John Mearsheimer, *The Tragedy of Great Power Politics*, 2nd edn, New York: W.W. Norton & Company, 2014.
21. Jeremy Page, 'Why Russia's president is "Putin the Great" in China,' *Wall Street Journal*, 1 October 2014, www.wsj.com/articles/why-russias-president-is-putin-the-great-in-china-1412217002.
22. For a strong refutation of at least four of the more comforting Western myths about the China–Russia relationship and why it will always fall foul of various obstacles according to this account, see Alexander Korolev, 'The strategic alignment between Russia and China: myths and reality', *The ASAN Forum*, 30 April 2015, www.theasanforum.orgithe-strategic-alignment-between-russia-and-china-myths-and-reality.

23 Rajan Menon, 'The limits of the Chinese-Russian partnership', *Survival*, 51:3, 2009, pp. 99–130.
24 Bobo Lo, *Axis of Convenience: Moscow, Beijing and the New Geopolitics*, Washington, DC: The Brookings Institution, 2008; and his *How the Chinese See Russia*, Russie.Nei. Reports no. 6, IFRI, Russia/NIS Center, December 2010, pp. 1–30, www.ifri.org/sitesidefault/filesiatoms/files/rnr6chinaloengdec2010.pdf.
25 'Russia and China: an uneasy friendship,' *The Economist*, 9 May 2015.
26 On some of the many problems facing economic relations between China and Russia, see Bjorn Alexander Duben, 'Why Russia's turn to China is a mirage', Reuters, 8 July 2015, www.reuters.com/article/duben-russia-idINL1N0ZO2ET20150708; Michael Schuman, 'Thaw in China–Russia relations hasn't trickled down,' *The New York Times*, 15 December 2015, www.nytimes.com/2015/12/16/business/international/thaw-in-china-russia-relations-hasnt-trickled-down.html; and Jacopo Dettoni, 'Trade misses targets despite political deals', *Nikkei Asia*, 20 January 2016, https://asia.nikkei.com/Politics/Trade-misses-targets-despite-political-deals.
27 Geoff Dyer, *The Contest of the Century: The New Era of Competition with China*, London: Allen Lane, 2014, p. 212.
28 For an exposition of a view close to the one expressed in this chapter, see, however, Gilbert Rozman, 'The Sino-Russia partnership is stronger than the West thinks', *HuffPost*, 11 January 2015, www.huffpost.com/entry/sino-russia-partnership_b_6140358.
29 Putin denies that 'China and Russia are […] creating any military blocs or alliances against anybody', but he does admit that 'we are in the process of building an alliance to safeguard our national interest'. See 'Russia, China do not form blocs against anyone: Putin,' *China Daily* [USA], 20 June 2015.
30 Daniel Drezner, 'The system worked: global economic governance during the Great Recession', *World Politics*, 66: January 2014, pp. 123–64.
31 Feng Zhang, 'China's new thinking on alliances', *Survival*, 54:5, 2012, pp. 129–48.
32 Gilbert Rozman, *The Sino-Russian Challenge to the World Order*, Stanford, CA: Stanford University Press, 2014.
33 Benni Avni, 'Vladimir Putin's budding bromance with China's Xi Jinping', *Newsweek*, 16 May 2015, www.newsweek.com/vladimir-putin-xi-jinping-332536.
34 Quotes from Fu Ying, 'How Russia sees China: Beijing and Moscow are close, but not allies', *Foreign Affairs*, 95:1, 2016, www.foreignaffairs.com/articles/china/2015-12-14/how-china-sees-russia.
35 Fidel Castro's statement can be found at 'Fidel Castro: Russia, China will do their best to preserve peace', *Sputnik News*, 12 December 2015, https://sputniknews.com/20151212/-castro-russia-china-peace-1031630092.html.
36 'China invites Russian troops to Second World War parade in Beijing', *The Guardian*, 11 May 2016, www.theguardian.com/world/2015/may/11/china-invites-russian-troops-to-second-world-war-parade-in-beijing; and 'Russia and China celebrate Japanese surrender in World War II,' *Moscow Times*, http://old.themoscowtimes.com/multimedia/photogalleries/russia-and-china-celebrate-japanese-surrender-in-world-war-ii/5859.html.
37 Michael Cox, 'The necessary partnership? The Clinton presidency and post-Soviet Russia', *International Affairs*, October 1994, pp. 635–58.
38 Stephen Kotkin, *Armageddon Averted: The Soviet Collapse 1970–2000*, New York: Oxford University Press, 2008.
39 Masha Gessen, *The Man without a Face: The Unlikely Rise of Vladimir Putin*, New York: Riverhead Books, 2012.
40 David Satter, *It Was a Long Time Ago, and It Never Happened Anyway: Russia and the Communist Past*, New Haven, CT: Yale University Press, 2012.

NOTES AND REFERENCES

41 Jonathan Fenby, *China: The Fall and Rise of a Great Power, 1850 to the Present*, London: Penguin Books, 2013, pp. 574–637.
42 Odd Arne Westad, *Restless Empire: China and the World since 1750*, London: The Bodley Head, 2012, pp. 427–8.
43 David Shambaugh, *China Goes Global: The Partial Power*, New York: Oxford University Press, 2013, p. 79.
44 David Shambaugh, *China's Communist Party: Atrophy and Adaptation*, Berkeley, CA: UC Press/Washington, DC: Woodrow Wilson Center Press, 2008.
45 Xi Jinping, Eighteenth National Congress of the Communist Party of China, 8 November 2012.
46 Amitai Etzioni, 'The air-sea battle "concept": a critique', *International Politics*, 51, September 2014, pp. 577–96.
47 Bonnie S. Glaser, 'Pivot to Asia: prepare for the unintended', *Center for Strategic and International Studies Forecast*, 2012, pp. 22–4, http://csis.org/files/publication/120413_gf_glaser.pdf.
48 See the comments delivered by Chinese Foreign Minister Wang Yi at the CSIS in Washington in February 2016. He noted, 'The surmise that China will become a major rival of the US and even supersede the US is a false proposition.' See USCNPM Staff, 'Wang: China won't be a rival to the US' [blog], US-China Perception Monitor, 26 February 2016, www.uscnpm.org/blog/2016/02/26/wang-china-wont-be-a-rival-to-us.
49 On partnership and rivalry in the US-China relationship, see Wendy Dobson, *Partners and Rivals: The Uneasy Future of China's Relationship with the United States*, Toronto: University of Toronto Press, 2013.
50 Deborah Welch Larson and Alexei Shevchenko, 'Status seekers: China and Russia's response to US primacy', *International Security*, 34:4, 2010, pp. 63–95.
51 Michael Cox, 'The empire's back in town: or America's imperial temptation – again', *Millennium*, 32:1, 2003, pp. 1–27.
52 On Russia, see Thomas Ambrosio, *Challenging America's Global Pre-Eminence: Russia's Quest for Multipolarity*, London: Ashgate, 2005. On China, see Jenny Clegg, *China's Global Strategy: Towards a Multipolar World*, London: Pluto Press, 2009; and Randall L. Schweller and Xiaoyu Pu, 'After unipolarity: China's visions of international order in an era of US decline,' *International Security*, 36:1, 2011, pp. 41–72.
53 Gregory Chin and Ramesh Thakur, 'Will China change the rules of the global order?', *Washington Quarterly*, 33:4, 2010, pp. 119–38.
54 Theresa Reinold, 'The responsibility to protect – much ado about nothing?', *Review of International Studies*, 36:1, 2010, pp. 55–78.
55 For a recent overview, see Alexander Gabuev, 'How China and Russia see the internet' [blog], World Economic Forum, 16 December 2015, www.weforum.org/agenda/2015/12/how-china-and-russia-see-the-internet.
56 On China, see 'Internet in China: government plans further tightening of controls on search engines and news outlets', Reuters, 7 May 2017, www.newsweek.com/china-internet-control-censorship-news-search-engine-595928.
57 On Russia, see Andrei Soldatov and Irina Borogan, 'Putin brings China's great firewall to Russia in cybersecurity pact', *The Guardian*, 29 November 2016, www.theguardian.com/world/2016/nov/29/putin-china-internet-great-firewall-russia-cybersecurity-pact.
58 Dmitry Sudakov, 'Russian FM Lavrov: USA's "exceptionalism" is a global threat', pravda.ru, 25 December 2014, http://english.pravda.ru/russia/kremlin/25-12-2014/129391-sergei_lavrov_usa-0.

59. Benjamin David Baker, 'Sino-Norwegian relations 5 years after Liu Xiaobo Nobel Peace Prize', *The Diplomat*, 4 January 2016, http://thediplomat.com/2016/01/sino-norwegian-relations-5-years-after-liu-xiaobos-nobel-peace-prize.
60. 'Lavrov outlines the way forward for relations,' *China Daily*, 14 April 2014, www.chinadaily.com.cn/world/2014-04/14/content_17433463.htm.
61. Fiona Hill and Bobo Lo, 'Putin's pivot: why Russia is looking East', *Foreign Affairs*, 31 July 2013, www.foreignaffairs.com/articles/russian-federation/2013-07-31/putins-pivot.
62. 'China's lesson for Putin in how to do diplomacy', *Financial Times*, 15 November 2014.
63. Ian Black, 'Russia and China veto UN move to refer Syria to International Criminal Court,' *The Guardian*, 22 May 2014.
64. George A. Lopez, 'Russia and China: sabotaging UN with vetoes,' CNN, 8 February 2012, http://edition.cnn.com/2012/02/08/opinion/lopez-russia-sanctions-cold-war/index.html.
65. On the SCO see Weiqing Song, 'Feeling safe, being strong: China's strategy of soft balancing through the Shanghai Cooperation Organization', *International Politics*, 50:5, 2013, pp. 664–85.
66. Richard Weitz, 'The Shanghai Cooperation Organization's growing pains,' *The Diplomat*, 18 September 2015, http://thediplomat.com/2015/09/the-shanghai-cooperation-organizations-growing-pains.
67. Jim O'Neill, *Growth Map: Economic Opportunity in the BRICS*, London: Penguin Books, 2011.
68. Zaki Laïdi, 'BRICS: sovereignty power and weakness', *International Politics*, 49:5, 2012, pp. 614–32.
69. Robert J. Lieber, 'The rise of the BRICS and American primacy,' *International Politics*, 51:1, 2014, pp. 137–54.
70. Alexey Timofeychev, 'BRICS now a full fledged organization', *Russia and India Report*, 10 July 2015, www.rbth.com/world/2015/07/10/brics_now_a_full_fledged_organization_44171.
71. Alexander Gabuev, 'Russia's uneasy relationship with China,' *The New York Times International Edition*, 26 November 2014.
72. 'US-backed TPP to be ineffective without Russia, China – Putin', *RT Business*, 6 November 2014.
73. Aurelia George Mulgan, 'Japan, US and the TPP: the view from China', East Asia Forum, 5 May 2013.
74. Gabriela Marin Thornton and Alexey Ilin, 'The real winner of the Ukraine crisis could be China', *The Washington Post*, 24 February 2015, www.washingtonpost.com/posteverything/wp/2015/02/24/the-real-winner-of-the-ukraine-crisis-could-be-china.
75. Lyle J. Goldstein, 'What does China really think about the Ukraine crisis?', *The National Interest*, 4 September 2014, http://nationalinterest.org/feature/what-does-china-really-think-about-the-ukraine-crisis-11196.
76. Wayne Ma, 'Why China is driving a hard bargain with Russia over gas', *The Wall Street Journal*, 19 May 2014, https://blogs.wsj.com/chinarealtime/2014/ 05/19/why-china-is-driving-a-hard-bargain-with-russia-over-gas.
77. Gideon Rachman, 'China, Russia and the Sinatra doctrine', *Financial Times*, 24 November 2014.
78. Roger Boyes, 'Why this old pals' act should alarm the West', *The Times*, 27 August 2014.
79. Ali Wyne, 'The limits of China-Russia cooperation', *Wall Street Journal*, 22 May 2014, www.wsj.com/articles/wyne-the-limits-of-china-russia-cooperation-1400776434.
80. Mark Landler, 'Obama, Xi and Putin: not buddies,' *The New York Times International Edition*, 1 November 2014.

81. Kathrin Hille, 'Russia: dangers of isolation,' *Financial Times*, 8 January 2015.
82. Jane Perlez and Neil MacFarquhar, 'Friendship between Putin and Xi becomes strained as economies falter', CNBC, 3 September 2015, www.cnbc.com/2015/09/03/friendship-between-putin-and-xi-becomes-strained-as-economies-falter.html.
83. 'Russia–China relations at "historic peak" despite "illegitimate Western restrictions" – Putin', RT, 1 September 2015, www.rt.com/news/313998-putin-china-visit-xinhua.
84. Andranik Migranyan, 'Washington's creation: a Russia–China alliance', *The National Interest*, 10 July 2014.

Part IV

1. Anthony Zurcher, 'US elections 2016: five reasons why Donald Trump won', BBC News, 9 November 2016.

Chapter 9

1. This article is based on the author's keynote address at the annual conference of the International Affairs Standing Committee of the Royal Irish Academy, titled 'Retreat from globalisation? Brexit, Trump and the new populism', which took place at the Royal Irish Academy, Dublin, on 31 May 2017. A version of this chapter was first published *Irish Studies in International Affairs*, 28, 2017, pp. 9–17, and appears here with permission.
2. Karl Marx and Friedrich Engels, *The Communist Manifesto*, Chicago, 1848.
3. Ghiţa Ionescu and Ernest Gellner (eds), *Populism: Its Meanings and National Characteristics*, London: Macmillan, 1969.
4. Matthew Goodwin, *Right Response: Understanding and Countering Populist Extremism in Europe*, Chatham House, Europe Programme report, September 2011, https://www.chathamhouse.org/sites/default/files/r0911_goodwin.pdf.
5. Lianna Brinded, 'The boss of one of the largest accounting firms in the world says his biggest concern for Europe isn't Brexit', *Business Insider*, 31 December 2017, http://uk.businessinsider.com/kpmg-global-chairman-john-veihmeyer-brexit-populism-europe-2016-12.
6. Gavin Esler, *The United States of Anger: People and the American Dream*, New York: 1997.
7. John Stepek, 'What's driving populism, and why it matters to investors', *MoneyWeek*, 4 April 2017, http://moneyweek.com/whats-driving-populism-and-why-it-matters-to-investors.
8. Frank Furedi, 'Populism on the ropes? Don't be so sure', *Spiked*, 15 May 2017, www.frankfuredi.com/article/populism_on_the_ropes_dont_be_so_sure; see also Furedi's 'From Europe to America: the populist moment has arrived', *Spiked*, 13 June 2005, www.frankfuredi.com/articles/Populist-20050613.shtml; and 'Populism: a defence', *Spiked*, 29 November 2016, www.frankfuredi.com/site/article/884.
9. Jan-Werner Müller, *What Is Populism?*, Philadelphia, PA: University of Pennsylvania Press, 2016.
10. Francis Fukuyama, 'The end of history?', *The National Interest*, 16, 1989, pp. 3–18; see also Ishaan Tharoor, 'The man who declared the "end of history" fears for democracy's future', *The Washington Post*, 9 February 2017, www.washingtonpost.com/news/worldviews/wp/2017/02/09/the-man-who-declared-the-end-of-history-fears-for-democracys-future.
11. David Goodhart, *The Road to Somewhere: The Populist Revolt and the Future of Politics*, London: C. Hurst & Co., 2017.
12. Moisés Naím, 'How to be a populist', *The Atlantic*, 21 April 2017, www.theatlantic.com/international/archive/2017/04/trump-populism-le-pen/523491.

13. Anthony Giddens, *Runaway World: How Globalization Is Reshaping Our Lives*, London: Profile Books, 1999.
14. Arvind Subramanian and Martin Kessler, 'The hyperglobalization of trade and its future', Peterson Institute for International Economics, Working Paper Series WP 13–6, July 2013, https://piie.com/publications/wp/wp13-6.pdf.
15. Thomas Piketty, *Capital in the 21st Century*, Paris, 2013.
16. James Montier and Philip Pilkington, 'The deep causes of secular stagnation and the rise of populism', GMO White Paper, March 2017.
17. Martin Wolf, 'The tide of globalisation is turning', *Financial Times*, 6 September 2016.
18. Simon Fraser, 'Bracing ourselves for Brexit', *The World Today*, 6 April 2017, www.chathamhouse.org/publications/the-world-today/2017-04/bracing-ourselves-brexit.

Chapter 10

1. www.eurotopics.net/en/169223/why-did-trump-win-the-election
2. Diana C. Mutz, 'Status threat not economic hardship explains the 2016 presidential vote', *PNAS*, 115:19, 23 April 2018.
3. www.pewresearch.org/fact-tank/2016/11/09/how-the-faithful-voted-a-preliminary-2016-analysis
4. www.militarytimes.com/news/2016/05/09/military-times-survey-troops-prefer-trump-to-clinton-by-a-huge-margin
5. Jon Henley, 'White and wealthy voters gave victory to Donald Trump, exit poll shows', *The Guardian*, 9 November 2016.
6. www.theatlantic.com/politics/archive/2016/11/why-hillary-clinton-lost/507704/
7. 58 per cent of white voters went for Trump in 2016 and 39 per cent for Hillary Clinton, thus making white people the only racial group in which a majority voted for Trump.
8. Nia-Malika Henderson, 'Race and racism in the 2016 campaign', CNN *Politics*, 1 September 2016.
9. Alec Baldwin and Kurt Andersen, *You Can't Spell America Without Me: The Really Tremendous Inside Story of My Fantastic First Year as President Donald J. Trump (A So-Called Parody)*, New York: Penguin Press, 2017.
10. Trump won the rural vote by 62 per cent to 34 per cent, and the suburban vote by 50 per cent to 45 per cent. Clinton won the urban vote by 59 per cent to 35 per cent.
11. www.cnbc.com/video/2016/07/21/trump-Americanism-not-globalism-is-our-credo.html
12. As the ever-reliable Pew Research Center reported in November 2020, of the 13 countries it surveyed no more than a quarter of adults expressed confidence in Trump, while in many (probably most) nations they discovered the lowest ratings ever for an outgoing president (www.pewresearch.org/fact-tank/2020/11/19/the-trump-era-has-seen-a-decline-in-Americas-global-reputation).
13. Donald Trump, speech to United Nations General Assembly, 19 September 2017.
14. Donald Trump, inaugural address, 20 January 2017.
15. Michael Crowley, 'Trump deal with Taliban criticized by some Republicans', *The New York Times International Edition*, 21 August 2021, p. 5.
16. Ben White and Lorraine Woellert, 'Trump's tweet shaming startles corporate America', *Politico*, 7 December 2016.
17. Louis Nelson, 'Hillary Clinton racks up business endorsements', *Politico*, 23 June 2016.
18. Jason Furman et al, 'The 2017 Economic Report of the President', 15 December 2016.
19. Martin Wolf, 'Donald Trump has been lucky with the economy, *Financial Times*, 30 January 2018.

NOTES AND REFERENCES

20. Daniele Palumbo, 'Donald Trump and the US economy in six charts', BBC News, 20 January 2018.
21. Kate Brannen, 'Trump's national security strategy is decidedly non-Trumpian', *The Atlantic*, 8 December 2017.
22. Max Boot, 'Trump security strategy: a study in contrasts', *Council on Foreign Relations*, 18 December 2017.
23. Frances Z. Brown and Thomas Carothers, 'Is the new US security strategy a step backward on democracy and human rights?', Carnegie Endowment for International Peace, 30 January 2018.
24. Kori Schake, 'How to grade Trump's national security on a curve', *Foreign Policy*, 19 December 2017, https://foreignpolicy.com/2017/12/19/how-to-grade-trumps-national-security-strategy-on-a-curve.
25. Trump on President Xi, quoted in Kevin Liptak, 'Trump on China's Xi consolidating power: "Maybe we'll give that a shot some day"', CNN Politics, 4 March 2018.
26. Ben Westcott, 'How China's Xi Jinping blew a golden opportunity with US President Donald Trump', CNN, 31 October 2020.
27. Matt Bevan and Scott Mitchell, 'How Donald Trump and Xi Jinping changed the US–China relationship forever', ABC News, 26 October 2020, www.abc.net.au/news/2020-10-27/donald-trump-xi-jinping-changed-relationship-us-china-forever/12765786.
28. For details see Chad P. Bown and Melina Kolb, 'Trump's trade war timeline: an up-to-date guide', Peterson Institute of Economics, 17 May 2021.
29. 'US–China trade deal: don't get overexcited', *ING*, 13 October 2019.
30. 'United States and China reach phase one trade agreement', 13 December 2019, https://ustr.gov/abneitherout-us/policy-offices/press-office/press-releases/2019/december/united-states-and-china-reach.
31. On 31 January 2020 Trump was warned by a national security adviser that the pandemic might easily become 'the biggest national security threat' he would be facing during his presidency. See Lawrence Wright, *The Sunday Times*, 'Trump's Covid catastrophe: what really happened inside the White House', 5 June 2021, www.thetimes.co.uk/article/trumps-covid-catastrophe-what-really-happened-inside-the-white-house-6hmlzvkr0.
32. Myah Ward, '15 times Trump praised China as coronavirus was spreading across the globe', *Politico*, 15 April 2020.
33. Eliot A. Cohen, 'How Trump is ending the American era', *The Atlantic*, October 2017.
34. https://origins.osu.edu/article/American-populism-and-persistence-paranoid-style
35. Peter Nicholas, 'There are no libertarians in an epidemic', *The Atlantic*, 10 March 2020.
36. John Harwood, 'Americans love social security but fear "socialism". Trump is exploiting that', *CNN Politics*, 30 August 2020.

Chapter 11

1. 'Globalization' is an extraordinary concept. It is a complicated concept that burst on the world relatively recently, but soon became a household concern. It is a concept that was rarely used until the 1990s, but processes of globalization had been happening for centuries. See Paul James and Manfred B. Steger, 'A genealogy of "globalization": the career of a concept', *Globalizations*, 11:4, 2014, pp. 417–34.
2. For Bush's speech on the 'new world order' in January 1991 see https://millercenter.org/the-presidency/presidential-speeches/january-29-1991-state-union-address.
3. Paul Kennedy, 'Europe's old laggards will never balance US power', *The Guardian*, 24 June 2003.
4. Amitav Acharya, *The End of the American World Order*, Cambridge: Polity, 2014.

5. Mark Steyn, *After America: Get Ready for Armageddon*, Washington, DC: Regnery Publishing, 2011.
6. Chris Hedges, *America: The Farewell Tour*, New York: Simon & Schuster, 2018.
7. Andrei Martyanov, *Disintegration: Indicators of the Coming American Collapse*, Atlanta, GA: Clarity Press, 2021.
8. Ed Luce, *Time to Start Thinking: America and the Spectre of Decline*, London: Abacus, 2013.
9. See, for example, Josef Joffe, *The Myth of America's Decline: Politics, Economics and a Half Century of False Prophecies*, New York: Liveright, 2013.
10. Nick Bryant, *When America Stopped Being Great: A History of the Present*, London: Bloomsbury Continuum, 2021.
11. Chris Evans, 'The American era is ending', *The Telegraph*, 19 August 2021.
12. Dina Smeltz and Emily Sullivan, 'US public supports withdrawal from Afghanistan', The Chicago Council on Global Affairs, 9 August 2021.
13. Allister Heath, 'Decadence and hubris have finally brought down the American empire', *The Telegraph*, 18 August 2021.
14. Charlie Kupchan, *Isolationism: A History of America's Efforts to Shield Itself from the World*, New York: Oxford University Press, 2020.
15. Kenneth Waltz predicted that the unipolar moment would not endure for long. As he put it: 'In the light of structural theory, unipolarity appears as the least durable of international configurations.' He also went on to add that 'as nature abhors a vacuum, so international politics abhors unbalanced power'. See his 'Structural realism after the Cold War', *International Security*, 25:1, 2000, pp. 27, 28.
16. John Mearsheimer, *The Great Delusion: Liberal Dreams and International Reality*, New Haven, CT: Yale University Press, 2018.
17. Robin Niblett, 'US allies know Washington needs them more than ever', *Foreign Affairs*, 19 August 2021.
18. Eric Toussaint, 'Domination of the United States on the World Bank', 2 April 2020, CADTM, www.cadtm.org/Domination-of-the-United-States-on-the-World-Bank.
19. Cissy Zhou, 'China's overseas investment fell 10 per cent last year, as government crackdown on capital flight continues', *South China Morning Post*, 13 September 2019.
20. See the essays 'Can China keep rising' in *Foreign Affairs*, www.foreignaffairs.com/issue-packages/2021-06-22/can-china-keep-rising.
21. See Joseph Nye's short but balanced assessment, *Is the American Century Over?*, Cambridge: Polity, 2015.
22. Figures from *The Economist*, 5 June 2021, pp. 13, 21.
23. Quote from an interview with Michael Beckley, https://now.tufts.edu/articles/why-united-states-only-superpower.
24. By 2030 China's dependency on foreign oil will be 80 per cent while its external dependence on key food products has steadily increased steadily over the past few years, with the greatest increases in imports in soybean, maize, sugar and dairy products. The US, on the other hand, now produces far more energy than it uses and annually exports close to $130 billion of agricultural products, thus making it the largest exporter of food stuffs in the world.
25. David Vine, *Base Nation: How US Military Bases Abroad Harm America and the World*, New York: Metropolitan Books, 2015.
26. Michael Beckley, *Unrivalled: Why America Will Remain the World's Sole Superpower*, Ithaca, NY: Cornell University Press, 2018.
27. Peter Trubowitz and Peter Harris, 'The end of the American century? Slow erosion of the domestic sources of usable power', *International Affairs*, 95:3, 2019, pp. 619–39.
28. 'Francis Fukuyama on the end of American hegemony', *The Economist*, 18 August 2021.

Acknowledgements

The author and publishers wish to thank the publishers of the following essays for permission to reproduce them, with changes, in this volume:

'From geopolitics to geo-economics?', from Michael Cox, *US Foreign Policy after the Cold War: Superpower without a Mission?*, 1995, pp. 21–37, 130–2, reproduced with permission of Chatham House.

'The Wilsonian moment? Promoting democracy', from Michael Cox, G. John Ikenberry and Takashi Inoguchi (eds), *American Democracy Promotion: Impulses, Strategies, and Impacts* 2000, pp. 218–39, reproduced by permission of Oxford University Press, https://global.oup.com/academic/product/American-democracy-promotion-9780199240975.

'Failed crusade? The US and post-communist Russia', from David Lane (ed.), *The Legacy of State Socialism and the Future of Transformation*, 2002, pp. 225–40, reproduced by permission of Rowman & Littlefield Publishers through PLSclear.

'American power after the towers', from Ken Booth and Tim Dunne (eds), *Worlds in Collision: Terror and the Future of Global Order*, 2002, pp. 152–61, reproduced by permission of Palgrave Macmillan.

'Empire, imperialism and the Bush doctrine', from *Review of International Studies*, 30:4, 2004, pp. 585–608, reproduced by permission of Cambridge University Press.

'Stresses across the Atlantic', originally published as 'Too big to fail? The transatlantic relationship from Bush to Obama', in *Global Policy*, 3:1, 2012, pp. 71–8, reproduced by permission of Wiley.

'Axis of opposition: China, Russia and the West', from Asle Toje (ed.), in *Will China's Rise Be Peaceful?*, 2018, pp. 321–48, reproduced by permission of Oxford University Press, https://global.oup.com/academic/product/will-chinas-rise-be-peaceful-9780190675394

'Populism, Trump and the crisis of globalization', originally published as 'The rise of populism and the crisis of globalisation: Brexit, Trump and beyond', *Irish Studies in International Affairs*, 28, 2017, pp. 9–17, and appears here with permission of the Royal Irish Academy.

Index

9/11 attacks *see* September 11 terrorist attacks

A
ABM (Anti-Ballistic Missile) Treaty (1972) 51
Acheson, Dean 63–4
Afghanistan
   intervention in 59–60
   withdrawal of US forces from 139, 155–6, 158
   see also Taliban
al-Qaeda 74, 100
Albright, Madeleine 26, 49, 50, 53, 62, 74
Altman, Roger 79–80
Ambrosius, Lloyd 37
'America First', Trump's key goal 137–41, 142
'America great again', Trump's goal to make 134, 137, 142, 147
American Economic Policy and National Security (Moran) 11
American Manifest Destiny, territorial expansion 69
Americanism vs globalism, Trump 136
'Americanization' of the world 59
Ames, Aldrich, arrest of 45
Arab Spring 89–90, 138–9
Argentina 19
   populism (Peronism) in 125
Asia-Pacific Economic Cooperation (APEC) 15–16, 120
Assad, Bashar al 90, 118
Attali, Jacques 33
'axis of evil' (Iraq, Iran and North Korea), Bush 60–1, 99, 100

B
Baldwin, Peter 102
Bannon, Steve 123, 130, 136
BEMs (big emerging markets) 19–21
   causing job losses in the West 132
   see also Argentina; Brazil; China; Mexico
Biden, Joe (2021–) 151, 153–8
bin Laden, Osama 58–9
Bohlen, Celestine 49
Bonner, Yelena, 'modernized Stalinism' 52
Brazil
   BRICS summit in (2014) 119, 121
   economic potential 19–20
Brennan, Kate 143
Brexit 126, 128, 130, 134, 135
   Trump's support for 140
BRICS (Brazil, Russia, India, China, and South Africa) 119–20
Brinkley, Douglas 25
Brittan, Sir Leon, GATT 16
Brown, Gordon, on globalization 84
Brown, Ron, national export strategy 17–18, 19–20
Brzezinski, Zbigniew 45, 46
Bush, George, Snr (1989–93) 5, 21, 23–4
   admired by Medvedev 91–2
   'new world order' 153
Bush, George W., Jnr (2001–09) 55, 57–8
   and American imperialism 67–8
   and American nationalism 60–1
   economic criticism of 74–5
   immediate response to 9/11 attacks 58–9
   long-term war against rogue states 61
   and the 'new' American empire 65

INDEX

short-term war against Taliban 59–60, 61
spending on defence 60
unilateralism 61–2
and the war on terror 98–100
Buzan, Barry, on the terrorist threat 101

C

Carr, E.H., inter-war crisis 39
Chechnya, Russian intervention in 47, 50, 51–2, 92
Cheney, Dick 90–1
Cherkesov, Viktor 52
China 21, 106–7, 156–7
  'anti-American sentiment' 114
  economic ascent 107–8
  membership of WTO 80, 154
  relationship with the US 108
    Obama's approach 85–6
    trade deals 86
    and Trump 87, 143–6
  relationship with Russia 108–10
    against US hegemony 114–17
    future of 122
    political cooperation 117–20
    supporting Russia in Ukraine crisis 121
    trade agreements 121
    united by history 110–13
  and US national security strategy (NSS) 143–4
Christopher, Warren 25–6, 29, 35
Civil War, US 1–2
climate change
  no mention in the NSS document 142
  Trump's views 87, 126, 138
Clinton, Bill (1993–2001)
  critics 12–14, 66–7
  government reforms 16–18
  key appointments 10–12
  political economy 8–10
  problems with economic strategy 21–2
  promoting democracy 24–35
  promotion of world trade expansion 14–16
  strategy towards post-Communist Russia 41–7
  support for research 18–19
  targeting BEMs 19–21
Clinton, Hillary 86, 103, 104, 127–8, 141
Cohen, Stephen 41
Cold Peace: America, Japan, Germany, and the Struggle for Supremacy (Garten) 11
Cold War 7–8, 34, 97
  debate over Russia 45
  'war on terror' as 'Cold War II' 97–102
communism 110–11
  effect on China of USSR collapse 112–13
  the US and post-communist Russia 40–54, 91, 92, 111–12
competitiveness, Clinton's economic policies 9–10, 13
  obsession with 14, 21–2
cooperation
  Clinton preaching 20, 22
  Russia and China 117–20
COVID-19 crisis
  Biden's recovery plan 155
  Trump's response 137, 146–7
Crimea, Russian annexation of 93
'crony capitalism' emergence of in Russia 52

D

D'Amato, Senator 45
de Gaulle, Charles 96–7
De Tocqueville, Alexis, *Democracy in America* 2
decline
  Russian economy 47–8
  of the Soviet system 107
  of the US 79–80, 84–5, 99, 154, 156
democracy promotion 23–39
  Clinton 24–6, 29–32
  depending on America fulfilling its promise as a nation 39
  and the economy 32–5
  not mentioned in the NSS document 142–3
  Wilson and 36–9
  see also 'enlargement' strategy
democratic enlargement *see* 'enlargement' strategy

Deng Xiaoping, on Gorbachev 113
Doyle, Michael 28, 69

E
economic crash (2008) 79, 81–4, 86, 133
economics as security, Moran 11–12
Economist, The, on US protectionism 13
Egypt 89–90
emerging markets 19–21
empire 63–5, 68–75
'enlargement' strategy 25–6
    hedged in by 'caveats', Lake 29–30
    link to economic renewal and the market 33–4
    reasons for promoting 28–9
Esler, Gavin, 'United States of anger' 126
Europe-US relations 96–7
    Obama and 102–5
    'war on terror' as a new Cold War 97–102
'exceptionalism', American 66, 116, 129

F
Federal Security Service (FSB), Russia 52
Ferguson, Niall, on US imperialism 67–8
financial crisis (2008) 81–4, 133
    China's reaction to 85
Financial Times, The, critique of Clinton's policies 13–14
Fiorina, Carly 87
foreign policy 7
    Clinton's 5, 8–9, 14, 25–6, 27, 30–1
    and ideology, Hunt 24
    impact of terrorist attacks on 58
    pursuit of imperial 55, 67
    Russian 45, 50
    utopianism 38–9
Founding Fathers 3, 37, 69
France 97
    anti-Americanism 102
    populism in 127
Fraser, Simon 134
free trade 22, 80, 84, 132, 132, 134, 136, 156
    ambivalence about benefits of 134
    Trump's views 136
Friedman, George 48

Friedman, Thomas 21
Fukuyama, Francis 48, 129, 153, 158

G
Gaddafi, Muammar, military action against 90
Gallagher, John, on imperialism 69
Gardner, Lloyd 36
Garten, Jeffrey E., on US trade policy 9, 11, 16
Gates, Robert 103
Gellner, Ernest, *Populism* 125
General Agreement on Tariffs and Trade (GATT) 16
Germany 11
    admired by Wilson 38
    and Clinton 103
    Trump's critique 140
Giddens, Tony 130–1
globalization
    Clinton's uncritical attitude towards 22
    enemies of American-style 57
    'hyper-globalization' 131, 156
    populism and future of 134
    'runaway world' of, Giddens 130–1
    under scrutiny following financial crisis 83–4
Goodhart, David, the 'somewheres' 129
Gorbachev, Mikhail 91, 112–13
Gore, Al 33–4, 43
Graham, Senator Lindsey 87
Grieco, Joseph M., 'second opinion' 74

H
Halliday, Fred 102
Havel, Václav 54
hegemonic power of America 96, 114–15
Howard, Michael, on the war on terror 100–1
Hu Jintao, President, trip to US 85
human rights
    China and Russia condoning abuses of 118
    Clinton and China 21
    doubts about Putin protecting 52
    Liu Xiaobo's winning of Nobel Peace Prize 117

NSS's strategy document failing to mention 142–3
Obama and Guantanamo 95
Trump and China 144
Hungary 46, 128
Hunt, Michael, ideology and US foreign policy 24
Huntington, Samuel 28
'hyper-globalization' 131, 156
hyper-partisanship, rise of 158

I

ideological contamination by the West 116
Ikenberry, John 69
IMF (International Monetary Fund) 47, 72, 119, 156
imperialism 63–5
   with American characteristics 65–8
   in American history 68–9
   British, outcomes of 69
   cost of 65, 74–5
   and discussion of empire 55, 68–72
   'new' imperial strategy weakening US empire 73
income
   inequality, exponential rise in 83, 136, 156
   rises in China 106
   stagnation 131
India, trade deal 20–1
Indonesia, oil deal 20
International Monetary Fund (IMF) 47, 72, 119, 156
internet censorship, China 116
Ionescu, Ghita, *Populism* 125
Iran 89, 90, 92, 94–5
   Obama's nuclear deal with 90, 95, 138, 139
Iraq war 55, 73
   aftermath, Obama's foreign policy 88, 89
   Europe's support for 100
   opposition to 80
   Trump's critique 133, 139
Islamic State (ISIS) 89, 138, 139
isolationism 3
   Clinton against 8, 9, 12

Russia 94
   and Wilson's foreign policy 32, 38
Israel 88–9, 138–9
Ivanov, Sergei 52

J

Japan
   black ships expedition to (1854) 3, 69
   and Clinton's trade policies 13
   high-technology trade conflict 11
   racial equality clause, Paris peace talks (1919) 37
   superseded by China economically 86
jihad, ideology of 101
job losses 83, 95, 138
   blamed on China 21, 86, 131, 144–5
   due to free trade economic policies 156
   due to technology and automation 132
John S. McCain National Defense Authorization Act 145

K

Kagan, Robert 100
Kantor, Mickey 7, 15, 16
Kennan, George. 'diplomacy of dilettantism' 23
Kennedy, Paul, and US decline 57–8, 84
KGB, Putin former member of 50, 91, 93
Kiriyenko, Sergei 47–8
Kissinger, Henry 39
Krauthammer, Charles 66
Krugman, Paul 14, 107
Kudlow, Larry 148

L

Lake, Anthony, democratic enlargement 26, 29–30, 31, 32, 33, 34
Latin America
   big emerging markets 19–20
   populism 125
   US intervention in 69
Lavrov, Sergei 138
Le Pen, Marine 127
Lee Kuan Yew 107
Lehman Brothers, collapse of 81–2
Levin, N. Gordon 36

liberation versus imperialism 67–8
Libya 90, 92, 103
Link, Arthur S. 36
Liu Xiaobo, activist winning Nobel Peace Prize 117
Luce, Henry, the 'American Century' 84
Lugar, Richard 45
Lynch, Allen 37–8

M

Macron, Emmanuel 127
Malia, Martin 48
market democracies, promoting 26, 34, 48
McKinley, President, war against Spain (1898) 3
Mearsheimer, John 86, 156
media censorship, Russia 116
Medvedev, Dmitry (2008–12) 91–2
Merkel, Angela 103
Mexico 14–15
   Trump's views 124, 136
   Trump's wall 138
Middle East
   Obama's approach 88–90
   Trump's policy towards 138–9
military cooperation, China and Russia 118
military force
   America's use of 59–61
   centrality of in world politics, Lake 31
   Obama's approach to 88
   Russia in Chechnya 51
   US history of conquest 68–9
military power, US 99, 157
military spending
   cuts in, Clinton 47
   increase in, Bush 60, 67
'modernized Stalinism', Putin's rise to power 52
Monrow Doctrine (1823) 69
Montier, James1, populism 31
Moran, Theodore 11–12
Morgenthau, Hans J. 1
Mubarak, Hosni 89–90
Müller, Werner, populism 128
multipolar power 115
Muslim Brotherhood 90

Muslims
   hatred of the Taliban 61
   non support for violence 101
   Trump's views 138

N

National Security Strategy (NSS) 142–4
nationalism
   of Chinese 85
   economic 11, 12–13
   following 9/11 attacks 60
   Russian 43, 44, 48–9, 51, 52, 54, 112
Native Americans, land taken from 1, 3, 69
NATO
   enlargement of (1990s) 45, 46, 93
   Russia's objections to 53
   Obama's attitude to Europe 103
   Trump's views of 140
'neoliberalism' 131–2
Netanyahu, Benjamin 89
Niblett, Robin, Chatham House 156
North American Free Trade Agreement (NAFTA) 14–15
North Korea 138, 142
NSS (National Security Strategy) 142–4
nuclear programme, Iran 90, 95, 118, 139
nuclear weapons 8, 44, 51, 94

O

O'Neill, Jim 119
O'Neill, Tip 158
Obama, Barack (2009–17) 77–81
   critique of presidency 94–5
   and the Europeans 102–5
   and the financial crisis (2008) 79–80, 81–4
   and the Middle East 88–90
   nuclear deal with Iran 90, 95, 138, 139
   relations with Putin 91–3
   tilt towards Asia 97, 114
   and Trump's opposition 138–9
   US–China relationship 85–7
Orbán, Viktor 128
Oren, Ido 38

INDEX

P

Panetta, Leon 103
Paris Climate Agreement 138
Paris peace talks (1919) 37
Patrushev, Nikolai 52
Peronism, Argentinian populism 125
Perry, Commodore Matthew C., black ships expedition to Japan (1854) 3, 69
Perry, William, Defense Secretary 46
Philippines, US takeover 38, 69
Pickering, Tom 52–3
Pilkington, Philip, populism 131
Poland, Trump's praise of 140
populism 125–6
    defining 129–32
    and the future of globalization 134
    liberal views of 127–9
    reflections on 132–4
    rise of in Europe 126–7
    and Trump 147
post-communist Russia, relations with US 40–54, 91, 92, 111–12
Powell, Colin 61
powerlessness and populism 133
pre-emption, Bush doctrine of 100
Primakov, Yevgeny 48–9
Prowse, Michael 13–14
Putin, Vladimir (2012–) 41, 90–4
    media censorship 116
    policies of 112
    'problem' of 50–4
    and the Russia–China partnership 108–9, 111, 120

R

R&D spending, Clinton administration 18–19
racism
    and Trump's election campaigns 128, 136, 148
    of Woodrow Wilson 37
Reagan, Ronald (1981–89) 99
Reich, Robert 12, 22
Rice, Condoleezza 98
Rice, Susan 142–3
Robinson, Ronald, on imperialism 69
Romney, Mitt 93
rule of law 35, 50
Rumsfeld, Donald 55, 62
Russett, Bruce 28
Russia
    relations with China 106–22
    relations with US 40–54, 91, 92, 111–12
    see also Putin, Vladimir; USSR, collapse of

S

Saddam Hussein, 61
Sanders, Bernie 126–7
Saudi Arabia
    arms deal, Trump 139
    trade with, Clinton 19
Schake, Kori 143
Schäuble, Wolfgang 126
SCO (Shanghai Co-operation Organization) 118–19
Security Council, UN 92, 117–18
Segal, Gerald, on China 107
self-determination, Wilson 37–8, 70
Sen, Amartya 28
September 11 terrorist attacks 55, 57
    future after 61–2
    and the idea of empire 65
    importance of 67
    response to 58–61, 98
    see also 'war on terror'
Shanghai Co-operation Organization (SCO) 118–19
'special relationship'
    Britain and America 64
    China and Russia 108
Stalin, Joseph 110–11
Stalinism 48, 52
Stelzer, Irwin 33
Stepek, John, on bias against populism 127
Subramanian, Arvind 131
Sudan, genocide 118
Sutherland, Peter, GATT 16
Syria 89, 90, 92, 118, 142

T

Talbott, Strobe 27, 28, 30, 32, 33, 34
    and crisis in Russian reform attempts 43–4

Talbott, Strobe (continued)
    on Putin's choice of security 53
    Republicans stance on 45
    Russia and NATO expansion 46
    on Russian democratization 49
Taliban 58
    little support from Muslim world 61
    Trump's deal with 139
    victory following pull-out of US forces 155
territorial expansion 68–9
terrorism
    counterterrorist role of SCO 118
    legislation 60
    response to 57–61
    'war on terror' 97–102
Thatcher, Margaret 58
Tiananmen Square events 35, 107
Tillerson, Rex 142
tilt towards Asia 97, 114, 120
Toynbee, Arnold 64
TPP (Trans Pacific Partnership) 94, 120
trade agreements 14–16
trade deals 86, 87, 134, 138, 144, 145–6
trade policy 9, 13–16
'trade war' with China, Trump 145
Trans-Pacific Partnership (TPP) 94, 120
transatlantic relationship 102–5
Trump, Donald (2017–21) 123–4
    America First 137–41
    and China 87, 144–7
    disruptive impact of 147–9
    election of 135–7
    and the national security strategy document 141–4
    populist 126–7, 129, 130
    Putin's support for 94
    and the US economy 141
Tyson, Laura D'Andrea 10–11

U

Ukrainian crisis 93, 110, 117, 120, 121
unilateralism of US 61–2
    Europeans attacking 100
    versus multilateralism 88
unipolar 'moment' 84, 115, 143, 156
unipolarity, dangers of 114–17

United Nations
    China–Russia cooperation 117–18
    Responsibility to Protect (R2P) 115
    Trump speech 138
USSR, collapse of 41, 91, 111
    Brzezinski's foreign policy following 45
    China's response 112–13
    long-term impact of 132

V

Veihmeyer, John 126
Vershbow, Alexander 50, 51, 53
Vietnam Syndrome 60–1, 75

W

Wade, Robert Hunter, on the US empire 72
Wall Street 72, 74–5, 79, 82–3
Wall Street Journal 13, 48
Walt, Steve 95
Wang Jisi, US's fear of a 'rising' China 157
'war on terror'
    as a new Cold War 97–102
    dividing the West 97
    support for, sustaining 74
Who's Bashing Whom? Trade Conflict in High-Technology Industries (Tyson) 10
Williams, Appleman William, moral purpose 70
Wilson, Woodrow (1913–21) 23, 24, 31–2
    search for the real 36–9
Wolf, Martin 134
World Bank, US and Europe dominance 119
world trade expansion, Clinton promoting 14–16
World Trade Organization (WTO) 80, 86, 92, 154

X

Xi Jinping (Nov 2012–)
    Trump's attacks on 146
    Trump's 'friendship' with 144
    visit to Russia (2015) 111

Y, Z

Yeltsin, Boris (1991–99) 43, 44–5, 47, 53, 91
Zhirinovsky, Vladimir, 'rise' of 43